International Law and U.S. Foreign Policy

Carl Q. Christol

UNIVERSITY PRESS OF AMERICA,® INC.
Lanham • Boulder • New York • Toronto • Oxford

4501 Forbes Boulevard
Suite 200
Lanham, Maryland 20706
UPA Acquisitions Department (301) 459-3366

PO Box 317
Oxford
OX2 9RU, UK

Printed in the United States of America
British Library Cataloging in Publication Information Available

Library of Congress Control Number: 2004106882
ISBN 0-7618-2875-3 (paperback : alk. ppr.)

™ The paper used in this publication meets the minimum requirements of American National Standard for Information Sciences—Permanence of Paper for Printed Library Materials, ANSI Z39.48—1992

Contents

Preface

My initial intention was to provide students with an analysis of the law and politics of the activities of Al Qaeda and Osama bin Laden. While developing that project it became apparent that there is a need to update the history of many other forms of violence to humans and to our natural environment. International law is applicable to these matters. But, first, a quick overview of the Osama bin Laden form of terrorism.

September 11, 2001 caused people everywhere to reconsider what was meant by "terrorism" and the action of "terrorists." Their attention was drawn to Osama bin Laden, his leadership role in Al Qaeda, its relationship to the Taliban and its governing of Afghanistan. His control over the Taliban, as the *de facto* government of Afghanistan was so dominant, in the days immediately following the attacks, that the United States addressed its demands to the Taliban to turn him over to the United States or suffer the consequences.

Osama bin Laden was not considered to be the Head of State in Afghanistan nor even the head of its *de facto* government. He was a private person who exercised an enormous amount of power. His design was to use the host State as the place where he would manage the widespread system of cohorts who, with him, conspired to destroy the perceived forces of evil that were in conflict with his beliefs and values.

In his view foreign influences and behavior had put at risk his way of life and all of the precepts upon which that way of life had been founded. In the minds of many in the West, he could be considered to be a religious zealot. His rather considerable talents were dedicated to destructive activity.

Under these circumstances the West, and thereafter much of the world, referred to his activity as "terrorist activity," and to him as a "terrorist." The U.S. government announced a plan for his capture, and if apprehended, to prosecute him in a suitable tribunal for his terrorist activity.

In 2001 the United States was bound by several international aviation conventions which made it a crime to hijack an aircraft or to sabotage it, and federal legislation had been adopted to make such conduct a crime. There are also federal statutes dealing with conspiracies and prohibiting murder.

Critical facts appear to prove quite conclusively that Osama bin Laden was a major conspirator in the attack of the Twin Towers in New York City and on the Pentagon. If the U.S. government had Osama bin Laden in custody, and subject to its jurisdiction, it is quite conceivable that he would be charged with many of the crimes attributable to Zacarias Moussaoui, the so-called 20th terrorist, who was apprehended in the United States, including conspiracy to hijack U.S. aircraft and to murder U.S. citizens. Under these circumstances it would appear that a wise course of action in the case of Osama bin Laden, if captured, would be to prosecute him under the same charges.

There is in fact a precedent for this approach, namely the prosecution and conviction in 2002 of persons charged with the bombing of the World Trade Center. Osama bin Laden was a named defendant, but was outside the territory of the United States at the time of the trial. In 2001 the Bush administration announced plans for the prosecutions of alleged terrorists by military commissions. However, pending their creation the prosecutions have taken place in Federal District Courts. Policies underlying the choice of a tribunal for terrorists, unlawful combatants, detainees, and prisoners of war are considered at length.

Courts of law have been proven to be acceptable institutions for the proof of innocence or guilt in criminal matters. The world has had more experience with domestic tribunals. At present it is learning that regional international criminal tribunals have the capacity to apply international law to cases coming before them. Although the International Criminal Tribunal for the Former Yugoslavia has not rendered its judgment in the case of President Slobodan Milosevic, other cases that have been decided by the court indicate that it can resolve matters in a fair and just manner. This is also true for the International Criminal Tribunal for Rwanda.

The court for former Yugoslavia has been invested with the power to deal with violations of international humanitarian law. This includes the subject of grave breaches of the Geneva Conventions of 1949, violations of the laws or customs of war, genocide, and crimes against humanity. Under these several headings there is an enumeration of many specific criminal acts, including willful killing and murder. These wrongdoings occurred during a period of armed conflict, and they were engaged in by persons who were parties to the armed conflict.

For present purposes it is important to observe that the charge against Osama bin Laden and President Milosevic are the same with respect to killings and murder. Osama bin Laden has been identified as a terrorist. Despite the identity of these two charges Milosevic has not. Osama bin Laden, as suggested, is a private person, while Milosevic held public office. Yet, the latter's conduct was clearly intended to terrorize, as well as destroy, those whom he caused to be or allowed to be attacked.

Terrorists are subject to the legal rule of universal jurisdiction, i.e., they can be prosecuted wherever and by whomever has them in possession. Despite the fact that there is the difference between a private person and a public official, one can support the view that Milosevic's conduct was so bad that he, also, should be subjected to the application of the principle of universal jurisdiction. The fact that President Milosevic was a public official should not prevent his being treated as a terrorist.

An assessment of the condition of President Slobodan Milosevic and Al Qaeda leader Osama bin Laden discloses similarities and differences. The former as President, and while in the dock at The Hague, receives the fierce political support of many of his fellow Serbs. The latter also is the recipient of the committed support of his followers, although they as Muslims, are the product of an assemblage of persons of many nationalities.

Both have been able to formulate and to carry into execution policies resulting in the wholesale killings of innocent nationals, although their victims come from quite different constituencies. Neither, at least so far as I am aware, has actually killed another person by his individual action. But, for groups of persons they have engaged in aggressive action. In both cases armed conflict has resulted. This conduct is a violation of the 1949 Geneva Convention because the killing has been willful.

Both have violated the laws or customs of war since their decisions have produced the wanton destruction of cities and villages. Moreover, each has engaged in crimes against humanity, although in different respects. Milosevic's actions have led to deportations and imprisonments. Both are responsible for the murders which they planned and saw executed.

There are also differences in their conduct. While Milosevic's targets have been Muslims and ethnic Albanians in Kosovo, Osama bin Laden's animosity has been directed at Americans, without regard to their ethnic inheritance or religious preferences. The former has been a Head of State, while the latter has been the leader of a conglomerate known as Al Qaeda. The authority of the former has been public; that of the latter private. The former was able to gather the support of citizens and military commanders. The latter was able to persuade his followers that the process of globalization, with its underpinnings derived from the progress of the West, was hostile to and would result in the destruction of their preferred values and way of life.

The crimes for which President Milosevic has been charged are genocide, commonly referred to now as "ethnic cleansing," as well as those mentioned above. The wide-ranging and indiscriminate killings produced by the Al Qaeda leader do not fit under the heading of genocide. The former is engaged in an emotional, imaginative, and wide-ranging defense before the International Criminal Tribunal for the Former Yugoslavia, an *ad hoc* regional body whose existence depends on a resolution adopted by the United Nations Security Council.

In the meantime Osama bin Laden has been on the run seeking safe haven in the mountain caves in Afghanistan and in friendly hands in Pakistan. He seems to have disappeared. Whether his successful illusiveness will continue is anyone's guess. If captured alive he could be prosecuted in one of several tribunals. From his view point the acceptance of a claim that he was a prisoner of war would be the most satisfactory. Much would depend on what country captured him. If he were to fall into the hands of the United States the probability would be that he would be prosecuted before a military commission following the procedures set forth by the Order of the Secretary of Defense on March 21, 2002.

Abselbasset al Megrahi, the Libyan intelligence agent accused of placing a bomb on Pan American flight 103 in 1988 was convicted of murder under Scottish law. Although he was charged with murder, his case is somewhat closer to that of Osama bin Laden than that of President Milosevic. His purpose appears to have been to create fear with regard to the use of American aircraft, and to serve as an armed reply to earlier bombings by U.S. aircraft in Libya. He was not involved in a condition of armed conflict.

Both regional international and national courts have been selected for the prosecution of the foregoing and many other defendants. Punishments and warnings against future misconduct appear to be the reasons for such prosecutions. Only the most serious violations of the worst offenders appear likely to come to trial, but they will set precedents. In the case of prosecutions for genocide in Rwanda the vast number of chargeable persons will restrict the number of cases that can be heard. Perhaps truth and reconciliation commissions will create the required balance of justice and public order.

Many believe that a permanent international criminal tribunal is required to deal with major violations of the international law of Human Rights. The 1998 Rome Treaty provides for such a court. It has received the overwhelming support of States, except for the United States and a handful of countries not known for their respect for Human Rights. An analysis of the Statute of this court, together with an assessment of reasons advanced or opposed will allow for forming an opinion on the subject.

A significant question for all of the above courts, as well as a tribunal to be created by the United States for the prosecution of Al Qaeda and Taliban members, is the means to assure a fair trial which will meet all requirements of the American system of justice. Here there will be the need to balance the so-called special circumstances associated with international terrorists and basic American traditions.

The link between international law and U.S. foreign policy is reflected in several other important matters in which there is considerable difference of opinion in the United States. Public policy in many foreign countries is also at variance with official U.S. pronouncements. Selected for analysis of these matters are the subjects dealt with in treaties on the human environment and climate change, anti-personnel land mines, arms control and disarmament, and the Middle East peace process. Grave charges have been made against Saddam Hussein. The application of international law to Iraq has excited great controversy. With the 2003 abrogation by North Korea of the non-proliferation of Nuclear Weapons Treaty foreign policy has become a critical issues for many Americans.

Shorter references will be made to the U.S. record of compliance with its treaty obligations, means to provide for a better understanding of international law by domestic decision makers, the international law of the sea, the international law of outer space, biological weapons, and the U.S. Constitution and the treaty process. Emphasis will be placed on the preference for multilateral approaches to the resolution of international differences. Here I shall be referring to the condition of globalization.

Acknowledgements

I wish to express my appreciation to the University of Southern California Emeriti Faculty-Undergraduate Research Program for its support. Through its auspices I was able to have the assistance of Miss Dara E. Purvis and Miss Jennifer Molayem, both of whom will be heard of in the future. I received the highly professional help of Ms. Gerlonda Battles of the Political Science staff. To these and the numerous persons who offered assistance and advice, I am most thankful.

Introduction

During the last half of the last century remarkable changes have taken place in international law. First, with the 1946 Declaration of Human Rights the individual became a primary beneficiary of international law. A process of devolution came into being in which the individual could make direct personal demands and experience duties derived from the existence of Human Rights. The person's rights and duties took on retail characteristics. The days of the person as a wholesale commodity have been challenged by the new international law and are long gone.

Second, in order to implement this new condition, it became necessary to revitalize international courts and dispute resolution procedures. More dramatically, a flood of new courts arrived on the scene, with one, the International Criminal Court, now engaged in formal activities. See *Chart 1. Recently Established Dispute Resolution Legal Bodies*.

Third, the rise of supranational structures of governance has been startling. Focused for the moment on trade and monetary subjects, these institutions are both the product of globalization and are contributing to it. They will change the habits of people.

International law, like all law, is able to respond to known problems. Frequently, a country's foreign policy and international law cooperate to gain valued objectives. Their paths are parallel as they move forward. On other occasions there may be substantial divergences.

International law can serve as a constraint upon a State's plan to seize the territory of a neighbor or to violate the Human Rights of its residents. While unable to prevent the outbreak of wars or the unlawful use of armed force, international law has restricted national conduct through the presence of the law of war.

Chart 1. Recently Established Dispute Resolution Legal Bodies (As Of December 2003)

Date	*Title or Source*	*Note Particularly*
1945	*International Court of Justice*	Reservations to jurisdiction
1945	*International Labor Organization*	Administrative tribunal for 46 international organizations
1946	*American Treaty on Pacific Settlement of Disputes*	
1950	*Council of Europe*	European Court of Human Rights
1950	*European Convention for the Protection of Human Rights and Fundamental Freedoms*	
1951	*Court of Justice for the European Coal and Steel Community*	
1957	*Court of Justice of the European Community*	Serves EEC and European Economic Community
1965	*Convention on the Settlement of Disputes Between States and Nationals of Other States*	
1969	*American Convention on Human Rights*	
1969	*Interamerican Court of Human Rights*	
1972	*Convention on International Liability for Damage Caused by Space Objects*	Articles XV–XX provide for Claims Commission
1975	*Final Act of Conference on Security and Cooperation in Europe*	
1975	*Judicial Tribunal of the Economic Community of West African States (ECOWAS)*	
1976	*Commission on International Trade Law* (UNCITRAL)	Provisions for court decisions and arbitral awards
1979	*Court of Justice of the Cartagena Agreement*	
1981	*African Convention on Human and People's Rights, Banjul Charter*	
1981	*Iran-U.S. Claims Tribunal, The Hague*	
1982	*Law of the Sea Convention, Annex VI, Statute of the International Tribunal for the Law of the Sea*	Became operational, 1996
1986	*European Free Trade Association Court*	
1992	*International Monetary Fund*	Administrative tribunal 1992
1992	*International Criminal Tribunal for the Former Yugoslavia*	
1994	*Common Market for Eastern and Southern Africa Court of Justice*	Modeled on European Court of Justice
1994	*International Criminal Tribunal for Rwanda*	Proposed tribunals for Sierra Leone, Cambodia, and East Timor
1994	*World Trade Organization Understanding on Rules and Procedures Governing the Settlement of Disputes*	Annex II, Uruguay Round Agreement

1997	*Claims Resolution Tribunal for Dormant Accounts in Switzerland*	Arbitration
1998	*International Commission on Holocaust Era Insurance Claims*	Private Persons, insurance companies, governmental agencies
2002	*Caribbean Court of Justice*	10 States as signatories
2003	*International Criminal Court*	United States not a Party

This book will appeal to those who believe that the interests of States can be realized by way of international cooperation and that a commitment to multilateralism will serve to achieve and protect such interests. Forces underlying the condition of globalism will continue to manifest themselves. No country, powerful or developing, can afford to adopt policies sponsored by proponents of unilateralism.

Following the last chapter I shall suggest opportunities for informed citizenry to influence the formation of U.S. foreign policy.

Chapter I

The Scope of International Law: A Definition and Treaties

1. A DEFINITION

Over the eons of history the nation-state has evolved as a preferred device for the management of interpersonal and international relations. Fortunate States possess a constitutional democracy with governmental powers distributed between the executive, the legislature, and the courts. In the less fortunate, the executive is dominant. Over centuries in totalitarian regimes, the Head of State has vigorously asserted sovereign prerogatives, contending he or she was above the law.

This contention, implemented by all manner of force and coercion, allowed the claimant to enjoy the benefits of wealth, to destroy his opponents, and to pass all the vestiges of authority to a family member, even though that person might be still an infant. These persons, exemplified in the crowned heads in Europe, constantly made grievous mistakes to the material detriment of their subjects, to the general well-being of their countries and empires, and to the peoples and other countries affected by their conduct.

More recently, totalitarian leaders, themselves the product of assaults on legitimate regimes, have regularly engaged in the same conduct as their royal predecessors, and with the same consequences. Their claim, framed as before, is: I am a Head of State and can do no wrong. Such assertions, in countries where the national courts have been but an extension of the executive prerogative, were frequently honored. Great injustice resulted.

With new forces alive in the world, and with the ordinary conduct occurring within a State having international ramifications, a newly emerging world conscience coupled with a new political will, have produced demands that unacceptable behavior be reviewed in judicial institutions. Traditional and contemporary courts are rendering informed and binding decisions. Thus, for his repressive conduct, General Augusto Pinochet of Chile in charges brought in Spain as genocide and terrorism and in England as torture and conspiracy to commit torture in the United Kingdom have been heard and decided in Spain and in England. President Slobodan Milosevic of the Federal Republic of Yugoslavia has been charged with war crimes, including slaying and persecution of ethnic Albanians in Kosovo, referred to as "ethnic cleansing," and the crime of genocide for conduct in Bosnia. He is being prosecuted before the new International Criminal Tribunal for the Former Yugoslavia. In 2002 Biljana Plavsic, former president of the Serb Republic of Bosnia and later Republica Srpska, entered a plea of guilty for crimes against humanity before the Court. With the apprehension of Saddam Hussein in 2003 plans were made for his early prosecution in a suitable court.

These illustrations identify the dynamic nature of international law. They reflect, under the heading of Human Rights, the subject matter of international law. The law's concern for Human Rights in present times stems from the trial and conviction of the Nazi war criminals at the close of World War II. The international law of Human Rights confirms that individuals possess certain inherent and fundamental rights that nation-states and their leaders must respect.

Until the middle of the 20th century, the textbook definition of international law was that it is a body of principles, standards, and rules governing the relationship between sovereign States. Reflecting this approach was the situation, where a citizen of the United States might have a valid legal claim against a foreign country for refusal to pay for goods sold to the foreign country. Since the foreign country could refuse to hear the claim on the basis of its asserted sovereign immunity from suits by aliens, the American would be obliged to ask his/her government to bring the claim in the name of the United States. In short, the private person not being a subject of international law, could not make international claims to vindicate his or her rights.

With the acknowledgment that human beings possess individual rights and the capacity to pursue such rights, a new definition of international law was required. Today the textbook definition is that this branch of law is a body of principles, standards, and rules governing the relations between States, individuals, and international organizations. With the great proliferation of public international organizations, such as the United Nations, it has become necessary, through treaties, to cope with such relationships. So, international law has been extended to encompass these relationships.

2. TREATIES

Professor J.L. Brierly in his *Law of Nations* introduces his analysis of treaties as a source of law with a quotation from J.W. Salmond. The latter wrote that "Agreement is a law for those who make it, which supersedes, supplements, or derogates from the ordinary law of the land. *Modus et convention vincunt legem*."[1] Treaties, often referred to as international agreements, or conventions, according to the Statute of the International Court of Justice constitute a major source of modern international law.[2] The United States under the Constitution is empowered to make treaties. Pursuant to Article VI treaties are, while subordinate to the Constitution, nonetheless the supreme law of the land. They enter into force following the advice and consent of the Senate and the ratification by the President.

Recognizing the importance of a code of treaty law, the United Nations in 1968 and 1969 conducted conferences which led to the Vienna Convention on the Law of Treaties. Having received the required number of ratifications it entered into force in 1980.[3] The Convention adopted the principle of *pacta sunt servanda*, namely that such agreements are to be entered into in good faith and are binding on signatories. The treaty allows treaty partners to file reservations and to make objections to reservations. Treaty practice allows for a signatory state to make declarations and to file understandings. The United States' acceptance of the 1948 Genocide Convention, for example, sets out declarations and understandings, which thereby measurably reduce its obligations under the agreement. This is also true for the 1984 Conventions on Torture. See *Chart 2. Scoreboard of a Core Group of Multilateral Treaties*.

In the United States, the entry into force of an important multilateral treaty is almost a miraculous event. Getting a treaty ratified has been likened to running an obstacle course through a field indiscriminately strewn with anti-personnel land mines. Cooking up an acceptable treaty involves perceptions of its constitutionality, the dynamics of political rivalries, the influence of lobbyists, the accommodations suggested by other treaty parties, the skills of the negotiators, the capacity to engage in extended (over many years) negotiations, and the importance of the subject, particularly as viewed by the Senate Committee on Foreign Relations, which jealously protects its authority to recommend to the full Senate and subsequently to the President that the terms of the agreement are consistent with the national interest. The separation of powers principle of the Constitution works to prevent an overly hasty or improvident treaty proposal by the Chief Executive.[4] This principle can also, particularly when the Office of the President is with one party, with a majority of the Senate Committee on Foreign Relations being held by the opposing party, result in almost complete deadlock.

Chart 2. Scorecard on a Core Group of Multilateral Treaties (as of December 2003)

Title & Date	*USA Signed*	*USA Ratified*	*Contracting Parties*
Genocide Convention, 9 Dec 1948	1948	1988	130
Elimination of All Forms of Racial Discrimination, 7 March 1966	1996	1994	156
International Covenant on Economic, Social, and Cultural Rights,16 Dec 1966	1977	No	142
International Covenant on Civil and Political Rights, 16 Dec 1966	1977	1992	144
Optional Protocol to the International Covenant on Civil and Political Rights, 16 Dec 1966 (Competence and access to Human Rights Committee)	No	No	95
Second Optional Protocol to the International Covenant on Civil and Political Rights, 15 Dec 1989 (Abolition of Death Penalty)	No	No	44
Convention on the Elimination of All Forms of Discrimination Against Women, 18 Dec 1979	1980	No	165
Optional Protocol to the Convention on the Elimination of All Forms of Discrimination Against Women, 6 Oct 1999 (Competence and Access to Human Rights Committee)	No	No	5
Convention Against Torture and Other Cruel, Inhuman or Degrading Treatment or Punishment, 1 Dec 1984	1988	1994	119
Convention on the Rights of the Child,	1955	No	191
20 Nov 1989 Convention Relating to the Status of Refugees, 28 July 1951	No	No	136
Protocol Relating to the Status of Refugees, 31 Jan 1967	No	1968	135
International Convention for the Suppression of Terrorist Bombing, 15 Dec 1997	1998	No	8 (58 signatories)
Rome Statute of the International Criminal Court, 17 July 1998	Dec 2000	No	89 (139 signatories)
Convention on Prohibitions or Restrictions on the Use of Certain Conventional Weapons Which May be Deemed to be Excessively Injurious or to Have Indiscriminate Effects, 10 Oct 1980	1982	1995	9
Convention on the Prohibition of the Development, Production, Stockpiling and Use of Chemical Weapons and Their Destruction, 30 Nov 1982	1992	1997	135
Comprehensive Nuclear Test-Ban Treaty, 10 Sept 1996	1996	No	56
Convention on the Prohibition of the Use, Stockpiling, Production and Transfer of Anti-Personnel Mines and on Their Destruction, 18 Sept 1997	No	No	96 (133 signatories)

Kyoto Protocol to the U.N. Framework Convention on Climate Change, 11 Dec 1997	1998	No	177 (84 signatories)
Rio de Janeiro Convention on Biological Diversity, 5 June 1992	1993	No	177
U.N. Convention to Combat Desertification in Those Countries Experiencing Serious Drought and/or Desertification, Particularly in Africa, 14 Oct 1994	1994	No	167
Treaty Banning Nuclear Weapon Tests in the Atmosphere, in Outer Space and Under Water, 5 August 1963	1963	1963	124
Treaty on Principles Governing the Activities of States in the Exploration and Use of Outer Space, Including the Moon and Other Celestial Bodies 27 Jan 1967	1967	1967	95
Agreement on Rescue of Astronauts, the Return of Astronauts and the Return of Objects Launched into Outer Space, 22 April 1968	1968	1968	87
Convention on International Liability for Damage Caused by Space Objects, 29 March 1972	1972	1973	80
Convention on Registration of Objects Launched into Outer Space, 14 Jan 1976	1976	1976	43
Agreement Governing the Activities of States on the Moon and Other Celestial Bodies, 18 Dec 1979	No	No	9
United Nations Convention on the Law of the Sea, Montego Bay, 10 Dec 1982	Yes 1994 (Part XI Revised: Seabed Mining)	No	144
Convention on the Prohibition of the Development, Production and Stockpiling of Bacteriological (Biological) and Toxin Weapons and in Their Destruction, 10 April 1972	1972	1975	143
Convention on Long-Range Transboundary Air Pollution, 13 Nov 1979	1979	1983	45
Inter-American Convention Against Terrorism, 3 June 2002	No	No	No
International Convention for the Suppression of Terrorist Bombings, 1997			Entered into Force 2001 with 22 Ratifications

It may be noted in passing that a cooperative President and Congress can avoid such a situation through the use of the legislative process. By a majority vote of both houses and the approval of the President, an "Executive Agreement" can neutralize the two-thirds vote rule governing the Senate's advise and consent power. This procedure replaces the need for a presidential ratification of a formal treaty. As in so many other issues involving the implementation of importance international issues, the political wisdom or justification of such an approach must be resolved.

The foregoing depends on what course of conduct at any particular time rises to the level of a "national interest." Since this term is characterized by its elasticity when applied domestically, it may also be employed, for want of a more precisely identified or carefully considered term, by a State as it perceives a real or an imaginary threat emanating from a foreign source.

3. OTHER SOURCES OF INTERNATIONAL LAW

It is easier to identify the other sources of international law than it is achieve agreement as to the substance of this area of law. The world community, unlike States, does not possess a formal legislative process. The United Nations, however, through the unanimous resolutions of the General Assembly and the Security Council, creates expectations that these decisions will be complied with. They have been identified as "soft law" as contrasted with the "hard law" of treaties.

Article 38 of the Statute of the International Court of Justice provides that customary international law and the general principles of law recognized by civilized nations constitute sources which may be considered by it. They are commonly treated as valid general sources. Since they do not speak for themselves it is necessary for practitioners to identify their content. As a result a great variety of views are expressed as to the substantive content of customary international law and of law's general principles. Even so, such common practices have evolved either other time or in some instances quite rapidly. When identified and accepted they serve as valid sources.

Uncertainly as to the substance of all international law irrespective of its source is clarified through the decisions of courts and the publications of highly qualified writers. These two resources have been identified as subsidiary means for determining the rules of law.

In many areas the rules of international law are sufficiently clear, such as the rights and duties of diplomatic and consular officials. They may be quite controversial as in the meaning of "armed attack" as used in Article 51 of the Charter. Different approaches are identified in Chapter IX.

International law has the capacity, like domestic or national law, to adjust to or cope with the conditions and circumstances of the times. The impact of science and technology has fashioned new international law for such subjects, among others, as outer space, the ocean, Antarctica, the human environment, warfare and armed conflict, national security (arms control and disarmament), business transactions, intellectual property, arbitration, civil and commercial litigation, claims of States for sovereign immunity from foreign demands, the diplomatic protection of persons and property, the accountability of international organizations, cultural heritage law, international law in national courts, international monetary law, the international regulation of securities, economic sanctions, international water resource law, and within the field of human rights law, such subjects as displaced persons, refugees, and the rights of women and children. (See *Chart 3. United States Department of State, Office of the Legal Advisor.*)

Chart 3. United States Department of State Office of the Legal Advisor: Functional Offices

Arms Control and Verification
Consular Affairs
Diplomatic Law and Litigation
Economic and Business Affairs
Human Rights and Refugees
International Crimes and Investment Disputes
- Extradition
- Narcotics
- Terrorism

Nonproliferation Affairs

Oceans, International Environmental and Scientific Affairs
- Outer Space
- Polar Areas
- Transboundary Air Pollution

Political-Military Affairs

Private International Law
- International Business Transactions
- Child Abduction

Public Diplomacy and Public Affairs
- Educational and Cultural Exchanges
- Holocaust Era Assets
- Protection of Cultural Patrimony

Treaty Affairs

United Nations Affairs
- Human Rights, International Criminal Tribunals, Peacekeeping, Rights of Women, Space Law, International Court of Justice (World Court)

All of the foregoing involve transnational activities. Such activities produced the modern condition of a globalization of sovereignty. In the real world States must look at these subjects from a global perspective. Multilateralism has replaced unilateralism as the preferred approach to the management of international relations.

DISCUSSION QUESTIONS

1. National sovereignty occupies a central place in identifying the rights and duties of States. Compare the way in which sovereignty was used and interpreted in the 17th Century with today.
2. What international documents, including but not limited to treaties, must be consulted to learn about "Human Rights"?
3. Several examples were provided in support of the view that international law is expanding to new areas. How do these, and others which you deem relevant, change the contours and direction of a nation's foreign policy?
4. Until the recent development of international and regional criminal courts there were great differences in the manner in which international and national laws were enforced. Does the problem of enforcement derogate from the existence of international law?
5. Why do international lawyers spend so much time examining the subject of "customary international law?"

NOTES

1. J.L. BRIERLY, THE LAW OF NATIONS, 6th ed., 57 (1963, SALMOND, JURISPUDENCE 31).

2. Article 38.

3. 1155 UNTS 331. The United States signed the treaty on 24 April 1970 but is not a party to this instrument. However, it contains much customary law with which the United States must comply. It entered into force on 27 January 1980.

4. For a recent assessment of the constitutional bases for a President's authority, see S.B. PRAKASH and M.D. RAMSEY, "The Executive Power over Foreign Affairs," 111 *Yale L.J.* No. 1, 231 (2001).

5. See, for example, "Multilateralism in International Law: Its Role and Limits: A United States—European Symposium," 11 EJIL, No. 1, 1 (2000).

Chapter II

U.S. Foreign Policy

1. BASIC POLICIES

United States foreign policy focuses, with different degrees of emphasis, on the following: First, a key concern is national security supported by a requisite military capability. Second, with diminishing nation-based natural resources, including both ocean-based and land-based, attention must be given to more distant resources. Third, the nation benefits from its commitment to democratically oriented essential civil and political rights and liberties. Suitable respect for internationally recognized Human Rights and for treaty obligations are essential elements.[1] Fourth, U.S. foreign policy must also take into account the roles assigned to the United Nations and other international intergovernmental organizations, including the well-considered views of the members, particularly those who share democratic values. Fifth, a successful U.S. foreign policy depends on an astute appraisal of the motivations and capabilities of other States possessing large populations and abundant resources, particularly when they may feel threatened by governmental actions carried on by the United States.

An influential advisor to President Bush, writing in February 2000, singled as key elements of American foreign policy: First, a strong military establishment. Second, economic growth with a stable monetary system. Third, the renewing of "strong and intimate relationships with allies who share American values and can thus share the burden of promoting peace, prosperity, and freedom."[2] Fourth, a focus on comprehensive relationships with such countries as Russia and China "that can and will mold the character of the international political system."[3] Fifth, dealing decisively with States protecting terrorists and engaging in the development of weapons of mass destruction.[4]

For another assessment, see U.S. Foreign Policies Goals Chart 4.

U.S. FOREIGN POLICY GOALS
Percentage who say the following should be a 'very important' goal of the United States.

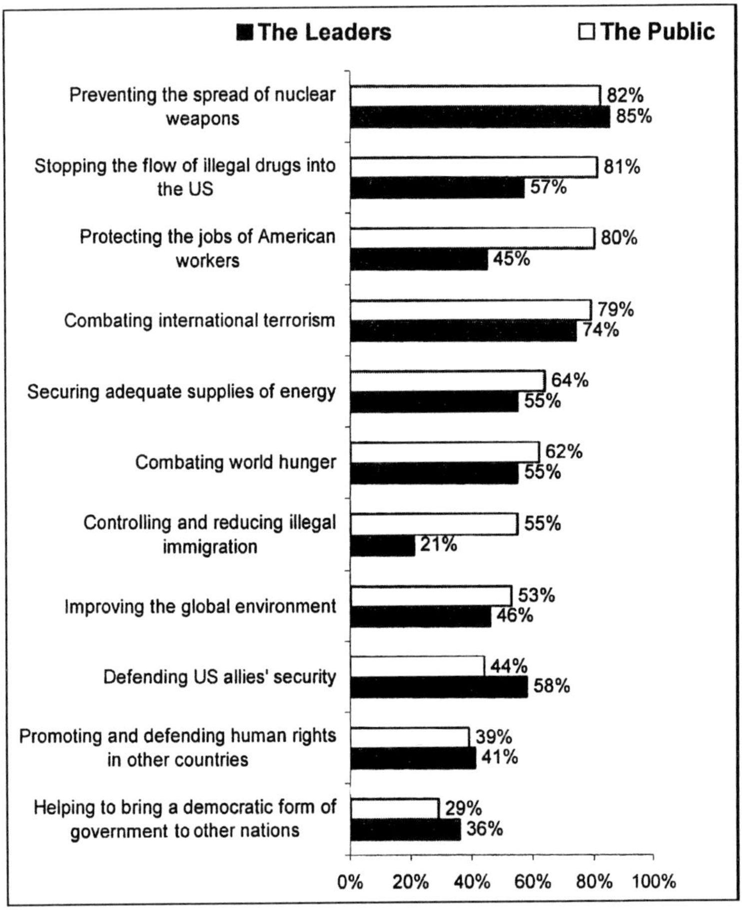

Chart 4.

Source: Chicago Council on Foreign Relations, November 1998 survey of 1,507 Citizens and 379 government leaders.

Foreign policy, like international law is not static. New threats to a nation's well-being may require a refocusing of foreign policy attention. The extent of the problem may bring into play new friends and foes. Following September 11, 2001 there was a major shift in direction. The United States made a critical effort to enlist Pakistan as a major ally, thereby causing new concerns in India. A new cast of "uneasy coalitionists" entered into the limelight.[5] While their motivations, the nature of their public expressions, and the degree of actual support varied, yet one could not casually dismiss the need for similar, and, common approaches.[6]

In recent years public leaders having an interest in foreign policy have been obliged to take into account the relationship between their States and the United Nations and the ever-growing numbers of other international intergovernmental organizations. For a State to play a meaningful role it is now obliged to adopt to the multilateral relationships that have, with increasing frequency, been referred to as globalization. Unilateral exponents, relying heavily on the expression "national sovereignty," have been restricted by the wants and needs and the interests and values of the times.[7]

The foregoing large-scale foreign policy goals may be viewed in the context of the use of the ocean. The interest in security is furthered by rules advancing freedom of navigation and freedom of over-flight in given areas and in given situations. The needs of commerce and economic security are also furthered by rules requiring freedom of navigation. Fisheries as an offshore resource, are also to be protected. Guarantees of access or limitations on access can be perceived as beneficial to both advanced States and those in the mode of development. The protection of marine ecosystems contributes to the promotion of environmental interests.

The considerations applicable to the ocean also apply to those who engage in the peaceful exploration, use, and exploitation of air space and outer space. For example, safe transit is a common need.

The implementation of a government's foreign policy is often delegated to lower level executive department officials. One example is the position taken recently by the Undersecretary of State on Oceans. His focus was on the 1982 Law of the Sea Convention, which has not been ratified by the United States. The Undersecretary in describing the terms of the agreement, referred to the fact that its implementation would cost money, would necessitate a new international bureaucracy, and would deprive signatory States of some of their sovereignty.

He asked, in determining U.S. policy, "whether costs outweigh the benefits?" whether signing a treaty "amounts to a net loss or a net gain in terms of our national interests?" and whether and how "do we convince a skeptical American public and the U.S. Congress that treaties sometimes represent the most efficient and cost-effective way of advancing and protecting those interests?"[8]

For international lawyers an important and formal proof of a State's foreign policy can be found in the signature and ratification of an intergovernmental agreement, followed by good faith implementation or its rejection. The agreement may be either multilateral or bilateral.

2. THE RELATIONSHIP BETWEEN FOREIGN POLICY AND INTERNATIONAL LAW

International lawyers, intrigued and even guided by the prospect of the world rule of law in foreign affairs, rely on the stabilizing effect of known principles, standards and rules. Exponents of a more free-wheeling approach to a nation's foreign policy, and relying upon periodic and novel assessments of asserted national interests, sometimes find it inconvenient to accept or apply international law. This constitutes a challenge to the proposition that conformity to basic and shared world interests also serves to further national interests. Thus, the objects identified with the rule of law in foreign affairs will vary from time to time.

If foreign policy is perceived as the carefully formulated, but loosely structured, engine of a State's internationally oriented activities, based often, but not always on continuity, then international law can be viewed as a built-in regulator imposing limits on the operation of the machine. The function of the regulator is to facilitate the effective operation of the engine, while at the same time preventing the machine from engaging in activities which are beyond its inherent capabilities.

Another way to compare the relationship between law and policy is to treat law as a football gridiron with its fixed boundaries within which play is governed by accepted rules. The contestants are expected to play according to the rules. Breaches negate gains. It may not, in a well-played game, by necessary to have recourse to inhibitory actions. Foreign policy and international law when seeking common goals may not require restraining influences. The difficulty, as observed by John Stewart Mill in *On Liberty*, has been "to induce men of strong bodies or minds to pay obedience to any rules which required them to control their impulses." When the law is violated an official may have to blow a whistle.

A nation's foreign policy, most respected when it is the product of a popular consensus, can result from narrower, dogmatic, partisan, and, in any event, authoritative decisions. In the last instance such policy can be quickly expressed, uncertainly identified, and wide-ranging in scope. Political figures operating on a daily basis find it easier to modify policy positions than to depart from international legal commitments. Law is characterized by a durability not expected of politics. For example, it would be more difficult to abandon the meaning of a treaty than to advance a new policy on global warming.

In any event foreign policies will require refinement, including the normal test of whether such policies conform to the norms of international law.

In today's world the regulator seeks to prevent the machine from trying to make claims based on out-dated and disappearing views of national sovereignty. Football players must stay within bounds. This is to say that a State, by reason of its sovereignty, may not assert that this legal condition enables it to pursue a self-selected course of conduct in disregard of the internationally recognized rights of other internationally recognized legal persons. Heads of State, by reason of their functions, are more inclined to be influenced by the theory of sovereignty than other governmental officials.

Though this legal restraint on national activities is not always immediately perceived, for example, by Heads of State, who, perhaps, are harboring plans to acquire by force territory belonging to another State, or who may have the intent and capability of killing persons entitled to Human Rights' guarantees, yet it is a fact that international law today does impose extensive restraints on such conduct. The law of humanitarian intervention is increasing in stature.

International law should not be perceived only as a means to prevent identified anti-social conduct, or to punish perpetrators. Modern international law contains principles and rules whereby a State acting alone or in cooperation with others can advance commonly supported highly beneficial activities. Protection of the earth's ecosystem is an example.

Nonetheless, there are informed persons who, self-describing themselves as "realists," minimize the role of international law (sometimes denying its existence) and denigrate its utility. Philosophically they support the freedom of action of States, which, in their opinion may justifiably determine what behavior is best suited to a States' "self-interest." This term, whose ambiguous and uncertain content is carefully guarded by the "realists," thus serves as the basis for adopting preferences between competing interests and favored policies. It is invoked to justify the claim of unilateralism.

Such unilateralistic behavior allows for *ad hoc* or selective courses of conduct with preferred material consequences. The problem with this is that such an approach does not contribute to the needs of society in general, and to States in their mutual relationships. The latter, no less than humans, need sufficiently clear guidance in the form of legal principles, standards, and rules. Through them there is a format for orderly, predictable, and socially cohesive relationships.

The case for international law is also based on the fact that people, without regard for boundary lines separating State from State, and without regard to their political, cultural, economic, and social outlooks, do accept that in many areas of human endeavor there are common or community-wide goals and interests.

This observation must be weighed in connection with international law's constantly enlarging area of governance, and particularly with respect to the international law of Human Rights. It must also be weighed in light of the constantly diminishing role of the Westphalian concept of sovereignty.

In the 17th Century, at a time of international anarchy, the concept of national sovereignty offered protection to the legal right of a State to continue its existence without foreign interference.[9]

Under the influence of globalization, including a perception of common inter-State interests, and the creation of such world institutions as the United Nations, States have seen fit to hold in abeyance or to give up some claims of sovereignty. There is no doubt as to the general direction being taken with respect to claims of unlimited national sovereignty. The present need, which will be the subject of many which follow, is to demonstrate to States, including the United States, the wisdom of adopting community perspectives.

The proposition is a simple one: In a world of increasing interrelatedness mutual accommodation is required. This can enhance benefits. Community well-being thereby reaches higher levels. The adoption of community perspectives best serves a State's realization of its own narrower preferences and its larger self-interest.

This concept was captured in the 19th Century by the American jurist, Joseph Story, who wrote:

> The true foundation on which the administration of international law must rest, is, that the rules which are to govern, are those which arise from mutual interest and utility, from a sense of the inconvenience which would result from a contrary doctrine, and from a sort of moral necessity to do justice, in order that justice may be done to us in return.[10]

From a historical perspective it is worth noting that the concept of sovereignty had foundations in the need for a Head of State to exercise unlimited power. This served to keep a royal person firmly seated on his or her majestic throne. It also enabled the State to fend off foreign enemies. With the development of national legislatures and independent courts, and with each having a measure of independence resulting from the lessening of the royal prerogative, the claim that a Head of State was above the law began to disappear. Even so, at the turn of the twenty-second century President Augusto Pinochet of Chile and President Slobadan Milosevic of Yugoslavia have asserted that they were above the law—a claim also asserted by the members of Adolph Hitler's cabinet when they were named as defendants at Nuremberg.

3. GLOBALIZATION AND THE DIRECTION TAKEN BY INTERNATIONAL LAW

At present the condition of globalization, driven by the world money markets, by advances in science and technology, and by the revolution of world information systems, has given direction to international law. This has been particularly noticeable in the areas of national security and communications. Somewhat earlier, and following World War II, a new and stronger sense of human values produced a concern for the protection and advancement of Human Rights, once marked largely by the anti-slavery movement. Growing out of these new developments has come an awareness of the need for new dispute resolving institutions. New courts are a totem of the time.

A sense of globalism has contributed to an understanding of policy choices. Policies result from the interplay of many competing preferences. They can be derived from a nation's positive vision of the future where such abstractions as national interest, well-being, security, harmonious relations, world order, and the universality of basic values are believed to exist and can be realized. In such a fashion general terms are employed to identify a country's outlook toward international relations.

Foreign policy is often identified as an element of domestic policy. Encompassed are the prospects that the two parties will have different outlooks and that within each party there may be differences. These differences exist despite the observation that "Politics ends at the waters edge." The nature and importance of any problem influenced by powerful lobbies, will provide answers.

A country's foreign policy can also be identified by examining its more specific "wish list," affirmative or negative. In the United States voters' preferences as understood, guided and implemented by the political branches of the national government, supply examples. Specific illustrations are in steady flux since they are bombarded constantly by changing conditions. Those which may appear to be fairly constant receive different emphasis over time.

Some of the affirmative specifics are the international exchange of goods, services, and ideas, access to and use of the world's natural resources, the exploration, use, and exploitation of common areas such as the ocean, international air space, and other space, and the preservation and protection of Human Rights. Others are considered in this book. They are the protection of the disarmament and arms control, elimination of land mines, establishment of international tribunals, control of terrorism, and the amelioration of the crisis in the Middle East.

A nation's foreign policy must take into account the means available for pursuing and achieving the desired goals. The choice will depend on the perceived gravity of a situation including the time-span believed to be available for decisions. In other instances, where the immediacy of a response is not critical, there still may be a national decision to "go-it-alone."

Countries are not entirely free to determine which mode best serves their interests. By agreement they may have limited their choices. Through memberships in international intergovernmental organizations, such as the United Nations, and regional organizations, unlimited freedom of action is foresworn.

In addition to the overarching legal obligations contained in the UN Charter there are scores of essentially universal international agreements as well as the customary norms of international law, such as laws or customs of war, that condition national choices.

These factors bring into focus the concepts of multilateralism and unilateralism as competing national options and the practical consequences resulting from the adoption of one or the other. In making choices it is noteworthy that a country frequently adopts one with reference to a given subject; it may take a different road when other specific policies are being determined and subsequently implemented. For example, States embark on unilateral policies when they consider their national security to be in peril and where they are persuaded, rightly or wrongly, that the principle of collective security has broken down. When the privileges and immunities of diplomats are under review, however, States find it desirable to proceed multilaterally.

The choice between multilateralism and unilateralism cannot be based entirely on utilitarian considerations even though they may appear to be dominant. A suitable respect for democratic principles including Human Rights opens a wider vista.

The following comparisons may be enlightening. Unilateralism, with its emphasis on national sovereignty, holds that States are free to choose their foreign policies. This outlook is favored by States well-positioned because of their economic, military, scientific, and technological attributes. Unilateral predispositions must be contemplated with considerable care when equally positioned countries holding opposing views and the give and take of diplomacy is unavailing.

Since no State is an island they have no hesitancy in seeking the help of a wider community, when they consider themselves to be at risk. Multinationalists believe that, while some national interests and needs are of vital importance others are not, and in order to avoid potential conflict they support diplomacy and accommodation.

Unilateralists, perhaps persuaded by illusions of hegemony, may consider that there is no particular need to be sensitive to the wishes and desires of much of the outside world. Sometimes labeled neoisolationists they tend to consider many portions of the globe as trouble prone, whose populations are resentful of American opulence, are too militant in requests for economic bailouts, and in any event lacking are lacking in gratitude for the benefits which have been received.

Multilateralists object to such a characterization of the real world. They assert that States benefit when they have the respect of their peers and that "strong-arm" diplomatic tactics are counterproductive. Nations as well as individuals have egos.

International organizations are not entirely accepted by the unilateralists. They are obliged to participate in such institutions in order to contest multilateral views which they deem prejudicial. When vast majorities of States arrive at international agreements, the unilateralists have endeavored to prevent the implementation of such accords and have entered to prevent the implementation of such accords and have entered into side agreements with participants in order to prevent their wide-ranging application. Multilateralists uphold the UN system and other international and regional intergovernmental organizations. They contend that collective judgments on foreign policies provide a more just and a more reliable basis for the conduct of international relations.

American advocates of unilateralism take the position that other countries, including members of the UN, have the burden of proving that world and regional organization are relevant to and beneficial to the interests of the United States. Multilateralists urge that the terms of the Charter and all major international agreements, particularly since the United States is a party, demonstrate quite clearly their relevance.

Unilateralism and multilateralism meet at a critical juncture when there is a challenge in particular cases to the UN's mandate to advance world order. This challenge is especially acute when it appears necessary to ideal with huge, but potential, harm.

The United States has promulgated and implemented multilateralism when the threat has come from terrorists and rogue States believed to possess WMD. The Iraq crisis brought the differences between the two to "High Noon." In that situation what at first was full support for the decisions of the Security Council later deteriorated into defeat for multilateralism leaving only the United States, the United Kingdom, Australia, and Spain as supporters of the Security Council Resolution 1441. The debates revealed substantial legal differences on matters of substance and procedure. The issues were fully drawn and the proponents took their stands.

Aside from the crisis at the UN as result of the Iraq conflict multilateralism may serve the interests of both "have" and "have not" States. The former may obtain the benefit of a more orderly world and enhance their globalist needs. The latter may be able to benefit from greater attention to their developmental aspirations.

Support for many particular globalist and multilateral policies has been revealed in polls taken in the United States. Such findings to be effective must be shown to be timely, supportive, and politically powerful. Polls, unlike voters, cast no ballots.

It is possible to argue that a State must keep open the option of either unilateralism or multilateralism. Theoretically multilateralism may be viewed as better suited then unilateralism to deal both with terrorism, possession of WMD, and massive violations of Human Rights, as well as more prosaic international issues. It in fact failed that test in 2002–2003 when unilateral responses on the part of States taking negative positions prevented the exercise of collective security.

The multilateral approach to Iraq in 2002–2003 was a mixed one. With regard to the application of collective military sanctions it did not prevail. However, following the military victory of the allied forces the Security Council remained the forum for the rebuilding of Iraq, including relief from oil export restrictions. The Iraq experience may point to an important fact, namely, whenever collective security based on multilateralism fails, recourse will be had to unilateral policies. Further, when collective security concerns are replaced by the need for humanitarian assistance and nation-building, multilateral policies will be resumed.

Unfortunately, a habit has developed in some States to engage in unilateral preferences even though the wisdom of such approaches may be suspect.

A. Concerns Respecting Judicial Training

This upwelling of international activity, with the ever-present prospect for international disputes, has raised concerns, including in the United States, whether tribunals, staffed with domestic personnel, were sufficiently trained in international law. The question is whether existing judges have the background to apply international law, both treaty-based and customary, in matters before them. In the United States the American Society of International Law, assisted by a grant from the Hauser Foundation, has enlisted the support of members of the profession, including U.S. Supreme Court Justice Sandra Day O'Connor, to conduct seminars for the judiciary. International law bench reference books have been distributed to more than 1200 judges. A more long-range project has been to encourage the study of international law and foreign policy in the colleges and law schools of the country.

The concern over judicial ineptitude respecting issues of international law and foreign policy is not reserved exclusively to the United States. In 1998 the Committee on International Law in National Courts of the International Law Association stated that there must be "ways and means of ensuring that national courts receive all necessary assistance in enabling them to identify and apply correctly rules of international law."[11]

There is, in addition, the need to affirm at the world level, and particularly in those countries which have experienced long periods of turmoil under autocratic leaders, a "sense of justice."[12] International lawyers can contribute to this goal by insisting on "accountability for war criminals and violators of fundamental human rights via criminal prosecution or other mechanisms of accountability."[13] The rehabilitation of national judicial systems will be facilitated by the constant reminder that their utility depends on the presence of a sense of justice.

B. Concerns Respecting National Leadership

Concerns of a different and equally important nature have been raised in the United States as to the wisdom of the political outlooks held by influential members of the Congress and by the President and his foreign policy and legal advisors. This relates to the emphasis placed, always assertedly, on the national interest, by such personages as they view alternative approaches—multilateral or unilateral. Often, and perhaps far too often, such leaders despite the availability of refined scientific information and thoughtful political advice, have failed to take positive leadership roles to mitigate or prevent dangerous man-made and natural hazards.

While admitting that governance is not an exact science, and acknowledging that political turmoil is often seen as the norm in American politics, yet it seems, with regard to many international law and foreign policy issues that the United States would be better served if it were to listen to world public opinion and take into account the wise observations of Joseph Story.

Further, the failures of the world's most powerful State to achieve world-community oriented policies are not restricted to either the Republican or Democratic party. The fault cannot lie in the American system of education, which at the University level is the highest in the world. Nor can the inadequacies be charged to a failure in communications, where, again the American competence and capability is unmatched in the rest of the world. In the United States unwise foreign policy, in the last analysis, is the fault of the party in power. The buck stops there.

In weighing the respective areas of responsible leadership, as well as those where defects are perceived to exist, the standard must be the mutuality of benefit that can flow only from a policy of world and regional cooperation. Mutuality of benefit does not mean a foreign policy in which American primary security interests are in any way imperiled. Moreover, such peril must be real and both long and short range. Further, the extent or measure of any peril must be capable of proof, both objective and subjective. In a *bona fide* examination of such proof the exclusive views of the

United States must be compared with and conditioned by the views of the other States, especially comparable States, that are confronted by the same challenges and circumstances.[14]

Several examples come to mind. The United States is clearly the world's major outer space-resource State, but it has its competitors. The relevant States have accommodated competing interests respecting the exploration, use, and exploitation of the space environment based on the agreed principle of equal access to it. The United States and other States, working with the International Telecommunication Union, have devised means whereby broadcasts from satellites can take place. Unreasonable interferences, though feared, have not occurred.

A national foreign policy balance sheet can identify the areas in which United States interests could be imperiled, but, where the United States after due consideration has determined that a multilateral policy of accommodation is in its true interest. A good balance depends on membership in universal international intergovernmental organizations, and in regional organizations, including the United Nations, the World Court, Latin American bodies, the Latin America Free Trade Association, NATO, the Conference on Security and Cooperation in Europe, Asian entities, and others. They include membership in and support for international legal regimes applicable to such non-sovereign areas as outer space, air space, the ocean, and Antarctica. There is support for stable diplomatic and consular procedures as reflected in ratification of the two relevant 1961 Vienna treaties. Although the United States has not ratified the 1969 Vienna Convention on the Law of Treaties, it is a signatory, and, through observable practice, can be considered to be supportive of its terms.

C. Human Rights

In the vast area of Human Rights, where it might have been expected that the United States would play a leading operational role, the record has been spotted. While it may be justifiably proud of its leadership role in the formulation of the 1948 Universal Declaration of Human Rights and the 1966 International Covenant of Civil and Political Rights, and, despite the numerous interpretations and conditioning statements made in 1988 when it ratified the 1948 Genocide Convention, it has failed to give its support to numerous other Human Rights Conventions which, in each case, have been ratified by well over 100 countries. These include the 1966 International Covenant on Economic, Social, and Cultural Rights (142), the 1979 Convention on the Elimination of All Forms of Discrimination Against Women (165), the 1951 Convention Relating to the Status of Refugees (136), as well as others.[15]

4. IS U.S. FOREIGN POLICY BENEFITING AMERICANS?

In assessing the issue of whether American foreign policy is serving the important interests of its citizens, there are strongly held views that it is not. Examples, which will be identified below, include dealing with terrorists, reaching international agreement on prohibiting land mines, demands for new international criminal tribunals, protection of the human environment from greenhouse gases, arms control and disarmament, and peace in the Middle East.

In each of these instances there have been long-ranging diplomatic negotiations. Because of the negative outlooks of essential leaders the potential benefits contained in proposed agreements have not been realized.

5. UNITED STATES COMPLIANCE WITH TREATY OBLIGATIONS AND INTERNATIONAL LAW

Moreover, the United States has engaged in outright violations of its treaty obligations and its own statutes.

A. The U.N. Annual Assessments

The United States has been for many years, and remains at the present, in violation of its treaty with the United Nations to pay annual assessments. In the minds of many Americans the deadbeat title given to describe the situation in 1999 was correct.[16] While recent efforts have been made to reduce the debt, which in 1999 exceeded $1 billion, the fact remains that the U.S. had failed to live up to its formal promise. It is perhaps the case that the U.S. was not reelected in 2001 to the U.N. Human Rights Commission because of its long-term delinquency in dues.[17]

B. 1961 Vienna Convention on Consular Procedures

Recently the United States was found guilty of violating its duty under the 1961 Vienna Convention dealing with consular procedures. In its June 27, 2001 decision the World Court ordered the United States to review all cases in which aliens were imprisoned in the United States to determine if the prisoners had been advised, as aliens, of their right to consult with a consular official of their country at the time of the prosecution. Germany has asked the Court to require the United States to promise to comply in the future with the treaty and to pay compensation to the families of the prisoners.[18]

In a prosecution in Arizona the accused, 10 years after their arrest, learned of their right to consular protections prior to trial. Having been convicted they raised this right on appeal. The appeals court held, under the U.S. judicial doctrine of "procedural default," that this right had been waived, since it had not been argued at the trial level.

In its decision of June 27, 2001, in the case of Germany against the United States, the World Court held that the foregoing rule of domestic law could not be used to justify violations of international law.

The World Court case established a rule as to the binding force of an order for provisional measures. The order of March 3, 1999 was received by the Governor of the state of Arizona on the day prior to the execution date. He disregarded it. In its June 2001 holding the World Court stated that its order was binding and that both Arizona, and the United States, as responsible for Arizona's conduct, was at fault.

In 2003 a similar case involving Mexican nationals who were facing death sentences in the United States was instituted. The government of Mexico asked the World Court to issue "provisional" or "interim" measures in order to prevent the execution of the accused prior to a final determination of the cases on their merits. In a unanimous decision the Court also held that the United States met inform it of "all measure taken in implementation" of the binding order. The Court stated that it was not passing judgment on the right of the United States to impose death sentences for serious crimes, and that the court was not acting as a court of criminal appeal. The foregoing holding was not, according to the Court, to be viewed as prejudging the sovereign right of the United States to determine the nature of its criminal justice system. Acceptance of the Court's ruling will affect the disposition of 48 other cases affecting Mexican nationals being prosecuted for murder in the United States.

C. Extraterritorial Kidnappings

In another case, decided in 2001 by the 9th Circuit Court of Appeals, it was held that the United States violated international law when it sent kidnappers to Mexico to apprehend and return to the United States a Mexican national, who was charged with killing an American citizen in Mexico. The American court held that this conduct violated international Human Rights conventions, and that the United States, as a sovereign nation could not claim sovereign immunity for the acts of its agents. The accused had a right to remain in his country as a Human Right, and his forcible removal violated international law which is a part of U.S. law.[19]

DISCUSSION QUESTIONS

1. Several examples have been given of U.S. foreign policies. Which appear to have the greatest durability?
2. Does international law restrain the choices available to States in the adoption of foreign policies?
3. List from one to five principles of U.S. foreign policy to which you would give your support, and explain the priority assigned to your choices.
4. Traditional allies of the United States have expressed dismay at a large number of the foreign policies implemented by the Clinton and Bush administrations. What can be done to ameliorate such concerns?
5. Review the proposal for seminars on international law for American judges and assess its validity. Should such seminars be conducted also for highly placed officials in the legislative and executive branches of federal government?

NOTES

1. See generally, HENRY J. STEINER and PHILIP ALSTON, INTERNATIONAL HUMAN RIGHTS IN CONTEXT: LAW, POLITICS, MORALS (2nd ed. 2000); and for an opposing position, J.S. WATSON, THEORY AND REALITY IN THE INTERNATIONAL PROTECTION OF HUMAN RIGHTS (1999).

2. Condoleezza Rice, "Promoting the National Interest," 79 *Foreign Affairs*, No. 1, 46–47 (January–February 2000).

3. *Ibid.*

4. *Ibid.*

5. John Hughes, "In New U.S. Foreign Policy, Unlikely Friends and Foes," *The Christian Science Monitor*, 9, December 5, 2001. He noted that Somalia, Sudan, and Yemen, which have harbored terrorists joined in denunciations of terrorism.

6. Steven Mufson, "American Foreign Policy Suddenly Shifts Course," *International Herald Tribune*, 3, September 28, 2001 (from *Washington Post* Service). He referred to new support by the United States for Russia's campaign against Chechnya.

7. J. Carey, "The Struggle for Law in the United Nations," *Proceedings of the American Branch of the International Law Association*, 1999–2000, p. 41 (2000).

8. Frank E. Loy, Undersecretary of State on Oceans. Speech given at the University of Virginia Conference on Oceans Law and Policy (May 11, 1999).

9. D. PHILPOTT, REVOLUTIONS IN SOVEREIGNTY (2001).

10. THE CONFLICT OF LAWS, 3rd edition, 45 (1864).

11. International Law Association, *Report of the Sixty-Eighth Conference* 677 (1998).

12. "Accountability and Judicial Response: Building Mechanisms for Post-Conflict Justice," 38th Strategy for Peace, U.S. Foreign Policy Policy Conference, *The Stanley Foundation*, 7 (1997).

13. *Ibid.*

14. W.H. Luers, "Choosing Engagement," 79 *Foreign Affairs*, 9 September/October 2000.

15. ANNE F. BAYEFSKY, THE U.N. HUMAN RIGHTS TREATY SYSTEM: UNIVERSALITY AT THE CROSSROADS (2001).

16. R. McMillion, "World's Biggest Deadbeat," *ABA Journal*, 88 (March 1999). The same concern has been expressed: "Isn't it tragic that our nation—the richest on Earth and with a long history of leadership at the United Nations—should be unable or unwilling to pay its fair share of the U.N. budget in a timely manner." A.P. Adams, Jr., President United Nations Association of the United States of America, 23 The *InterDependent* 2, No. 4 (Winter 1997–98).

17. In 2002 the United States was reelected to membership.

18. W. Hwang, "World Court Faults U.S. For Flouting Consular Treaty," 27 *The InterDependent*, No. 2, 10 (Summer 2001).

19. *Los Angeles Times*, A1, September 13, 2001.

Chapter III

Terrorism, Foreign Policy, and Law

1. INTRODUCTION

This Chapter deals with terrorism's threat to our way of life. We must decide how to be secure and how to enjoy the constitutional protections that have shaped our past.

The gravity of the threat has resulted in legislation allowing the use of armed force. Governmental officials, and the public at large, have consistently referred to the "war against terrorism."

New criminal statutes have been adopted and governmental orders have been issued calling for a variety of procedures for prosecuting alleged terrorists. It has become necessary to determine if international law, with its historic content dealing with the laws or customs of war, and international agreements to which the United States is a party, have application to those charged with acts of terrorism. As will be seen, the United States has not been consistent in the selection of its national courts for the prosecution of persons referred to as "unlawful combatants."

The United States in attacking terrorism has pursued a multilateral or global approach. For other key foreign policy issues the United States has opted for a unilateral approach. Should American foreign policy be consistent? Are there reasons why inconsistency may best serve our national interest? Will other countries accept such inconsistencies? The information provided in this and following chapters may assist you in deciding what is best for the United States as it examines the two approaches.

2. POSITIVE DISARRAY AS A RESPONSE TO GLOBALIZATION

It is unrealistic to think that the forces driving the conditions leading to globalization would not meet resistance. Change threatens ingrained preferences and ways of doing things. Globalization may be seen as the enemy of those who have much to lose from reconstituted circumstances.

Terrorism is clearly one response to globalization.[1] At this moment, Osama bin Laden can claim to be the primary and most notorious exponent of violent change. It is quite remarkable that one person could, with relatively limited immediate support from other persons, effectively challenge the larger flow of events and his formidable adversaries.

This "king of terror" is a private but privileged revolutionary. His claim to authority is not based on national sovereignty but upon the possession of a vast and passionate hatred of opposing values. He rallied his cohorts under the cry "let America leave the holy places of Islam." With the support of religious zealots, with organizational cohesiveness, and with skill in the selection of weaponry for his time and place he has engendered responses extending well beyond the imaginable limits of unintended consequences.

For the average American, it is difficult to understand what motivates people to become terrorists. The shocking events of September 11, 2001 created an abrupt awareness of their presence, their organizational capabilities, their multinational composition, the extent of their malice, and their ongoing capacity to produce enormous, and possibly unrivaled, harm. In the intervening months it has become evident that such terrorist leaders as Osama bin Laden have at least contemplated catastrophic harm to both persons, who held views contrary to theirs, and to property. Formed into relatively small but cohesive units, terrorists have demonstrated that they possess both the means and the will to act. Their deep-seated purpose is to obtain publicity for their cause and to acquire cohorts for future activities. The proliferation of home-grown terrorists has resulted from local conditions. The successes of the Al Qaeda have been a source of encouragement. Local leaders have had the responsibility for building their own infrastructures. The local successes, and there have been many in Asia, Europe, the United States, and in November 2002 in Kenya, and in May 2003 in Saudi Arabia, have been the product of a decentralized approach. These successes have, on the whole, been in democratically oriented countries; not in totalitarian States.

Theoretically all countries can be made the targets of terrorists, particularly if CBN weapons fall into the hands of desperate persons. However, the better targets are to be found in more permissive and wealthier countries. These are the countries which have produced, shared in, and benefited from globalism.

The events of September 11, 2001 galvanized the attention of the world on the role of the Taliban government in Afghanistan in providing support for Osama bin Laden's Al Qaeda. The latter through its domination of the Taliban, for all intents and purposes, was the country's government. It is a fact that the Taliban in the name of Afghanistan sent to and received diplomatic representatives from several States.

Although the role of Al Qaeda has caught the attention of people and has become singularly recognizable, this should not disguise the fact of the worldwide phenomenon of terrorism, with strong local institutional structures and goals, and with evident resources in personnel, money, and materials. Its global reach is expanding. It would be a monumental error to consider terrorists merely as a temporary, unrelated, loosely structured, and generally disorganized band of brigands, whose time will pass.

In addressing the dangers flowing from terrorism and the means for bringing it under control it is necessary to be aware of the social and political structure of terrorism. Al Qaeda's most notorious member is an expatriate national of Saudi Arabia, but high leadership positions have been held by Egyptians and by citizens of other countries.

Of those who were directly involved in the attacks which took place on September 11, 2001, almost all were nationals of Saudi Arabia. These had received technical training in Germany and in the United States. They were members of the relatively small Salafist (orWahhabi) sect of Islam, which recently has been expanding on a world-wide basis with assistance from Saudi officials and Osama bin Laden. While he has been the most dominant member of Al Qaeda, he does not have a hierarchal control of Muslim and other terrorists in far-flung portions of the globe. Al Qaeda is a loosely organized collection of extremists. It was never a monolithic organization.

Further, it would be wrong to assume that terrorism is an exclusive or even a primary concern of any single, ethnic, religious, or national group. A claim that terroristic activity is more likely to be exercised by persons because of such affiliations has been described as "racist."

President Bush has stated that "tens of thousands of trained terrorists are still at large. These enemies view the entire world as a battlefield, and we must pursue them wherever they are."[2] The enormity of the threat must be taken as the primary reason for dealing with present-day terrorism. This is not a situation where a normal "business as usual" approach has validity. A critically new outlook is required which is consistent with the termination of the on-going dangers of terrorism.

The problem for those who have been targeted for terroristic attacks, or who have experienced them, is to know how to cope with this phenomenon. If, as is believed, terrorism is one response to the fact of globalism, and since today's myriad of influences giving meaning and direction to globalism have shown no signs of abating, it is hard to believe that, both in the short and in the long run, globalism will fail to prevail. This fact, however, will not eliminate the real or imaginary grievances of those who engage in terrorism. They will maintain their beliefs and will seek to advance them through the application of force and violence on their targets of choice.

There are several options available to those who fear that their way of life is threatened by the conduct of terrorists. They may be pursued one at a time or collectively. The most dramatic is the American war on terrorists. Prosecutions are taking place in U.S. Federal District Courts. Plans for the ultimate disposition of "detainees" held at Guatanomo Bay are moving forward. Illegal aliens have been deported in large numbers. One of the grounds for engaging in the use of armed force against Iraq has been the presence in that country of supporters of Al Qaeda, although this has undergone serious challenge.

Another approach is to use peaceful means to improve the economic, political, and social conditions in areas which are underdeveloped and have experienced large-scale harms. Included would be the nation-building procedures now employed in Kosovo, Afghanistan, Pakistan, and Iraq.

One can only speculate as to the possibility, costs, and timeframe of such activities. It should be evident that such long-range changes are beyond the means of any one or a small group of countries. To be successful it would have to be an undertaking of the UN. Educational programs with exchanges of technicians, professionals, and teachers would be helpful. A clearer understanding of the world's religions evolved after 9/11. Changing outlooks, including an effort to cope with the economic exploitation of individuals living in the developing world, will have to be encouraged.

Those who embrace terrorism, as a response to their discontent, will seek to continue their activities, even though profound humanitarian and economic benefits can be made available to them. At this time there is a need to deal with terrorists, per se. How to proceed with individuals held by the United States, in particular, and other countries in general, must be analyzed and resolved.

There is much truth to the observation that issues which at the outset have strong political, and in the present situation, both historical, cultural, and religious facets, end up in a legal context. Since organized political authority maintains institutions to protect itself against threats to governments and to people who owe allegiance to such governments, the most immediate and the most probable response to the acts of terrorists is to seek their punishment. This response, which is a normal one, then raises further questions: by whom, where, and under what set of legal and moral principles, standards and rules? All will be influenced by factors of expediency and practicality.

When it comes to terrorists and terrorism special legal problems arise. This issue will be dealt with below. The problem is to determine in the context of September 11, 2001, whether the legal concepts of "war" or "the use of international armed force by a State" applies to "private persons" (if this describes those who staged the attacks on New York and the Pentagon). The perpetrators are clearly chargeable as common criminals under the law of the United States. Under international law should they be allowed to claim prisoner of war status under the laws or customs of war? Or, should prosecutions be based on both approaches?

Alternatively, and based on South Africa's approach to apartheid, should corrective actions follow the course of commissions of cooperation and reconciliation?

The harm has been done by "persons." From this wide and generic expression it becomes necessary to seek a more specific term. In the context of the September 11 event, a number have been employed, each with its own legal consequences. The popular term, which also has international and national legal meaning, is the one that has been used above, e.g., terrorist. The mission of terrorists is to produce the condition of terrorism.

3. DEFINITIONAL PROBLEMS

In order to cope with the present danger, efforts have been made to define "terrorist" and "terrorism." Clarity is required for the meaning of such terms if criminal prosecutions are to occur. It seems only fair that a person to be subject to prosecution as a terrorist or for terrorism should have advance knowledge of the elements of such crimes.

The definitional efforts have been based on the assumption that both constitute separate situations, and, as such, both can be made the subject of prosecutions. The problem with this is that law is more comfortable in addressing specific courses of conduct. Thus, an act, such as murder, can be identified as the act of a terrorist. To be acceptable the definition would have to couple the prohibited conduct and the intent to engage in such conduct with resultant harm. Penalties would assigned for such an intentional act.

Terrorism, on the other hand, is not so much an overt act but a condition. Harms are produced by the acts of terrorists. In order to overcome a definitional problem, States, including the United States have adopted statutes referring to "acts of terrorism." In this manner the acts of the individual terrorist become the prosecutable "acts of terrorism."

This national approach can also be employed internationally for terrorism. In each case terroristic acts or acts of terrorism can be used to describe the forbidden conduct. In both cases there would have to be a concordance of intention and observable conduct.

Terroristic activity, rather than the abstract term "terrorism", challenges western values. It allow for focus on the evil acts. In identifying conduct as the basis for societal responses prosecutions can be based on murder, mayhem, arson, aerial sabotage, hijacking of aircraft, provision of monetary support, and conspiracies to engage in such conduct. It is not abundantly clear that there is a need for a definition of terrorism. As suggested, terrorism, per se, may be treated as a condition which, while important to understand, would serve as an obstacle to rather than aid in the prosecution for provable facts like the crimes enumerated above.

Responding to the attack of September 11, 2001, the United States on September 18 declared war and a condition of armed conflict exists.[3] When the U.N. General Assembly invoked Article 51 of its Charter, it approved of the U.S. response as based on the right of self-defense. In this manner the General Assembly determined that terrorist activity constituted an armed attack. President Bush has consistently referred to the situation as one of "war." With the general acceptance of a state of war, the international law of armed conflict became applicable.

On September 25, 2001, the President of the United States issued Executive Order 23114 dealing with "Blocking and prohibiting transactions with persons who commit, threaten to commit, or support terrorism." For the purposes of the order, which linked intent with conduct, terrorism was described as an activity that "(i) involves a violent act or an act dangerous to human life, property, or infrastructure; and (ii) appears to be intended (A) to intimidate or coerce a civilian population; (B) to influence the policy of a government by intimidation or coercion; or (C) to affect the conduct of government by mass destruction, assassination, kidnapping, or hostage-taking." Its focus was on activities and not on a condition.

This was followed on October 6, 2001 by the USA Patriot Act.[4]This statute repeated the terms appearing in the foregoing. It redefined international terrorism so as to include activities of mass destruction intended to affect the conduct of government. It defined domestic terrorism to include activities that occur primarily within U.S. jurisdiction that involve criminal acts dangerous to human life, and that appear to be intended to intimidate or coerce a civilian population, to influence government policy by intimidation or coercion, or to affect government conduct by mass destruction, assassination, or kidnapping.[5] Among its numerous provisions was the imposition of penalties for attempting to and engaging in conspiracies relating to acts of terrorism. The statute took note of the fact that acts of terrorism can be both national and international. The statute set an eight year statute of limitations for prosecutions and provided for up to life imprisonment upon conviction. Conviction could also result in heavy fines.

This wide-ranging statute was supplemented in 2002 by the "Suppression of the Financing of Terrorism Implementation Act." It referred to nine international agreements designed to deal with terrorists. Included were hijacking of aircraft, aircraft piracy, use of biological and chemical weapons, possession of nuclear materials, arson and bombing of government property, an attack on an energy facility, impeding maritime navigation, possession of weapons of mass destruction, sabotage of nuclear facilities or fuels, and acts of terrorism transcending national boundaries. Federal District Courts were given jurisdiction.

The issue of terrorist bombings has been of long-standing concern at the United Nations. In 1994 the General Assembly adopted a Declaration on Measures to Eliminate International Terrorism. Following studies by its Sixth Committee the General Assembly on December 15, 1997 adopted Resolution 52/164 to which was annexed an International Convention for the Suppression of Terrorist Bombings. This crime was based on the existence of an intent to cause death or serious bodily injury or the intent to cause extensive destruction to identified objects, including major economic losses. Article 2 1. stated: "Any person commits an offense within the meaning of this Convention if that person unlawfully and intentionally delivers, places, discharges or detonates an explosive or other lethal device in, into or against a place of public use, a State or government facility, a public transportation system or an infrastructure facility." This comprehensive definition dealt with attempts as well as an organizing or directing others to act in "any other way" while contributing to the commission of one of the described offenses.[6]

This draft convention, which had not been ratified by the required 22 parties on September 11, 2001, provided an acceptable definition or description of the use of bombs by terrorists. As the title indicated the subject was bombings, and not the concept of terrorism, per se.[7]

An effective national statute on terrorism would be designed to protect the security and military needs of a country, and, based on the present anti-terrorism statutes would range widely over almost every aspect of human behavior. Institutional changes and greater individual awareness will be necessary.

One response was the establishment of the Homeland Security Office on October 8, 2001 which became the Department of Homeland Security on March 1, 2003. Consolidated in one Department were numerous security-oriented agencies. It will be obliged to coordinate with foreign police organizations. To be effective America's policies must be both proactive and defensive in nature. Americans must accept that they exist in the world and are subject to global forces.

Both long range and short range all Americans must be aware that in times of crisis constitutional guarantees are subject to challenge under the heading of protecting national security. It is in this area that wise leaders will find ways both to preserve our national traditions and to deal effectively with the ongoing problems described as "terrorism." Quite obviously there would have to be a suitable balance between the need to fight terrorism and the protection of the democratic traditions in a free society.

It is also evident that a satisfactory definition of terrorism is a highly complex and, perhaps, at least at the international level, an unsatisfactory undertaking. For example, at the world level the definition of "aggression" was agreed to by the UN General Assembly in its 1974 Resolution 3314 (XXIX) after years of effort. At present there are questions as to the adequacy of the 1974 definition and debates continue at the United Nations and at the International Criminal Court.

The international definition of "terrorism" will have to meet the challenges posed by opposing ideological and cultural outlooks, as influenced by different responses to multilateralism and unilateralism. Thus, for the globalists, terrorists and acts of terrorism are threats to civilized society. The often voiced opposing response is that such persons are "freedom fighters," and, as such, true heroes and martyrs endowed by justifiable moral convictions and commitments. Despite these claims it is necessary to reject the self-appointed and self-serving term "freedom fighter." To accept it would enable all political dissidents to justify violent conduct.

Several noteworthy attempts to define international terrorism have been made. Thus, the Mitchell Committee, appointed in 2000 to seek conciliatory outlooks on the part of Israeli and Palestinian leaders stated that terrorism "Involves the deliberate killing and injuring of randomly selected noncombatants for political ends. It seeks to promote a political outcome by spreading terror and demoralization throughout a population."

The European Union Council of Ministers of Justice and Home Affairs in December 2001, suggested as a definition: "Offenses intentionally committed by an individual or a group against one or more countries, their institutions or people, with the aim of intimidating them and seriously altering or destroying the political, economic, or social structures of a country."

At the end of January 2002, the members of the UN debated the terrorist-definition problem. It became clear that groups of States were far apart on the issue of the meaning and legality of terrorism. Advanced Western States favored the outlawing of terrorism using definitional terms of the kind identified above.[8] Express disapproval was voiced by the 56-member Organization of Islamic Conference. In their view any definition that might impede the activities of "national liberation movements," in itself an undefined term, would be unacceptable. The same outlook was confirmed by references to "resistance to foreign occupation."

Founded in concerns over violations of national sovereignty because of foreign interventionary activities, the political convictions of these protesting States are hard to overcome. That the notion of national sovereignty has been much eroded by the forces of globalism has not been sufficient to modify the survival instincts of these states. They consider "good" terrorists to be instruments suited to their needs to stay in power. Those who see "good" terrorists as weapons against the interventionary conduct of others, undoubtedly are morally blind to the deliberate taking of innocent lives, and not necessarily on the huge scale of 2001.

These deep-seated political differences constitute a major threat to any hope for a truly just and orderly universe. In the short run there may be occasional gains on the part of the supporters of terrorist activities. In a longer perspective, since their power-bases are limited, and since the more powerful have now become more focused on a common resolve, the sponsors of terrorism will suffer incalculable harm. Unfortunately, foreign aid for the impoverished cannot satisfy the needs of constantly expanding populations. They are attentive to charges of capitalistic exploitation. Moreover, a higher degree of material well-being does not in itself reduce historic animosities.

The absence of an internationally acceptable definition of terrorism does not deny to States which have been hurt by terroristic activities the right to have recourse against such harms.

In the meantime those States with global perspectives will be able to proceed on a selective basis by identifying new and old activities as sufficiently threatening to require new international agreements. A principal provision of such agreements will be the duty on the part of signatories to prosecute or to extradite an accused to a State claiming a primary interest.

A treaty is not necessary to make it clear that acts of violence are critical elements of terrorism. States which allow terrorists to live within their boundaries need to be put on notice that their presence is unacceptable. This notice could be made by resolutions adopted by international governmental organizations, and through diplomatic channels. Following such notice it would be possible for signatories to a new treaty to declare that a State's failure to remedy such a situation would allow the signatories to engage in collective remedial action. The act of giving sanctuary would provide a satisfactory basis for taking collective action. Specific activity would be treated both as terrorism and unlawful.

Terrorism, today as in the past, constitutes a hidden or unsuspected threat to the safety and well-being of persons and their possessions. Historically the general threat has been acknowledged. In the past low-key plans and responses have been directed toward overt actions. Considering that terrorists have the same scientific and technical skills as those who may become their targets, is not unreasonable to assign a very high priority to the "war against terrorism."

The acts of terrorists do not fit readily into the international law governing the conduct of war and armed conflict. Traditional international law does not deal with conflicts between States and individual terrorists. One way to overcome this situation is to treat such persons as combatants and as terrorists. In this way they could be punished under the laws or customs of war because of their military activities and under national legislation as criminals.

Since the attack on the United States was followed by a declaration of war, the persons engaging in the armed conflict have been identified as combatants, detainees, non-combatants, and unlawful combatants. According to the Third 1949 Geneva Convention, combatants are entitled, if captured, to prisoner of war status.

Persons whose principal loyalty was to Afghanistan, namely members of the Taliban, and who were captured outside the United States, might be accorded prisoner of war status, pursuant to the laws or customs of war. This means that interrogation can be limited to the person's name, rank, and military serial number. Prisoners are guaranteed appropriate food, clothing, housing, health care, bathing facilities, continuance of compensation, access to financial accounts, special privileges depending on rank, mail privileges, and in the event of crimes committed while in POW status to have a fair trial. If they had not committed any crimes during the period of their detention as POWs they are to be released by the detaining power in Afghanistan at the end of the conflict.

The term "detainee" was employed intentionally by the United States to describe the status of an unlawful combatant who engaged in acts of terrorism. If guilt were established the accused would be treated under national law as a terrorist and not as a military person under international law. From a domestic perspective those participating in the events in Afghanistan have been identified as citizens, aliens, traitors, and murderers.

The label affixed to any particular person will extend to that person certain legal rights and duties. This applies to the availability and application of substantive law. It would also apply to the choice of a court or tribunal that may be called upon to exercise jurisdiction over the above persons.

4. AL QAEDA, TALIBAN, AFGHANISTAN

Certain facts stand out in arriving at how to deal with the terrorists or military personnel captured in Afghanistan, where the Taliban was the *de facto* government in September of 2001. As such, its membership has been composed, on the whole, of nationals of the country with a permanent residence there. The government has not actively engaged in terroristic conduct or mischief in foreign countries.

By contrast, Al Qaeda in Afghanistan has consisted generally of non-nationals, whose residency has been transient. It has carried out its own plans through persons having primary allegiance to it and not to Afghanistan. This is particularly true regarding its foreign operations. Osama bin Laden was the dominant authority in Al Qaeda.

Al Qaeda has been an elite clique which usurped the governing authority of the Taliban. Its principal purpose was to advance on a world-wide basis the many facets of terrorism. Governance of Afghanistan was incidental to its central motivation.

On February 7, 2002, the Bush administration, following internal debates in which Secretary of State Powell reportedly urged the application of the Third 1949 Geneva Convention to the detainees, issued a two-page press release disposing of the matter.[9] The release, identifying United States *policy*, contains two key provisions which are inconsistent: "neither the Taliban or al-Qaida detainees are *entitled* to POW status."[10]

It then recites that "even though the detainees are not entitled to POW privileges they will be provided many POW privileges as a matter of policy." Further, the United States is to treat "all of the *individuals* detained at Guantanamo humanely and, to the extent appropriate and consistent with the principles of the Third Geneva Convention of 1949."[11] But, at the same time, the statement reads: "The President has determined that the Geneva Convention applies to the Taliban detainees, but not to the al-Qaida detainees," even though the "Taliban detainees do not *qualify* as POWs."[12] This appears to be based on treating Taliban personnel as combatants and Al Qaeda personnel as terrorists. This would mean that neither the Taliban nor members of Al Qaeda achieved POW status because they did not wear distinctive uniforms, and, also since they are not POWs they are subject to full scale interrogation.

Apparently the foregoing position, applicable to individuals held at Guantanamo, depends on questioning of captured persons to determine who is an Al Qaeda member. Once a person is found to be only a member of the Taliban, then this person would be accorded POW benefits, but not status, and would not be subject to further interrogation, while, if the person is determined to be a member of Al Qaeda, further questioning would take place both as a matter of law and as a matter of policy.

Al Qaeda are to be accorded the same basic rights as POWs for food, housing, health care, and general maintenance. They are not entitled to all of the Geneva Convention privileges, but is to be expected that they will be treated fairly. Undoubtedly their religious preferences will be honored.

The decision of the U.S. government, though based on apparently practical considerations, including a justifiable distinction between members of the Taliban and Al Qaeda, is subject to criticism. A major purpose of the Geneva Convention is to identify who must be treated as a prisoner of war. The U.S. position in giving Taliban fighters the benefits of the Geneva Convention, while entitled to approval, but failing to assure their status as POWs, detracts from the rights accorded to such persons under the terms of the Convention. The United States has come under heavy criticism as a result of its initial handling of the Taliban prisoners at Guantanamo Naval Station in Cuba, including the interrogation procedures.

The International Committee of the Red Cross, charged under the Geneva Convention with the protection of the rights of POWs, has been allowed to visit the detainees at Guantanamo. This may have resulted in the decision by the United States to return those identified as only members of the Taliban to Afghanistan. Upon their return to Afghanistan, if they were wearing a distinctive uniform at the time of their capture, they would be entitled to POW status. Or, they could be simply released if the United States did not wish to bear the burden of keeping them in detention.

Article 4.A. (1) of the Third Geneva Convention identifies prisoners of war as "Members of the armed forces of a Party to the conflict, as well as members of militias or volunteer corps, forming part of such armed forces." Article 4.A. (2) refers to "other militias and members of other volunteer corps." They also are entitled to prisoner or war status. As lawful combatants they must meet four conditions. He or she must be a part of a unit with an organized command structure, with the commander being responsible for his/her subordinates. Arms must be carried openly. A distinctive uniform or means of identification recognizable at a distance must be worn. There must be compliance with the laws or customs of war.

Those falling into the "other" category during World War II included the French Forces of the Interior, who were treated as members of a resistance movement, and commandos. German officers, who followed orders from Hitler and killed commandos who were in compliance with the foregoing conditions, were tried and convicted in military tribunals by allied forces for having violated the laws of war.

Applying the foregoing to Taliban soldiers they would be treated as members of the armed forces of Afghanistan. When captured they are to be accorded prisoner of war status.

The soldiers serving Al Qaeda fall into a different category, either "militias or volunteer corps," or "other militias and members of other volunteer corps," since they were not a part of the regular Afghanistan army. To achieve such status they would have to prove that in taking up arms they were giving their support to the Taliban government. In resolving this issue it would have to be determined whether, in fact, Al Qaeda had taken over the Taliban authorities and was the de facto government of Afghanistan. Also to be resolved, if Al Qaeda were to be classified under the "other" categories, would be meeting the four conditions identified above. Responses to these questions would provide guidance as to whom the "prisoner of war" status can be applied. To avoid such inquiries would present a dangerous situation, since it would thwart the humanitarian goal of obtaining clear-cut criteria for according "prisoner of war" status. All countries have a vested interest in protecting their armed combatants, including militias and volunteer corps.

The response in the case of Al Qaeda is complicated by their primary support for terrorism and engaging in terroristic actions. Thus, if they failed the prisoner of war test, they could, when apprehended, by prosecuted for such terroristic activities. If it were to be assumed that such persons could fall into both categories, the policy of the United States appears to be to treat them as terrorists.

From statements made in January, 2002 by President Bush and Secretary of Defense Rumsfeld, and the President's press release of February 23, 2002, it is clear that they want to treat members of Al Qaeda for purposes of prosecution as terrorists or unlawful combatants and to identify them as detainees and not as prisoners of war. This characterization would allow for the creation of military tribunals. It would avoid the Geneva Convention provisions applicable to prisoners of war. One of the products of the "detainee" classification is to determine if an individual qualifies as a prisoner of war. In short, despite the U.S. position that it is at war against Al Qaeda, if their conduct is not seen as the legal equivalent of war, then Al Qaeda members cannot be prisoners of war. As terrorists they would be subject to criminal prosecutions.

The Bush administration has had to respond to the fact that in this war a lawful distinction had to be made between lawful POWs and persons such as members of Al Qaeda, who were principally engaged in world-wide terroristic activities. The distinction flows from the fact that a war against terrorists is a unique form of armed conflict. It does not fall within the traditional concept of war, where the international law of armed conflict applies to lawful combatants. This is because the terrorist entity is not a State. Its principal opponent is not a State but rather the innocent members of a civilian population.

Since terrorism has become a critical issue in recent times, it is important that new international agreements be formulated to determine if terrorists are entitled to an international legal status. The International Committee of the Red Cross should convene a conference to engage the issue.

5. THE PRESIDENTIAL ORDER OF NOVEMBER 13, 2001

The prospect of detaining and prosecuting Al Qaeda terrorists in the United States or elsewhere has excited controversy. The Presidential Order of November 13, 2001, authorized the Secretary of Defense to detain in the United States or abroad "terrorists" as defined in that Order.[13] It applied to non-citizens. The need for such detention was based on the existence of a "state of armed conflict."

Pursuant to the Bush Military Order, based on the finding of a national emergency, the prosecutions of terrorists involved in the terroristic attacks of September 11, 2001 are to take place in military tribunals under the "laws of war and other applicable laws."[14]

Penalties are to be subject to applicable law, including life imprisonment or death.[15] The Secretary of Defense is granted authority to specify the practices and procedures for the conduct of trials. He is given specific authority to determine the time and place of trials, including both in the United States and abroad.[16]The directive makes no mention of "secret" trials but does indicate that there is a need to protect classified information from unauthorized disclosure, and that this would be considered in connection with "the conduct, closure of, and access to proceedings."[17]

Unlike cases in Federal District Courts, but like proceedings in court martials, the court would be an investigator of both fact and law and base its decisions on evidence having "probative value to a reasonable person."[18] Provision is made for the appointment of defense counsel, with sentencing to be based on a ⅔ vote of a majority of the judges serving on the tribunal, review by the President of the findings of the tribunal, and the granting of reprieves and pardons.

The military tribunal is granted exclusive jurisdiction. An accused is specifically denied the privilege "to seek any remedy or maintain any proceeding, directly or indirectly, or to have any remedy or proceeding sought on the individual's behalf, in (i) any court of the United States, or any State thereof, (ii) any court of any foreign nations, or (iii) any international tribunal."[19] An accused is not granted all of the trial guarantees afforded under the U.S. Constitution, although there is the requirement that throughout the proceedings an accused is to be given a "full and fair trial."[20]

Pursuant to Sec. 6.(a) of the Order, the Secretary of Defense was authorized to fill in details so as to make the proposed procedures effective. Pending the issuance of such rules and regulations it became necessary to determine whether the prosecution of terrorist Zacarias Moussaoui, a French citizen, who was apprehended in the United States, should be prosecuted before a military tribunal. There was also the possibility, as later determined, that he would be tried in Federal District Court.

In formulating such rules and regulations it became necessary to determine how to classify members of Al Qaeda, who have been referred to as "detainees," rather than prisoners of war by the U.S. armed forces based on their description as "bands of people" whose conduct "would not meet the criteria of organized military activity."[21] This was a result of the type of military uniform worn by the Taliban. If distinctive uniforms, the wearers are entitled to the 1949 Geneva Convention protection. In early January 2002, three months after the Bush Order, Secretary of Defense Rumsfeld remarked that Department of Defense lawyers "are looking at all these treaties and conventions and everything, trying to figure out what is appropriate."[22]

6. THE DEPARTMENT OF DEFENSE "MILITARY COMMISSION ORDER NO. 1"

On March 21, 2002, the Secretary of Defense issued Military Commission Order No. 1, following advice from leading members of the legal profession as well as a careful analysis on the part of governmental lawyers. Consultations with private attorneys, including the American Bar Association leadership, resulted in approval of the terms of the order. There was negative criticism, but not as embracing as those directed at the Presidential Order of November 13, 2001.

The Secretary's Order made it clear that jurisdiction over members of Al Qaeda, other persons involved in acts of international terrorism against the United States, and those persons who knowingly harbored such terrorists would be prosecuted before military commissions. The language contained in the Bush Order denying an accused access to "any court of the United States or any State thereof, any court of any foreign nations, or any international tribunal" was not repeated. The Secretary's Order stated that an accused would receive a fair trial before a military commission. Further, the procedures set forth in it "and no others shall govern such trials."

Under the Bush Order triable offenses are those falling under "the laws of war and other applicable laws." This was changed in the Secretary's Order to read: "violations of the laws of war and all other offenses triable by military commission." Charges can be brought only against an individual or individuals.

It is clear from the Order that the commission is to be a military tribunal staffed by military personnel. In this respect it is much more like a court martial proceeding than a Federal District Court. Among the terms of the Order is the presumption of the innocence of an accused, the test of evidence being that which "would have probative value to a reasonable person," protection of witnesses against the fear of recrimination, open proceedings unless secrecy is required, the availability of counsel, provided either by the government or employed by an accused, the right of an accused to testify, and the use of cross examination. The members of the commission will determine facts and apply the law identified in the order in specific cases. Provision was made for post-trial procedures, including an appellate review by three persons. On these both civilians and military personnel can serve. One of them must have had experience as a judge. There is to be an automatic review by the Secretary of Defense. The President has the power to grant pardons or reprieves.

Practical considerations, including the vital need to begin processing the terrorists held by both civilian and military authorities, could not wait the issuance of the above order. As a result Federal District Courts have been selected for prosecutions of U.S. citizens, and for aliens living in the United States at the time of their alleged criminality.

On April 30, 2003 the Department of Defense issued Military Commission Instruction No. 2 dealing with "Crimes and Elements for Trials by Military Commissions." Prior to its publication a draft of it had been circulated widely in order to provide comment on possible constitutional imperfections. The Instruction purports to deal with "guidance with respect to crimes that may be tried by military commissions," and, "the elements of those crimes."

The crimes and elements referred to in the Instruction are derived from existing principles of the law of armed conflict. Convictions will depend on conduct that is both wrongful and intentional, The Instruction will affect the disposition of the detainees held at the Guantanamo Naval Station, unless previously released following interrogation.

The jurisdiction of the commission will extend to 25 enumerated crimes. It is not a definitive list. Among the identified crimes are the willful killing of protected persons, rape, hijacking or hazarding a vessel or aircraft, terrorism, which was defined as the killing or inflicting bodily harm, or engaging in inherently dangerous conduct when such harm or destruction was "intended to intimidate or coerce a civilian population, or to influence the policy of a government by intimidation or coercion," aiding the enemy, and engaging in a conspiracy to commit a substantive offence identified in the Instruction.[23]

To insure fairness in prosecutions an accused is entitled to all of the defenses "available under the law of armed conflict." The burden of presenting "evidence of lawful justification or excuse or any applicable defense" rests with the accused. Once this has been demonstrated "the burden is on the prosecution to establish beyond a reasonable doubt that the conduct was wrongful or that the defense does not apply."

Reliance on the defense of a severe mental disease or defect must be proven by an accused by clear and convincing evidence, not beyond a reasonable doubt. Violations of the listed laws of war are not subject to any statute of limitations.

The Instruction maintained the distinction between "lawful" and "unlawful" combatant immunity or "belligerent privilege." The term enemy was broadly described. Included is "an entity" with which the United States or allied forces may be engaged in armed conflict, or which is "preparing to attack the United States." Enemy "specifically includes an organization of terrorists with international reach."

Seemingly any organization would include a "domestic" organization of terrorists sponsored by an international terrorist body. If so, it would be subject to the jurisdiction of a military commission.

The Department of Defense moved slowly in setting up the tribunals. At the end of 2003 it had established an appointing authority to approve charges, refer cases to trial, and supervise prosecutions. A review panel of distinguished American civilian jurists was named. With these procedural steps completed the long awaited prosecutions will be able to get under way.

7. COURTS AND TERRORISTS

The Bush Order of November 13, 2001, with its emphasis on trials before military tribunals, revived interest in the prosecutions of saboteurs in the United States during World War II. In the 1942 *Ex Parte Quirin* case a distinction had been made between wartime lawful combatants and unlawful combatants.[24] Eight German soldiers had entered the United States, equipped with explosives, with the mission of destroying weapon factories. They shed their military uniforms and blended into the U.S. civilian population.

Upon their capture the question arose whether they were to be treated as ordinary prisoners of war and prosecuted in accordance with established treaty procedures or whether they were to be considered to be "unlawful combatants" subject to prosecution in a separately and statutorily based U.S. military tribunal. Cases before this court did not include the right to a jury. The court was authorized to meet in secret. With the creation of this new court a new jurisdictional issue was presented to the United States, namely, whether the prosecution should occur in a regular Federal District Court, with full constitutional protections, or before a newly created military tribunal. Following the conviction by a military tribunal their appeal was heard by the U.S. Supreme Court. It concluded that the accused, one of whom was a U.S. citizen, were "unlawful combatants" under the laws of war and enjoyed no constitutional rights to a jury trial.

The *Quirin* case was criticized on the ground that it should have been decided in accordance with the 1867 Supreme Court case of *Ex parte Milligan*.[25]

Civilian courts were in operation during and following the Civil War. The accused journalist was prosecuted in a military tribunal after hostilities had ended. He was freed on appeal on the ground that the civilian tribunal had priority over the military. The federal government had failed to show why it was necessary for the prosecution to take place in a military tribunal.

These two cases are different, however. *Quirin* was an alien engaged in war against the United States. He had given up the right to be treated as a lawful combatant when he substituted civilian clothing for his military uniform, e.g., had become an unlawful combatant. In the *Milligan* case the accused was a civilian newspaper editor and was not a combatant of any kind.

When a terrorist is detained by the United States the place of detention and the person's nationality may resolve the issue of where the trial is to occur. Such an approach, foreseen in the Presidential Order of November 13, 2001, may soften the concern that trials before military tribunals sitting in the United States would not conform to constitutional guarantees.

Trials of terrorists arrested in the United States should be conducted in civilian courts, unless the government can demonstrate that necessity requires military trials. This would follow the reasoning advanced in the *Milligan* case. The *Quirin* approach, although followed in the current Presidential Order, should not be employed. Federal District Courts, experienced in the prosecution of terrorists, are available. Accused appearing before them are entitled to all constitutional guarantees. Terrorists outside the United States can be prosecuted as prisoners of war, if they can meet the definitional requirements. If they fail to meet such requirements, their prosecutions can take place under the "laws of war and other applicable laws" in foreign based military tribunals, pursuant to the Bush Order. Under present court review is the question whether foreign detainees at the U.S. Naval Station in Cuba are entitled to constitutional guarantees.

It is more convenient to prosecute a foreign terrorist who is not within the United States in the place where he is held. Jurisdiction would vest in a military tribunal and the conviction rate might be even lower than were he tried under civilian law in the United States. With American military officers serving as judges in war crimes cases after World War II, the rate of conviction of German and Japanese defendants was 85%. In 2000 the rate of convictions for civilians in cases involving felonies tried in U.S. Federal District Courts was 88%.[26]

The Bush approach has been emphatically rejected by Mary Robinson, Chairman of the United Nations Human Rights Commission. She has stated with regard to the Al Qaeda and Taliban combatants that "They were combatants in an international conflict. It may be that some of them have also been involved in the Al Qaeda conspiracy, that's quite likely, but they are entitled to POW status or, if that is defeated, there is a provision in the Geneva Convention that it goes before a tribunal."[27] Article 5 of the 1949 Geneva POW Convention provides with respect to persons having committed "a belligerent act and having fallen into the hands of the enemy," and whose status as a "prisoner of war" is not clear, pursuant to the manner a prisoner of war is identified in Article 4 of the Convention, are to be protected by the treaty "until such time as their status has been determined by a competent tribunal."

A "competent tribunal" was interpreted by the United States Department of the Army in 1956 to mean a United States "board of not less than three officers acting according to such procedure as may be prescribed for tribunals of this nature."[28] There could be further proceedings. Thus, "Persons who have been determined by a competent tribunal not to be entitled to prisoner-of-war status may not be executed, prosecuted, otherwise penalized without further judicial proceedings to determine what acts they have committed and what penalty should be imposed therefore."[29]

Probably such tribunals would determine both fact and law. At first it was possible that the procedural guarantees of the U.S. Constitution would not be available, since both past practice and the terms of the Bush Order of November 13, 2001 are based only on the standard of a fair trial. This was modified in Military Commission Instruction No. 2, of April 30, 2003, which provided that "the burden is on the prosecution to establish beyond a reasonable doubt that the conduct was wrongful or that the defense does not apply."

Support for the "fair trial" approach was based on the view that a terrorist engages in a form of murder not normally associated with prisoner of war status under the Third Geneva Convention, that the trial process would be simpler if the terrorist were prosecuted in his place of residence, or, at least outside the United States, that a sufficiently large number of such tribunals could be created and get to work which would be preferred to the limited number of available Federal District Courts in the United States, and that early convictions would have the greater preventive impact on terrorism.

The initial governmental position generated enormous popular and professional outpourings, with the discussants not always clear as to the distinction to be made between events occurring within the United States and abroad. At the heart of the matter, from the domestic point of view, has been concern that the President has exceeded his executive authority under the Constitution.

Reliance on broad presidential authority was implicit in his Order of November 13, 2001 and in Military Commission Instruction Order No. 2 of March 21, 2002. Those urging an overreaching by the President, relying on the basic constitutional concept of separation of powers, have argued that the Congress and ultimately the constitutional courts of the United States must be allowed to have a hand in determining the rules to be applied by military tribunals, including determining whether a given person is to be treated as a prisoner of war or as a terrorist detainee. In February, 2002, the American Bar Association reviewed the matter over the objection of the Department of Justice which had not at that time completed its draft code for the prosecution of terrorists.[30]

8. THE ATTORNEY GENERAL'S DRAFT STATUTE

The Attorney General on September 24, 2001, in order to clarify the procedures for the prosecution of terrorists, submitted a draft Mobilization Against Terrorism Act to Congress. In Title III of the proposal it was suggested that existing federal criminal law be modified in several respects. First, it was indicated that "terrorism should be considered no less than murder,"[31] since murder already constituted a violation of the criminal law of the United States. Thus, the proposed legislation dealt with the elimination of the statute of limitations, with alternative maximum sentences, rules on conspiracy to conceal terrorists, and giving support to terrorist organizations. The proposed legislation did not call for the creation of a new statutory criminal tribunal to sit in the United States; it specifically stated that the proposed changes in the existing federal law met the very highest standards, namely, in the "law of crimes and criminal procedure, the constitutional rights of the accused are respected."[32]

The draft act did not contain a provision requiring that terrorists in the United States were to be subject to prosecution exclusively in the United States District Courts. Failure to take this approach has created strong opposition from proponents of the use of such courts, in which an accused is entitled to claim all available federal fair trial guarantees. Support for their claim can be found in the decision of the United States District Court in 2000 involving the bombing of the World Trade Center and U.S. embassies.[33]

9. THE DECISION TO PROSECUTE ZACARIAS MOUSSAOUI

In early December 2001 Attorney General John Ashcroft authorized the filing in the Federal District Court in Alexandria, Virginia, of a case against French national, Zacarias Moussaoui, for terroristic activity, specifically for hijacking of aircraft and involving a conspiracy to kill and maim persons present in the Twin Towers in New York and in the Pentagon on September 11, 2001. According to the Attorney General the accused was one of the 20 persons who actively participated in and engaged in the disaster. At the time of the attack Moussaoui was in custody in Minnesota as an illegal alien following his arrest on August 16, 2001.

The charges included his having been trained in Afghanistan in a camp operated by Al Qaeda, being a member of Al Qaeda, preparing himself for piloting aircraft by enrolling in a Boeing 747 simulator flight training program, puchasing flight-training videos, navigation equipment, knives and other equipment used in hand-to-hand combat, and researching crop dusting procedures.

He received over $14,000 from an established terrorist cell located in Hamburg, Germany. It is the government's position that, while each of the above would not necessarily reflect preparing for acts of terrorism, when viewed as a whole they readily serve as the basis for conspiracy charges, particularly since they reflect the pattern of conduct of the terrorists who died on September 11. The U.S. Supreme Court has characterized conspiracy by its difficulty in detection, and often necessitating a long time for discovery.

The government after having engaged in detailed factual searches, and with an awareness that convictions on conspiracy charges have traditionally resulted in severe penalties in July 2002 added a third indictment. It stated that the accused had acted in "an especially heinous, cruel and depraved manner" with premeditation to cause death and to commit terrorism. Since the act of one of the 20 terrorists is the act of all, the accused, if convicted could be sentenced to death.

The federal death penalty statute allows the imposition of a death sentence in two situations. First, a jury would have to find that the accused intentionally participated in an act, contemplating that the life of a person would be taken or intending that lethal force would be used. Second, the jury could find that the accused intentionally and specifically engaged in an act of violence, knowing that the act created "a grave risk of death to a person . . . such that participation in the act constituted a reckless disregard for human life." Both provide that a victim's death must be the direct result of that conspiratorial act.

The choice of a Federal District Court came as a surprise in light of the earlier attention given to military tribunals. Among the reasons initially advanced for a District Court were that the accused was in detention in Minneapolis on September 11, was already in the criminal justice system, that military prosecutions should be reserved for persons suspected of crimes committed after September 11 and who are captured during a period of hostilities, that witnesses were available in the U.S., that a trial in an open court would not compromise critical national security information, and there was no danger that evidence would endanger the working of the U.S. intelligence gathering process.[34] Further, it was not evident that a military tribunal was necessary to dispose of the matter. These propositions later were seriously disputed. When the case first got under way in April, 2002, Moussaoui described himself as a "slave of Allah," asked to represent himself, and stated that his court appointed lawyers and the judge were engaged in a vendetta to obtain his conviction. The accused has continued to serve as his own lawyer. However, when the government indicated it would seek the death penalty the trial judge appointed a "defense" team to represent the interests of the accused.

In all criminal prosecutions in a Federal District Court an accused possesses the constitutional right to a fair trial. Included are rights to representation by independent counsel, confrontation by adverse witnesses including cross-examination, and the testimony of witnesses who are able to demonstrate innocence or mitigating circumstances. The accused has contended that his defense depends on testimony in open court of three Al Qaeda prisoners held by the United States in foreign prisons. The three have been identified as organizers, masterminders, and a paymaster for the dead terrorists. The government has classified the three as enemy combatants. The Attorney General has taken the position that the three potential witnesses are not to be allowed to testify. He has based his decision on the view their open testimony would disclose secret intelligence sources. It has also been urged that such testimony would be highlighted by the media and would provide an incitement to virulent Al Qaeda elements now having footholes in many parts of the world. This outlook is claimed to be justified by the policy of a full-fledged attack on terrorism.

The prosecution of Zacarias Moussaoui as the alleged 20th conspirator in the September 11, 2001 attacks will undoubtedly be recorded as both historic and ironic. It will be historic since the case has presented a conflict between the exercise of presidential authority to deny to an accused access to witnesses believed to possess information beneficial to his defense. The basis for the president's position is found in his constitutional authority as Chief Executive, Commander-in-Chief, statutory provisions, and the presence of a "war against terrorism."

On the other side of the "separation of powers coin" is the constitutional provision guaranteeing criminal defendants in Federal District Courts a fair trial as set forth in the Bill of Rights. The federal prosecution has resulted in numerous hearings at Federal District Courts and in the U.S. Court of Appeals. In December 2003 the issue had not been resolved, with one prospect being an appeal to the United States Supreme Court.

Under these circumstances the issue of a death penalty for the accused has become a vital concern. In October 2003 the trial judge responded to the government's position by prohibiting the government from seeking the death penalty and also barred any trial evidence linking the accused to the terrorist strikes. At the same time the judge rejected a motion made by counsel for the accused to dismiss all charges. This motion was not contested by the government. The judge concluded that the case should be heard in an "open and public forum." The judge also noted that if the government were not to proceed with conspiracy charges and if it were to confine its case to the lesser allegations made against the accused there remained the possibility of his being exposed to a sentence of life imprisonment.

The Attorney General's position is that if an Appeals Court were to decide that the accused is to be accorded the right to interrogate his preferred witnesses the United States will ask that the case be dismissed. If that were to occur the accused would be turned over to a federal military tribunal where, although the principle of fair trial would also apply, there would presumably be a decision not to make the witnesses available for security reasons.

The case is more than unusually ironic. From its inception the accused, despite abundant advice to the contrary, insisted that he would conduct his defense by himself.

Nevertheless, the accused, having persuaded the trial court judge of his constitutional right to interrogate witnesses, and because of the governments continuing refusal to make them available, has positioned himself to obtain a dismissal and to avoid the death penalty.

In her ruling the judge stated that "it would simply be unfair to require Moussaoui to defend against such prejudicial accusations while being denied the ability to present testimony from witnesses who could assist him in contradicting those accusations."

Following the refusal of the U.S. Attorney to provide the accused with access to the latter's witnesses the trial judge on October 2, 2003 banned prosecutors from using evidence or testimony linking the accused to the September attacks. At the same time she ruled that the prosecutors could not seek the death penalty. This was based on the view that it could not be demonstrated that the accused could be a major participant while he was being held in prison in Minnesota. However, the trial judge ruled that the trial could go forward on the government's claim of conspiracy, through membership in Al Qaeda not involving the 2001 attacks, and that a finding of guilt could result in a life prison sentence.

The federal prosecutor appealed to the U.S. Court of Appeals, stating that the judge had not dismissed the entire case and seeking a ruling that the case could proceed without the testimony of Moussaoui's three defense witnesses. In its starkest form the contest was between the Constitutional guarantee of an accused to have access to witnesses on his or her behalf and whether security considerations resulting from on-going threats of terrorism could produce an exception. If the government remains steadfast this will result in a new prosecution before a military tribunal having greater discretion to deny access by the accused to friendly witnesses. It remains to be seen whether an appeal from the holding of a military tribunal to the Supreme Court will overturn a conviction. Much will depend on the view of an appellate tribunal on whether under the circumstances it is necessary for a civilian court to be prevented from exercising jurisdiction.

It is evident that the United States, in at least this case, initially favored a trial in a District Court rather than a military commission. It has been reported that President Bush, after consultation with Attorney-General Ashcroft and Secretary of Defense Rumsfeld, decided to forego the use of a military commission based on the *Quirin* example.

This approach taken to the prosecution of Zacarias Moussaoui, the first trial for the terroristic planning culminating in the September 11 event, has been hailed by those fearing the exceptional approach of military commissions. The political ramifications of the initial Ashcroft decision have been applauded, because in this time of crisis the United States was willing to accord an alien and alleged terrorist the statutory and constitutional protections enjoyed by residents of the United States in time of peace. This approach, which is not mandated by the U.S. Constitution, according to the *Quirin* case, at first was deemed as expedient because the government's evidence was readily available in the United States. The government's position became moot when the accused insisted on the testimony of foreign terrorists.

International law and practice, as well as fair trial considerations, because the evidence will be more immediately available, will allow foreign prosecutions of terrorists abroad when captured abroad. Military commissions, no less than civilian juries, seek to apportion penalties based on wrongful conduct. The Nuremberg Tribunal ranged in its penalties from 10 years of imprisonment, to life-time imprisonment and hanging.

The initial approach taken in the Moussaoui case, with the approval of the President, if pursued in the trial of all terrorists found in the United States, will limit the application of the terms of Section 1(e) of the Military Order of November 13, 2001. Its provision for military tribunals would be applied only to terrorists apprehended and prosecuted overseas, and would be justified by reliance on all of the executive powers granted to the President in the Constitution.

Commentators have supported keeping an option open for the use of military commissions. Such courts could sit in the prosecution of defendants who gave overseas support to the events of September 11. Such tribunals served effectively for the lesser defendants in Germany and Japan at the close of World War II.[35] Such courts were seen as a "flexible forum . . . more readily adaptable to large numbers of defendents."[36]

10. THE CASE OF JOHN WALKER LINDH

During the first week of December, 2001, American forces in Afghanistan captured a group of Taliban and Al Qaeda soldiers. Among them was a 20-

year old American citizen named John Walker Lindh, who at the time of his capture used several Islamic names. With the other soldiers he was interrogated by military personnel. He also responded to questions during interviews with the FBI and put to him by newspaper reporters covering the war. These more detailed disclosures identified an active participation with the terrorists.

In the interviews he stated that he had trained with Al Qaeda, was committed to fighting against India in the Kasmir region long before September 11, 2001, and had been with Taliban troops for about six months before being first captured at Kunduz by Northern Alliance troops.

His disclosures suggested that he had engaged in warfare against the United States. If such acts could be proven on the testimony of two credible witnesses, he could be charged with treason. Alternatively, his activities as a soldier made him a candidate for prosecution for terroristic activities. This, in turn, raised the huge question whether he should be prosecuted before a military tribunal of the kind proposed in the Presidential Order of November 13, 2001. The same issue was being considered at that time regarding the prosecution of Zacarias Moussaoui. Although there are many differences in the two cases, wiser heads in the Bush administration also opted to initiate Lindh's prosecution for terroristic activity in the Federal District Court. His U.S. citizenship appears to have influenced the decision.

In January, 2002 he was charged with violations of federal laws including conspiracy to kill U.S. citizens overseas, providing material support and resources to Osama bin Laden and Al Qaeda, and engaging in prohibited transactions with the Taliban and Al Qaeda, including the use of fire arms at their request.

On February 5 the first criminal complaint, resulting from a new inquiry by a grand jury, was restated. To the initial three charges were added seven more. Included were the allegations that Lindh had been a house guest of Osama bin Laden and had received training at an Al Qaeda facility; while at the facility he learned that bin Laden had sent terrorists operatives to the United States and Israel; had met with a senior Al Qaeda official who offered him the opportunity to join in such efforts; had sworn allegiance to jihad; following training was sent to Kabul where he was equipped with a long-range AKM rifle, as well as an RPK rifle, and hand grenades; and after learning of the September 11 attacks, he remained with his military unit "despite having been told that Bin Laden had ordered the attacks, that additional Al Qaeda personnel were being sent from the training camps to the front lines to protect Bin Laden and defend against an anticipated military response by the United States."[37]

When deciding to proceed in a district court, the government implicitly determined that the accused was not a POW and thus avoided having to deal with the 1949 Geneva Convention. One reason for prosecution before a military commission is to exclude the public from highly classified intelligence information, including those who provide it. It was concluded that this 20-year old boy, despite his extended participation in terroristic activities, was not in a position to formulate or influence foreign policy. His counsel argued that his immaturity, made him an easier target for interrogations, and that he was deprived of basic rights because of the manner and circumstances of his interrogations, including deprivations and punishments.

If convicted he would face multiple life terms but not the death penalty. In accordance with District Court trial procedures, his counsel may be entitled to view classified information gathered by the government. In order to comply with fair trial standards his counsel obtained court delays in order to search for favorable witnesses. Ultimately, as a result of plea bargaining he was given a 20 year imprisonment.

Although having used essentially different means, both Moussaoui and Lindh took part in the terroristic activities initiated by Osama bin Laden. If the approach identified in the Presidential Order of November 13, 2001, had been pursued, both would be subject to prosecution before military rather than civilian courts. If the deciding factor were the place where their crimes were committed, a stronger case exists for the prosecution of Lindh before a military tribunal of the kind identified in the Bush order, or held as a prisoner of war.

If the aim of the U.S. government were to obtain a severe punishment, since in the case of Lindh the charge of treason had been ruled out, prosecution in a District Court was the alternative. In making this election the U.S. government opened the door to an accused to have a much wider range of fundamental procedural rights. The prosecution of both defendants represented a firm resolve on the part of the United States to pursue the evil of terrorism. It is a matter for speculation whether more or less publicity would have resulted from the venue in which the prosecutions could have taken place.

11. THE CASES OF YASER ESAM HAMDI AND JOSE PADILLA

Mr. Hamdi is a U.S. citizen by birth. When young he was taken by parents to Saudi Arabia. He fought with Taliban forces in Afghanistan. At the time of his capture he was wielding an assault rifle. He was returned to the United States as an alleged enemy combatant and held in a military jail. On June 11, 2002 his father obtained an order from a Federal District Court which provided that the detainee was entitled to counsel and that the Public Defender be allowed unmonitored access to his client. On appeal by the government to the United

States Court of Appeals the order calling for unmonitored access to counsel was reversed.

In its July 12, 2002 decision the court cited precedents holding that the courts must accord "great deference" to a President's "wartime detention decisions." The appellate tribunal also rejected the government's contention that "with no meaningful judicial review, any American citizen alleged to be an enemy combatant could be detained indefinitely without charges or counsel on the government's say-so." The court also ruled that if Hamdi were an "enemy combatant" that the government's detention of him was a lawful one. The matter was remanded to the trial court to determine if the accused were an enemy combatant. He was to have the aid of counsel in presenting his case. The Federal District Court in August 2002 examined a governmental declaration designed to prove that the accused was an enemy combatant. The judge determined that the declaration failed to demonstrate that the accused fell into this category. The appellate court reviewed the lower court's holding on October 22. At that time it had before it *amici curie* briefs from about 400 lawyers and organizations on behalf of Hamdi and seven supporting the government.

On January 8, 2003 the Court of Appeals ruled against Hamdi and dismissed the appeal. In its decision reference was made to the fact that "detention of enemy combatants serves critical functions." The target is to obtain foreign military information and the knowledge of conspiracies.

Of much vaster importance, however, was the view that the case raised separation of powers issues. Thus, the court stated that "the review of executive branch decisions premised on military determinations made in the field carries an inordinate risk of a constitutionally problematic intrusion into the most basic responsibilities of a coordinate branch." And "The constitutional allocations of war powers affords the President extraordinarily broad authority as Commander in Chief and compels courts to assume a deferential posture in reviewing exercises of this authority."

To Hamdi's contention that his ongoing detention was unlawful since "the relevant hostilities have reached an end," the court responded: "Whether and when it would be open to this Court to find that a war through merely formally kept alive had in fact ended, is a question too fraught with gravity even to be adequately formulated when not compelled." With the nation under attack special significance was accorded to the principle of separation of powers.

The accused was able to have the benefit of counsel in seeking habeas corpus relief. However, since he was considered to be an enemy combatant and was being held in detention rather than being prosecuted he was not entitled to counsel. The court stated: "As an American citizen, Hamdi would be entitled to the due process protections normally found in the criminal justice system, including the right to meet with counsel, if he had been charged with a crime.

Hamdi's citizenship rightfully entitles him to file this petition to challenge his detention, but the fact that he is a citizen does not affect the legality of his detention as an enemy combatant." Since he was not charged with a crime he was not entitled to counsel. This holding produced a great outcry with much sentiment favoring an appeal to the United States Supreme Court.[38]

In December 2003 the case took on a new meaning. A public defender had petitioned the U.S. Supreme Court to obtain rulings on whether Hamdi could be imprisoned without access to counsel and without charges being filed against him. On the day before the administration filed its response the government decided that Hamdi was entitled to be represented by counsel. This statement was conditioned by the claim that such access was "not required by domestic or international law and should not be treated as a precedent."[39] The government added that it was acting only "as a matter of discretion and military policy," that there was "no general right to counsel under the laws and customs of war," and that it had the power to detain alleged combatants "at least for the duration of the conflict" without having to file charges against them.[40] The government contended the matter had to be interpreted in the light of the wartime detention of combatants, including U.S. citizens, rather than as a normal criminal prosecution. The powers of a commander-in-chief were urged in the face of the due process rights guaranteed by the constitution. Observers have noted that the government's statement followed its interrogation of Hamdi and its conclusion that a lawyer would not interfere with its intelligence gathering activities. The case is pending before the Supreme Court.

Mr. Padilla was born in Brooklyn. As a civilian he was arrested in Chicago in May, 2002, following a flight from Cairo. He had been under surveillance following contacts with an Al Qaeda official in Pakistan. According to the government he had been learning how to construct a nuclear "dirty bomb" designed to spread radiation without a nuclear explosion. His arrest was based on the suspicion that he intended to steal radioactive material for use in the proposed weapons in the United States.

He was jailed but no charges were brought. His detention was based on his having associated with terrorists with whom the United States was at war and that he was a security threat to the United States. Detention was deemed necessary to prevent him from aiding Al Qaeda. It was the government's position that when Padilla became involved in terrorist activities he violated the laws of war and became an unlawful enemy combatant.[41]

He obtained counsel who filed a petition for a writ of habeas corpus in the Federal District Court. Padilla's theory was that he should be formally charged with violation of American laws and international law or be released. If charged he would claim all of his constitutional rights to a fair trial.

The court in a holding dated December 4, 2002 determined that the President possessed the authority to classify Padilla as an unlawful enemy combatant under the laws of war and could be detained. However, it ordered the government to submit "evidence" to substantiate that conclusion. Continued incarceration was supported by the need to prevent Padilla from rejoining the enemy, that detention is an important tool in a war against terrorism, and that interrogation while in custody would provide intelligence information which could aid military and anti-terrorist operations.

In its holding the District Court rejected the contention of Padilla that the President as Commander in Chief had exceeded his authority in establishing a class of persons referred to as unlawful enemy combatants.

Padilla's right to counsel must be addressed at two levels. First counsel appeared in support of the petition for the writ of habeas corpus. Second, it was determined that Padilla by reason of his status was not entitled to counsel in determining his guilt or innocence. A distinction was made between the ordinary right of citizens to have counsel, and that of terrorists as members of groups with international roots and intent on using their characteristically violent measures. It was contended that they could not be treated as ordinary criminals. To support such a distinction the court would be obliged to accept the extreme gravity of terroristic capabilities.

The President had another option. He could have, in light of the contention that there is an existing "war" against terrorism treat Padilla as a prisoner of war. As such he would be detained without any access whatever to a Federal District Court and would be released when the war was over. Such an approach would have to demonstrate some kind of lawful military activity by Padilla.

In order to clarify the holding of the District Court the matter on April 10, 2003 was certified to the Court of Appeals for review. The principal issue was whether the President was authorized under the Constitution and by law to direct the military authorities to detain illegal enemy combatants. At issue, also, will be whether the terrorist type of detainee will be entitled to consult with counsel, and, if so, under what circumstances.

Although Hamdi was serving in the Taliban armed forces, and Padilla was a civilian, both have been identified as "enemy combatants." Both remain in military custody. However, Padilla, through counsel, was able to obtain a habeas corpus hearing in a Federal District Court which ruled he had the right to consult with counsel and to contest his detention status. The Court of Appeals announced its decision on December 18, 2003. The majority held that the "detention was not authorized by Congress, and absent such authorization, the President does not have the power under Article II of the Constitution to detain as an enemy combatant an American citizen seized on American soil outside a zone of combat." The court ruled that the 1971 federal Non-Detention Act established the conditions for detentions of U.S. citizens on American soil and that the 2001 War Powers Act did not create an exception. Citing Youngstown Sheet & Tube Co. V. Sawyer, 343 U.S. 579, 637-38, which restricted President Truman's effort to sieze steel mills during the Korean War, the majority held the President did not have the inherent power to detain Padilla. Hamdi will not benefit from the ruling since he was apprehended in Afghanistan.

In examining the above cases some unique patterns exist. John Walker Lindh, an American citizen, who was a prisoner of war and a terrorist, was convicted in a Federal District Court. Yaser Esam Hamdi and Jose Padilla, also U.S. citizens, following litigation, have established the right to habeas corpus proceedings and to counsel. Terrorist Richard Reid, and alleged terrorist Zacharias Moussaoui, both of whom are aliens, have been prosecuted in Federal District Courts on criminal charges leading in the case of Reid to a conviction. He was sentenced to three consecutive life-time terms in prison.

Although much attention has been given to the foregoing cases many other alleged terrorists have been apprehended in the United States. In each case the accused had been connected with the Taliban or Al Qaeda or both, and had been involved in terrorism directed again the United States, were noncitizens, with some being identified as enemy combatants. In each instance the prosecution took place in a Federal District Court where all constitutional protections were present. Sentences ranged up to 18 years imprisonment. In one case the Attorney General obtained a dismissal. The accused was transferred to the Navy brig in South Carolina for holding until the war against terrorism has been won. Many other alleged terrorists, some of whom may qualify also as prisoners of war, are being held outside the United States, and will fall under the jurisdiction of military courts or commissions. At the present time the Attorney General's criteria for prosecution in a military tribunal are the accused must be a non-citizen, must have been declared to be an enemy combatant, and must either through membership in Al Qaeda or otherwise here engaged in terroristic acts against the United States.

In sum, for those who engage in military activities the most favored status is to be treated as an ordinary prisoner of war. Where POW status is combined with terroristic activity, because of the perceived critical gravity of such activities, the status of terrorist has overridden that of prisoner of war. This would account for the treatment accorded to Lindh, Hamdi, and Padilla, except for the forum in which their innocence or guilt are to be determined. For the last two they may be prosecuted before a military commission.

In the Reid and Moussaoui cases prosecutions occurred in Federal District Courts because their conduct occurred in the United States, even though both were aliens. However, because the latter has demanded access to witnesses whose identity the government has asserted cannot be revealed, the matter may ultimately be referred to a military commission.

If terroristic activity is the overriding consideration of the process to be followed, then both Hamdi and Padilla should be tried in a Federal District Court. At that time the exact nature of the terroristic activity of an accused could be considered. Moussaoui's alleged conspiracy to destroy the Trade Towers in New York City could then be contrasted with Hamdi's possession of an automatic weapon in Afghanistan and Padilla's association with members of Al Qaeda.

The apprehension and prosecution of terrorists and unlawful enemy combatants ranks high as an American foreign policy. Different judicial tribunals have been or may be employed with the use of military commissions looming in the future. Much concern has been expressed over the non-availability of all constitutional rights for the accused except for bona fide POWs where the Third Geneva Convention provides many safeguards.

Following almost three years of investigation of the bombing of the U.S. destroyer Cole in Yemen a grand jury in Washington, DC in May 2003 returned sealed indictments against two Yemeni nationals. The government benefited during its investigation from facts provided by two senior Al Qaeda operatives who were named as unindicted co-conspirators. They provided information allowing for inquiries to take place at undisclosed overseas locations.

With the Department of Justice responsible for gathering essential facts the prosecutions will take place in a Federal District Court. This means that the large emphasis given to the "war" against terrorists will not result in prosecution of the Cole defendants in a military commission. With this matter to be pursued in a District Court the Department of Justice rather than the Department of Defense appears to have determined the process for the trial of terrorists, although it will be necessary to assess the preferred approach on a case by case basis.

The disposition of these matters is subject to varying interpretations. Supporters of a high level of security contend that detentions are an important tool in the war against terrorism, and that they serve security needs. In opposition is the view that it is not necessary to hold a person incommunicado for the duration, and especially without a clearly applicable federal statute overriding the 1971 non-detention statute. Those who emphasize civil liberties fear that harmful precedents will be established and that they will find their way into more normal times.

12. THE GUANTANAMO DETAINEES

By December, 2002, approximately 600 prisoners from 43 countries had been transported for safekeeping to the U.S. Naval Base in Cuba. They were captured in Afghanistan. They have been labeled "detainees" in order to avoid their claim that they are prisoners of war under the Third Geneva Convention. Underlying this form of detention is the opportunity to carry on intensive interrogation in order to obtain information concerning the location of terrorists and their plans.

Several law suits have been filed in the federal courts challenging the legality of the detentions. In California a coalition of clergy, lawyers, and faculty members asked the Federal District Court to order the release of the detainees. The trial judge ruled in 2002 that the individuals who had initiated the suit did not possess the "next-friend" standing necessary for them to represent the detainees. The detainees claimed the government was depriving them of their liberty without due process of law since they had not been informed of the nature of the accusations against them and by not affording them assistance of counsel. These claims were made in a habeas corpus proceeding.

On appeal to the Court of Appeals it was ruled that the lawyers for the detainees did not possess the "significant relationship" with the detainees to allow for representation. It also held that the trial court had gone too far in ruling that the writ of habeas corpus could be suspended by the federal government. Regarding the due process contention the higher court referred to *Zadvydas v. Davis*, 533 U.S. 678, 693 (2001) where the U.S. Supreme Court stated: "It is well established that certain constitutional protections available to persons outside the United States are unavailable to aliens outside of our geographic borders." This was based on the view that Cuba holds territorial sovereignty over the U.S. naval base which is leased to the United States by Cuba.

In a Washington, D.C. case the Court of Appeals, also in December, 2002, was asked to rule on the detention at Guantanamo of specifically identified prisoners, who are nationals of Kuwait, the United Kingdom, and Australia. Counsel argued that in the absence of access to United States courts the prisoners would fall into a "black hole" and would be unable to perfect their rights under the U.S. Constitution and the Third Geneva Convention. Among the litigant's contentions was that Guantanamo Bay Naval Base is under the complete jurisdiction and control of the United States, while Cuba's sovereignty is merely nominal. This was in response to the trial court's holding that the base was "abroad," and that federal courts had no power review the treatment of the detainees.

The government also repeated its contention that the persons being detained were "unlawful enemy combatants" because of their commitment to terrorism. The United States attorney pointed out that an extended detention facilitated the gathering of intelligence information; that the detainees were receiving humanitarian treatment; that some had been released to Afghanistan as prisoners of war; and that they had been freed after returning home. Following diplomatic interventions British and Australian detainees were released.

In November 2003 the Supreme Court agreed to hear the cases of *Al Oda v. United States* and *Rasul v. Bush*. In the first the issue was whether federal courts possess jurisdiction in cases involving aliens who were captured abroad in connection with hostilities and are presently incarcerated at Guantanamo. The second was an appeal from a holding that the detainees could not be released because of alleged violations by the government of the Constitution, treaties, and statutes.

In December 2003 federal courts issued rulings in Cuban detainee cases. In *Gherebi v. Bush*, decided by the U.S. Court of Appeals located in California, the relative of a Libyan, who had been captured in Afghanistan, sought the release of the detainee. The court, in a habeas corpus proceeding, ruled that indefinite detention was unlawful and that the detainee was entitled to the benefit of counsel. This ruling was based on the view that, despite the terms of the lease between the United States and Cuba, which confirms Cuban sovereignty over the land occupied by the Guantanamo Naval Station, that the United States was, in effect the sovereign. The decision urged that substance should take precedence over form.

The response of the Department of Justice was that the U.S. Supreme Court had held that U.S. courts have no jurisdiction over non-U.S. citizens being held in military control abroad. Attention was also called to a recent U.S. Court of Appeals decision handed down in Washington, D.C. It held unanimously that detainees in military control at Guantanamo Bay could not meet the jurisdictional requirements for access to U.S. courts.

The California decision with its unusual holding that national sovereignty and jurisdiction and control were legal equivalents has been appealed to the Supreme Court. Pending its decision the California decision will not be implemented. When the matter comes to the Supreme Court it will have to determine if the term "ultimate sovereignty" as employed in the lease is to be substantially affected by the nature of the power exercised by the U.S. government in Cuba. In doing so it will take into account that the United States, and other countries, regularly exercise jurisdiction and control over persons in areas in which they are not sovereign. The government will have to demonstrate that national security is so paramount that civil tribunals should not be allowed to exercise jurisdiction.

The result of the Cuban cases and those involving enemy combatants, such as Hamdi and Padilla is the same. Pending appeal all Cuban detainees and this category of combatants are being held for unstated periods.

The U.S. policy has been severely criticized by Human Rights groups, which have demanded that such persons be charged with crimes, prosecuted, and either convicted or found not guilty. Charges have also been made that the living conditions at Guantanamo do not meet the standards required by the laws or customs of war. The United States has been criticized on the ground that in November 2001 the President authorized the establishment of military commissions for the prosecution of terrorists and that such courts had not been established in May 2003.

13. INS DEPORTATIONS AND MANDATORY DETENTIONS

The INS, recently renamed the Bureau of Citizenship and Immigration Services, as an active participant in the war against terrorism, has reviewed cases where a visa holder had violated the terms of entry into the United States. Many persons left the country voluntarily. Others have been held for extended periods pending a final determination of their status. Hearings, when conducted, were conducted rapidly resulting in many summary deportations.

The Bush administration in a case now pending before the United States Supreme Court has asked the court to rule that deportable immigrants have no due process right to a public hearing. The Attorney General has urged that security considerations justify questioning alien detainees in secret.

Many believe that the First Amendment gives the public and the press the right to attend deportation hearings. To this the government has responded that the primary national policy must be self-preservation. The question remains whether there should be a rule allowing for unrestricted closure or whether in each case there might be a determination as to the precise security issue that is present. Also to be determined is whether a deportation hearing is sufficiently like a criminal proceeding to require the application of the rules required in such cases. As in so many other situations involving terrorism there is a need to balance security interests against the public's right to know.

14. THE FOREIGN INTELLIGENCE SURVEILLANCE COURTS

In 1978 Congress passed the Foreign Intelligence Surveillance Act to meet Cold War challenges. Two courts were created. One is the Foreign Intelligence Surveillance Court; the other the Foreign Intelligence Surveillance Court of Review. This statute was amended in the wake of 9/11. In the USA Patriot Act there is a provision that allows federal prosecutors to apply for a wire-tap order where the collection of foreign intelligence information was a "significant purpose" of the search. This can be compared with the original statute's provision that the target was "an agent of a foreign power." The act calls for eleven federal judges to serve on the court. In late 2002 a request was made to this body for permission to wiretap conversations where the significant purpose was to search for and apprehend persons who were believed to be engaged in terroristic activities. It was granted.

15. A LONGER-RANGE RESPONSE TO INTERNATIONAL TERRORISM

Aside from the need for guaranteeing a "fair trial" no matter what court hears the charges of terroristic activity, the ultimate question is how to deal with terrorism. What will be a multilateral policy to manage the convicted and respond to those who unremittingly pursue their violence?[42]

If responses to terrorism are to be effective there will have to be a very high degree of collaboration and cooperation between experts on numerous subjects. These areas include bio-terrorism, cyber-terrorism affecting computers and e-commerce, financial controls, and homeland security. Additionally, effective responses will require the use of diplomacy, the gathering of intelligence information, and formidable humanitarian activities, including food, clothing, shelter, medical care, and educational opportunities. All of these responses involve domestic and international activities.

16. DEALING WITH BIO-TERRORISM

The United States had been involved in all of the foregoing areas prior to the September 2001 bombings, and international organizations had provided working papers, adopted resolutions, and proposed international agreements. More immediate practical responses are now taking place.

In the area of bio-terrorism the 2003 federal budget adds $2.4 billion "to develop new test protocols and new treatments for bio-terrorist weapons."[43] The goal was to have "enough antibiotics on hand to treat up to 20 million people for anthrax, plague and other bio-terrorist diseases."[44] The 2003 proposed budget to fight biological terrorism increased $5.9 billion, a 319 percent increase over the 2002 level.[45]

The events surrounding the anthrax scare in the United States in September 2001 have caused the United States to review the 1972 Biological and Toxic Weapons Convention.[46] This agreement prohibits all offensive biological and toxin weapons. It has been signed by more than 140 States. Until 1998 the treaty was dormant, since the major signatories were not able to agree to an inspection system. While the United States had abandoned its germ-weapons programs in 1969, it had also called for a procedure for verification of non-manufacture that would include private companies. As late as 1998 American companies and the U.S. government had failed to establish a common position.

In 1998, at a time when the U.S. did not have a position allowing domestic verification, it accepted the importance of the international monitoring of the biological weapons program of Iraq. In his State of the Union Address in January 1998 President Clinton, put forward the basics for a new U.S. policy. It would allow for an international monitoring system to make inspections following a prior notification. He also suggested that such a body investigate formal charges of treaty violations. In such inquiries the U.S. indicated that proprietary secrets would have to be guarded.

All signatories then began negotiations to obtain an enforcement procedure including on-the-spot verifications. When this proposal was presented to the Bush administration it was rejected. It was thought that the powers given to inspectors were too limited and that it would provide Iraq a "veneer" of respectability while it continued manufacturing these weapons, and that it would prove to be too burdensome on the U.S. biotechnology industry.[47] The United States was content in suggesting a voluntary code of conduct for manufacturing laboratories, limitations on shipments, and further inquiry into an international agreement allowing for the prosecution of biological terrorists.

The subject has received much attention in the press. On September 6, 2000 it was revealed that, despite the 1969 order by President Nixon not to produce biological weapons, the Department of Energy was engaged in the study of different means for the delivery of dangerous microorganisms.[48] Reference also was made to "the construction and testing of a germ production plant."[49] In November of 2001 a representative of the Department of State announced publicly that some States, sometimes referred to as "rogue States," namely, Iran, Iraq, North Korea, Libya, and Syria were engaged in the manufacture of biological weapons. At this time no mention was made of China, Egypt, and Russia, which have similar capabilities, since they have been somewhat supportive of America's presence in Afghanistan.[50]

A quieter form of diplomacy on this subject has been carried out between the United States and Russia. In November, 2001, Presidents Bush and Putin in a joint statement referred to national efforts, by both military and civilian personnel, to prevent and defend against the threat of bioterrorism. They confirmed their strong support for the 1972 Biological and Toxic Weapons treaty.[51]

Also in November 2001, President Bush offered a new approach with regard to the 1972 treaty. Because of the anthrax incidents in the United States, he urged that individuals engaging in prohibited biological warfare activities should be prosecuted.[52] Other proposals called for a more active role by the UN in investigating suspicious outbreaks of disease and allegations of biological weapons use, the establishment of a code of ethics for bioscientists, rapid scientific on-the-spot investigations of the outbreak of diseases, and greater care, with accompanying procedures, in the genetic engineering of pathogenic organisms.[53] Implicit in the view that only States should monitor and prosecute those persons who are engaged in the production of germ weapons was the conclusion that it would not be possible to establish the criteria for an international monitoring agency, or, if established, to rely on the integrity of its findings.

17. CYBER-TERRORISM

Cyber-terrorism is the term applied to the hostile and unlawful invasion of computers to destroy existing information or to introduce commands designed to advance the goals of terrorists. Through the use of computers, the internet, and other high-tech tools the terrorist would attempt to take down power grids, networks used for communication, and all of the specialized scientific and technological equipment constituting the nation's critical infrastructure. Through such means the terrorist would attempt to spread false information, prevent access to means to verify the falsity of the messages, cause fear, uncertainty, and panic, with the result that normal, including defensive measures, could not be taken to redress dangerous situations.

One of the responsibilities of the Department of Homeland Security is to devise means to make government and private computers more secure against breaches. More advanced security measures are contemplated to protect against unlawful access to intelligence and military secrets. Underlying this need is the fact that in past years there has been a fairly high level of laxness in maintaining security for governmental computers and their programs, including the theft of a computer from a protected area in the U.S. Department of State. Larger concerns relate to the theft of nuclear materials.

18. FLATTENING THE POCKET BOOKS OF THE TERRORISTS

Control over the financial resources of terrorists can play a critical role. To this end the United States, many foreign States, and the United Nations, as well as a host of other international organizations, can impose certain limitations. To be effective such policies must prevent the movement of valuable resources across national boundaries for the benefit of resident terrorists.

On September 23, 2001 the President signed executive order 13224 blocking the transfer of funds to the Al Qaeda terrorists. By January, 2002, the U.S.

government had identified 168 organizations and individuals as financiers of terrorism and blocked $34.2 million. On January 9, 2002, the Secretary of Treasury reported that America's "coalition partners have blocked another $33.9 million. 196 nations have expressed support for disrupting terrorist financing and 144 have blocking orders in force."[54] On April 20, 2003 Secretary of State Powell announced that since 9/11 more than $134 million of terrorist assets in the United States had been frozen.

On October 26, 2001 the International Money Laundering Abatement Act of 2001, was signed into law.[55] Important provisions dealt with due diligence measures, bank secrecy, and money laundering provisions. The statute gave the government many new weapons to combat international terrorism, and adopted increased sanctions. With regard to money laundering, long-arm jurisdiction was established over foreign money launderers including financial institutions, which were redefined to include foreign banks. The civil and criminal penalties for laundering were increased from $100,000 to $1,000,000.[56]Just as there has been a dramatic increase in security regulations applicable to air travel, so also have there been huge restrictions on the transfer of money and other assets to suspected terrorists.

The United Nations has taken a key interest in this subject. On January 10, 2000 it opened for signature the International Convention for the Suppression of Financing of Terrorism, which was signed by the United States on January 20, 2002. On September 28, 2001 the Security Council adopted Resolution 1373 entitled Prevention and Suppression of Financing Terrorist Acts with a Definition of Terrorism.

As further evidence of the Security Council's active interest in preventing Al Qaeda, and any country where it may find refuge, from having assets for terroristic purposes is its Resolution 1390 of January 28, 2002. The Security Council decided that "all States" should

> Freeze without delay the funds and other financial assets or economic resources of these individuals, groups, undertakings and entities, including funds derived from property owned or controlled, directly or indirectly, by them or by persons acting on their behalf or at their direction, and ensure that neither these nor any other funds, financial assets or economic resources are made available, directly or indirectly, for such persons' benefit, by their nationals or by any persons within their territory.[57]

The 2002 Resolution called for the interdiction of travel of identified terrorists through a member's territory. It also called for the withholding of military supplies or the delivery of such materials to identified terrorists.

Relying on existing statutes, including the 2001 Patriot Act, the government began its special war against accountants, auditors, and bankers who served as conduits between U.S. residents and terrorist organization. One such body was the Chicago-based Global Relief Organization. It had been under surveillance since 2001. This body had links to Osama bin Laden and Al Qaeda networks. In the prosecution of this organization in a Federal District Court the government was asked to produce its evidence and the sources of its information. It declined to do so because of its secret sources. Officers of the organization were convicted and appealed to the Court of Appeal in Chicago. It upheld the secrecy provisions of the statutes and sustained the conviction of the officers of the organization.

Providing funds to terrorist organizations may constitute one of several unlawful acts. Earnest James Usama, an American citizen residing in Seattle, received training at an Al Qaeda camp in Afghanistan, where he installed computer software programs for Taliban officials. Following his arrest in the United States he was refused bail and was charged with terroristic activities including the provision of money, goods, services, and technical assistance to the enemy. He received a two year prison sentence which was based on his willingness to cooperate with federal authorities in tracking down terrorists. The outcome met with the approval of the Attorney General who stated that a part of the war on terrorism consisted in gaining the "cooperation of insiders who have direct knowledge of activities" of terrorists.

In a separate case a Chicago resident who was a naturalized American citizen created the Benevolence International Foundation devoted to humanitarian purposes. He was charged with illegally bankrolling Muslim fighters in Chechnya and Bosnia-Herzegovina. He denied assisting Al Qaeda. Following a guilty plea to a single count of racketeering he was convicted. The plea-bargaining required that the accused cooperate with the government in identifying terrorists.

Further governmental investigations have disclosed the terrorist use of so-called charitable or educational organizations which have collected funds in the United States and transmitted them to foreign militants. The Department of Justice has been given the green light to proceed with prosecutions. In proceeding in this fashion the court hearings will be aired publicly and Americans will be provided with a deeper understanding of the activities of terrorists. Preference for prosecution will be given to Federal District Courts rather than to military commissions.

19. CONCLUSION

The defining characteristic of terrorism is the means employed to obtain a specifically and carefully identified goal causing catastrophic harm to persons and property. The means range all the way from the killing of one person to the enormous destruction of civilian persons and property hitherto not seen by civilized persons in recent centuries. The magnitude of the harm distinguishes terrorism from the kind of force equated with the conduct of persons engaged in freeing themselves from the domination of authoritarian regimes. Profound grievances underlie commitments to use vast violence.

A subordinate but important characteristic of terrorism is its world-wide presence. Local and world-wide conditions produce reasons for its existence.

Up to this point no reference has been made to the religious preference of those charged with recent terrorist activities, except to say that members of Al Qaeda have been commonly referred to as religious zealots. That many are Muslims appears to be true, and certainly those who were captured in Afghanistan and removed to the Guantanamo Naval Base have asked for and have been granted the opportunity to consult with a United States military chaplain who is himself a Muslim. But, in other areas of world where terrorism exists, the militants subscribe to other faiths.

In the United States two major issues relating to terrorism have arisen. First, there has been the choice of judicial bodies for the prosecution of terroristic activities. The Bush Order of November 13, 2001 applied to "noncitizens." Since Zacarias Moussaoui and Richard C. Reid are aliens they were candidates for prosecution in military commissions rather than in the Federal District Courts. Since the Guantanamo Bay detainees are non-citizens the commissions would have jurisdiction.

Alleged terrorists such as Yaser Esam Hamdi, John Walker Lindh, Jose Padilla, and Earnest James Usama are United States citizens. All six of these individuals have been prosecuted in a District court with full constitutional protections. The pattern is clear. However, for other non-citizens, including those held at Guantanamo Bay, their trial before a commission is probable. Their constitutional rights, if any, are currently under review.

In the event of the conviction of a major defendant in a military tribunal, such as Zacarias Moussaoui, with perhaps a sentence of death, there will have to be a complete explanation to the worldwide observers of the trial. A review of the theories of punishment will have to be made. The purpose underlying the punishment will have to be explained. The manner in which the trial or trials are conducted will have to be portrayed. Proof of guilt must be demonstrated as having been arrived at in accordance with the very highest demands of a civilized system of justice. Findings of guilt based on such standards will have to be related to convictions of heads of State, such as Bijana Plavsic, President of the Serb portion of Bosnia-Herzegonia, and possibly Slobodan Milosevic.

In the case of a Head of State prosecuted for different crimes, a major question is will a conviction and meaningful sentence deter other Heads of State and their subordinates. The same question must be asked about terrorists.

The September 11 acts of terrorism have been so gross that America's search for a globalistic approach to fight terrorism has been readily supported. Will America acknowledge the presence, not only in these present circumstances, of common interests? Or, because of America's frequent adoption of unilateralist approaches which would seem frequently against its best interest, the question must be, how much of a threat to America must there be to allow it to cross the threshold of multilateralism?

Although the United States suffered the immediate brunt of terrorism in September, it is evident that in different degrees of intensity, fears and acts of terrorism have been experienced on a world-wide basis. All now know it can erode national infrastructures as well as incinerate people and structures. Will it take a particularistic and increasingly devastating turn as in the Middle East?

At the beginning of the Chapter these circumstances were addressed from a legal, including a choice of courts, perspective. Toward the close of the Chapter other considerations were mentioned, which may have more of an international coloration than at the beginning. If terrorists are to spread anthrax, engage in cyber-terrorism, transit across national boundaries, and obtain the delivery for their survival of funds held in foreign banks, there is manifestly a need for international professional assistance. It should also be noted that a number of countries have made available elite military units for use against the terrorists of Afghanistan and Iraq.

There was a general awareness of terrorists and their goals prior to September 11, 2001. Some specific international and national protection measures had been promulgated and enforced. But, it took the massive attack of September to galvanize suitable responses. It is now evident that wide-ranging, cooperative and continuing international attention must be given to this phenomenon. This will require high costs and many inconveniences. Over time, following a globalist approach, the benefits may exceed costs.

DISCUSSION QUESTIONS

1. Analyze the prospect for a very widely accepted international agreement including a definition of terrorism.
2. Within the United States, who, at the national level of government, appears to have the most influential role in post-combat decision making relating to the legal disposition of member of the Taliban and Al Qaeda? Why?

3. Under what conditions can members of the Taliban and Al Qaeda be treated as prisoners of war and claim the protection of the 1949 Geneva Convention?
4. What are the characteristics of terrorists which distinguish them from militants who engage in force and violence to achieve their goals?
5. On a scale of one to ten, where does terrorism fit in as a subject of U.S. foreign policy?
6. On what grounds can the United States justify the summary deportation of individuals who have overstayed the time set in their visas?
7. How can the Federal government justify the use of the anti-racketeering law to prosecute and convict terrorists for sending funds to oversees charitable or educational institutions?
8. Under what circumstances can a writ of habeas corpus proceeding be useful in obtaining the release of a person being held as a terrorist?
9. What are the critical difference between the *Quirin* and the *Milligan* cases?
10. To what extent has the United Nations contributed to the effort to bring terrorism under control?

NOTES

1. Terrorism, in the sense of intentional harms to civilians, is not a modern phenomenon. C. CARR, THE LESSONS OF TERROR: A HISTORY OF WARFARE AGAINST CIVILIANS (2002). A general reference is the Department of State publication PATTERNS OF GLOBAL TERRORISM. For recent symposiums of "Terrorism," see "Terrorism's Burdens on Globalization," 36 *The Int'l Law*, No. 1, 1-119 (Spring 2002) 82 *Phi Kappa Phi Forum*, No. 2, 10-48 (Spring 2002), and L. Walter and others, TERRORISM AS A CHALLENGE FOR NATIONAL AND INTERNATIONAL LAW, SECURITY VERSUS LIBERTY (2003).

2. George Bush, "State of the Union Address," January 29, 2002, *Los Angeles Times*, A20, January 30, 2002.

3. Authoritization for the Use of Military Force, Public Law No. 107-40, 115 Stat. 224, September 18, 2001.

4. Public Law 107-56, 115 Stat. 296-342, October 24, 2001. The statute's wide-ranging provisions calling for record keeping and reports have been criticized as imposing constraints on freedom of expression and the circulation of ideas.

5. *Ibid.*

6. International Convention for the Suppression of Terrorist Bombings, Art. 2 3. (c).

7. For a comprehensive republication of documents addressing terrorism, see 40 *ILM*. 1254-1286, Sept. 2001. Included are U.S. statutes, Executive Orders, and decisions taken by the UN, OAS, European Union, NATO, and the OECD. For a list of 12 international conventions and other treaties relating to terrorism where the United

States is a party or signatory, see www.state/gov/r/pa/ho/pubs/fs/6093.htm. For a list of 20 conventions on terrorism, which includes regional agreements, see www .untreaty.un.org/English/Terrorism.asp.

8. The most recent effort to promote international responses to terrorism is the June 3, 2002 Inter-American Convention Against Terrorism. 42 *ILM* 19 (2003).

9. *Fact Sheet, Status of Detainees at Guantanamo*, Department of State, Office of the Press Secretary (2002).

10. *Id.* at p.1, italics added.

11. *Id.*, italics added.

12. *Id.*, italics added.

13. "Detention, Treatment, and Trial of Certain Non-Citizens in the War Against Terrorism" 66 F.R. 57833 (Nov. 16, 2001); (http://www.whitehouse.gov/news/releases/2002/11/20011113-27.html). Public Law 102-40, 115 Stat 224 (2001).

14. *Ibid.*

15. *Id.* at Sec. 4.(a).

16. *Id.* at Sec. 4.(c)(1).

17. *Id.* at Sec. 4.(c)(4).

18. *Id.* at Sec. 4.(c)(3)(4).

19. *Id.* at Sec. 7.(b)(2).

20. *Id.* at Sec. 4.(c)(1).

21. *The Christian Science Monitor*, 10, January 17, 2002. The quoted words were attributed to a Pentagon source.

22. 317. U.S. 1 (1942).

23. Only "wrongful conduct" is subject to prosecution. With regard to terrorism this requirement prescribes that an act does not constitute terrorism when there is "an attack against a lawful military objective undertaken by military forces of a State in the exercise of their official duties." This means that members of Al Qaeda must prove that they are part of the military forces of Afghanistan in order to escape prosecution.

24. 317 U.S. 1(1942).

25. 18 L.Ed. 281 (1866).

26. "Military Tribunals," *Los Angeles Times*, A10, December 5, 2001. In the domestic cases a vast proportion of defendants entered pleas of guilty.

27. *Los Angeles Times*, A22, January 18, 2002. Federal District Courts have been asked to rule on the rights of the Guantanamo detainees. On January 20, 2002, a Los Angeles Court was told that they were held in violation of the U.S. Constitution and the Third Geneva Convention. *Los Angeles Times*, A5, February 1, 2002.

In a case entitled Coalition of Clergy, Lawyers, and Professors vs. Bush the Court of Appeals ruled on November 18, 2002 that the plaintiffs, who had asserted that they were "next friends" of the detainees or had "third-party standing," did not meet those conditions. The coalition had alleged that the detainees were being deprived of their liberty without due process of law, had not been informed of the nature and cause of the accusations against them, and had not been provided with counsel. 310 F. 3d. 1153 (2003). On February 19, 2002, similar allegations were made in Washington for Australian and British citizens who were serving with the Taliban at the time of their capture in Afghanistan, *Los Angeles Times*, A12, February 20, 2002. "Military

Tribunals," Los Angeles Times, A10, December 5, 2001. N.K. Katyal and L.H. Tribe, "Waging War, Deciding Guilt: Trying the Military Tribunals," 111 *Yale L.J.* 1259 (April 2002). See also articles by Jordan J. Paust in 23 *Mich. J. Int'l L.* at 1 and 677 (2001–2002).

28. *The Law of Land Warfare*, FM 27-20, Department of the Army Field Manual, 30 (1956).*Los Angeles Times*, A22, January 18, 2002.

29. *Id.* at 30–31.

30. Of particular concern to the ABA was an administrative rule issued by the Attorney General and published on October 31, 2001 in the Federal Register. It was designed to apply within the United States. It would allow the Attorney General to monitor conversations between terrorist-detainees and their lawyers. The president of the ABA indicated that the ruling went "too far" in addressing the "delicate balance between protecting our own security and protecting our own civil rights." *ABA Journal*, January 2002 at p. 21. Constitutional law experts have supported and criticized this outlook. An assessment of the Order has been made by the Human Rights Committee of the American Branch of the International Law Association. Entitled "International Law and Constitutional Law Ramifications of the President's Military Order of November 13, 2001." It was addressed to the U.S. Senate Judiciary Committee. J.E. Noyes, ed., *Proceedings of the American Branch of the International Law Association*, 2001–2002, 141 (2002).

31. Press Release #492, http://www.usdoj.gov/opa/pr/2001/September/492ag.htm.)

32. *Id.* at p.2.

33. *United States v. Bin Laden*, 92F. Supp. 2d 225 (S.D.N.Y. 2000). The court gave careful scrutiny to 4th and 5th Amendment claims. 95 *AJIL* 637 (2001).

34. *Los Angeles Times*, A12, December 13, 2001.

35. M. Glennon, *The Washington Post National Weekly Edition*, 23, January 7–13, 2002.

36. *Ibid.*

37. "Lindh Faces Added Grand Jury Charges," *Los Angeles Times*, A1, February 5, 2002.

38. S.I. Vladeck, "A Small Problem of Precedent: 18 U.S.C. #4001 (9) and the Detention of U.S. Citizen 'Enemy Combatants'" 112 *Yale L.J.*, No. 4, 961 (January 2003).

39. *Los Angeles Times*, A30, December 3, 2003.

40. *Los Angeles Times*, A16, December 4, 2003.

41. Directive, President Bush to Secretary of Defense Rumsfeld June 9, 2002. www.findlaw.com

42. Assessments of these issues are contained in the annual "Patterns of Global Terrorism" prepared by the Coordinator of Counterterrorism in the Department of State. The 2002 Report was issued on April 30, 2003. Extraordinary measures will be required to bring continuing high levels of terrorism under control. It is a persistent virus.

43. President Bush, "Defending Against Biological Terrorism," *White House Press Release*, p. 4 February 5, 2002.

44. *Ibid.*

45. *Ibid.*, p.1. Further detail on how such sums are to be spent can be found in "President Increases Funding for Bioterrorism by 319 Percent," *White House Press Release*, pp. 3–5, February 5, 2002.

46. 26 UST 583; TIAS 8062; 1015 UNTS 163.

47. *Los Angeles Times*, A3, July 25, 2001.

48. *Los Angeles Times*, B14, September 6, 2001.

49. *Ibid.*

50. *Los Angeles Times*, A1, November 20, 2001.

51. *White House Press Releases*, p. 1. November 13, 2001.

52. *Los Angeles Times*, A5, November 2, 2001.

53. *Ibid.*

54. U.S. Department of the Treasury, *Treasury News*, Office of Public Affairs, Fact Sheet, p.2. January 9, 2002.

55. It is a section of the USA Patriot Act, Pub. L. No. 107-56, 115 Stat 296-342, October 24, 2001.

56. E.J. Krauland and S. Lagonico, "The Counter-Money Laundering and Anti-Terrorists Financing Law," 31 *International Law News*, No. 1, p. 16 (Winter 2002).

57. S/RES/1390 (2002), p. 2, January 28, 2002. Reprinted in 41 *ILM* 511 (2002). In an earlier Resolution the Security Council had called on all States to "freeze funds and other financial resources" belonging to the Taliban until Usama bin Laden had been turned over to a State where he had been indicted or to other interested countries. S/RES/1267, p. 2, October 15, 1999. An assessment of Security Council resolutions appears in M. Kantor, "Effectively Enforcement of International Obligations to Suppress the Financing of Terror," The American Society of International Law Task Force on Terrorism, 5–8 (September 2002).

Chapter IV

International Criminal Tribunals

In fairly recent years the idea of creating international criminal courts has gathered much interest. The successful roles of the International Military Tribunal, popularly known as the Nuremberg Tribunal, and the World War II prosecutions of Japanese war criminals have influenced this development.

Following World War II there had been a very large advance in the area of Human Rights. Why, it has been asked, should there not be a formal international institution to which violations of basic Human Rights might be referred for adjudication?

The International Court of Justice in The Hague is limited in its jurisdiction to civil matters. The establishment of a permanent international criminal court would, in the minds of many, eliminate a "missing link" in an evolving international legal system.

Great forces lie behind the establishment of a more advanced international legal order. At the United Nations the General Assembly has the legislative function and the Security Council the executive function. The creation of a permanent international criminal tribunal would augment the role of the world judicial process.

At present there are permanent regional courts dealing with Human Right's violations, such as European and Latin American Human Right's courts. Additionally, there are two major *ad hoc* regional international criminal courts, the International Criminal Tribunal for the Former Yugoslavia (ICTFY) and the International Criminal Tribunal for Rwanda (ICTR). The substantial roles of these would be considerably enhanced with the formation of a permanent International Criminal Court (ICC).

It is possible to devise an ICC compatible with the foreign policy objectives of the United States?

1. A PERMANENT INTERNATIONAL CRIMINAL COURT (ICC)

Following years of intense efforts at the United Nations and by international law experts an international conference met in Rome in June 1998 to draft a convention for a permanent international criminal court. It would deal with the crime of genocide, crimes against humanity, war crimes, and after agreement was reached on "aggression," with that subject also. It had the support of Americans generally, and international lawyers, in particular. Yet, Presidents Clinton and Bush were not so sure. Positions advanced by Clinton administration's delegates were derided. The Bush administration has repeatedly indicated its disapproval. Their fears have been grounded in national sovereignty, and the belief that matters subject to the jurisdiction of the new court could be better disposed of via diplomatic negotiations.

A particularly objectionable provision of the Convention according to the United States was the adoption of a territorial basis for the exercise of jurisdiction over an accused. Thus, if an American military person were arrested in a ratifying country for an unlawful act occurring in that country, its courts would have the right to prosecute. The two administrations argued that charges could be politically motivated, and, in any event, the United States would not have jurisdiction. Particularly offensive to the United States was a treaty provision allowing a territorial State to prosecute, even though the United States was not a party to the agreement.

As with all courts there will have to be the requisite amount of confidence in the structure and purpose of the tribunal before it can become a reality. Of vast importance in gaining the required confidence in the court are such traditional matters as its competence, its jurisdiction, procedures for securing the appointment of judges and their qualifications, the manner of selecting the chief prosecutor, the manner in which cases are selected for prosecution, rules of evidence, sentences that could be imposed, places of incarceration, the appellate process, funding, provisions for the acquisition of an accused, protections for witnesses, the publication of opinions, and all of the day-to-day matters required to be dealt with in order to have an efficient institution. In short, there must be clear rules, procedures, and criteria, equally applied, for its ultimate function, which is the ascertainment in individual cases of innocence or guilt.

American presidents have to decide what position to take regarding foreign policies as they try to advance the well-being of Americans. Some policies receive more support than others. High in the scale of importance is national security. Other matters are considered to have a lower priority and receive less attention.

Proponents of preferred American policies are obliged to consider what other countries deem of importance to them. At this point the United States has a choice. It may be supportive and cooperate in finding means to implement such policies. On the other hand, the United States may oppose foreign proposals and mount a campaign to defeat them. In doing so American leaders are obliged to weigh political constituencies that are believed to be the most influential on the subject. In short there can be American foreign policies which are supportive and consistent with world proposals; there can be policies which seek to negate such proposals. Both sides urge that their views are consistent with the national interest.

This applies to the American position on the ICC. The tribunal, with its potential for improving the quality of world order, has been rejected by the Bush administration on the broadly based charge that its operation would threaten elements of American sovereignty. The question has been raised as to the possible bias of the prosecutor. These concerns have been opposed by Americans supportive of the world rule of law and rejected by the countries which have ratified the Convention. Their objections have been vigorous. Differences in this area have contributed to a minimization of America's leadership potential in other areas.

In the United States those of its international lawyers who take comfort in the concept of a world community influenced by the forces of globalism regard the formation of the ICC as an important issue of foreign policy. Whether their views will or will not prevail will depend on popular opinion. This will be influenced over time by the manner in which the Court conducts its business. The fact that Presidents Clinton and Bush have rejected the Convention does not remove this issue from the field of American foreign policy.

With this overview of policy considerations affecting the establishment of the ICC, one can turn to characteristics of the tribunal. Are these characteristics conducive to the success of the court? Will an operative court advance the cause of world order? Can the legal processes of the Court deal successfully with the international crimes identified in its Statute? Or, is the tribunal destined to fail because of the tyranny of the judges who serve it?

A. Drafting the Statute

The need for an international criminal tribunal resulted from the resurgence of violations of basic Human Rights, including the crime of genocide, which has taken place in the former Yugoslavia in the late 1980s and early 1990s. With the outbreak of civil war in Rwanda at the same time there were atrocities on a grand scale. Awareness of constant killings was reflected in newspaper and TV coverage. Human Rights organizations were active in their portrayal of what was going on. Non-governmental organizations, equipped with detailed knowledge of particular situations, reported these facts to governmental officials.

Another important influence, probably the foremost, has been the post-World War emergence of international intergovernmental organizations, which, over time, have come to focus on humanitarian matters. Without the 1948 Universal Declaration of Human Rights and the U.N. Human Rights Commission, daily public attention could not have been called to the discriminative practices affecting women and children, attacks on minorities, the plight of refugees and displaced persons, torture, and a whole host of attacks on civil and political rights and liberties. These were frequently instigated, and even more often encouraged by the very Heads of State, who were bound by their oaths of office to advance the cause of domestic tranquility.

The United Nations has been joined by regional intergovernmental institutions in the effort to protect Human Rights. These are the American Commission and the American Court on Human Rights, NATO, the European Court of Human rights, which has absorbed the work of the former Commission, the Organization for Economic Cooperation and Development in Europe, and the African Union.

The United Nations has had a long-standing interest in the creation of an international criminal tribunal. On December 8, 1948, the General Assembly asked the International Law Commission to study the subject. That body in 1951 arrived at a draft statute, which was revised in 1953. It referred to "aggression" as a major crime citing the 1928 Kellogg-Briand Pact and the holding of the Nuremberg Tribunal. In 1954 the General Assembly was engaged in a politicized debate on a definition of "aggression." The Commission considered it expedient to defer its work until the General Assembly had arrived at a decision.

In 1993 the General Assembly renewed its request to the International Law Commission. In 1994 the Commission completed a 60-article draft convention.

The General Assembly then created an *Ad Hoc* Committee on the Establishment of the court. Its report led to the General Assembly's establishment in 1995 of a Preparatory Commission (Prep-Com), which met in increasingly intensive sessions until 1998. Its work was sufficiently complete at the end of 1997 for the General Assembly to announce the convening of the Rome Conference. However, the extended efforts fell far short of anything like a final draft.

Delegates met in Rome between June 13 and July 16, 1998. They came from 160 countries. They had before them the draft articles of the Preparatory Committee. They were debated, amended, and approved by a vast majority of States on July 16, 1998. The Statute consists of 128 articles.[1] As the conference proceeded it became evident that the United States was opposed to certain proposals. It became common knowledge that the United States was seeking to "control" the court. The principal U.S. negotiator in a statement to the members of the Committee on Foreign Relations of the U.S. Senate said that the Statute would have to contain a provision that Security Council, where the United States has a veto power, "has an unfettered right and power under the U.N. Charter to halt the Court's work if it deems that is necessary."[2] The United States initially proposed that the Court could deal only with cases referred to it by the Security Council.

When the United States failed to gain support for certain of its proposals, it employed tactics that did not endear it to the majority. It was reported that the United States indicated that it could cut off financial assistance, might reconsider its military alliances, and that it would reserve the right to lobby signatory states against final ratification of the agreement.

Nonetheless, the treaty was adopted by a vote of 120 to 7. Voting against the statute were the United States, China, Iran, Iraq, Israel, Libya, and Yemen. Twenty-one countries abstained.

On the last day of the Rome Conference the United States also proposed a limitation on the Court's jurisdiction over persons, designed to protect officials of countries which were not parties to the Statute. It is evident that this proposal was made because the United States had been unable to obtain a "weak" version of the statute or to "control" the functioning of the Court. The proposal stated that the Court would not exercise jurisdiction over "acts . . . committed by officials or agents of a State not a party in the course of official duties and acknowledged by the State as such," unless that State had consented.

This would allow any country to veto the prosecution of any of its citizens. Under the procedures of the conference motions of non-action were used. 112 countries voted against the U.S. proposal. 17 were in favor. 25 abstained. Among those joining the United States were Algeria, China, Indonesia, Iraq, Israel, Libya, Mexico, Qatar, Sudan, Turkey, and Yemen.

The American proposal was "viewed by nearly all the other delegations as inconsistent with the main purpose of the treaty, i.e., to deprive war criminals of the impunity they have heretofore enjoyed by virtue of the protection of their states of nationality."[3] The U.S. proposal seemingly was based on the proposition that if the ICC were not to come into existence, or if the United States refused to ratify the Statute, that U.S. citizens could not be prosecuted by foreign countries. As has been noted "The fatal misconception in this line of reasoning is that, in the absence of some kind of agreement, the jurisdiction of the state in which the offense is committed will prevail over any other claim of jurisdiction. Territorial jurisdiction prevails over jurisdiction based on nationality."[4]

On the same day a proposal was made by India. It dealt with the manner in which the Court would exercise its jurisdiction. It sought to override the provisions of Article 16 of the Statute, which was entitled "Deferral of investigation or prosecution." The article provided "No investigation or prosecution may be commenced or proceeded with under this Statute for a period of 12 months after the Security Council, in a resolution adopted under Chapter VII of the Charter of the United Nations, has requested the Court to that effect; that request may be renewed by the Council under the same conditions." 114 countries voted against the Indian proposal, 16 were in favor, 20 abstained. At issue in this proposal, as in the one put forward by the United States, was the extent of the powers of the Court and the restraints to be retained by the members of the Security Council, or whether the Court was to be independent and not subject to Security Council domination.

On February 8, 2003 eighty-eight of the 139 countries that had signed the Convention met at The Hague to elect the Court's 18 judges. Seven of the judges are women. Seven judges are nationals of European and other Western nations. The election of the judges set the stage for the election of the Prosecutor and the appointment of a registrar. The first President will be Philippe Kirsch of Canada who chaired the Rome Conference. No U.S. citizen was elected to the Tribunal. It is expected that the trial of the first case will occur in 2004.

The Convention as agreed to in 1998, was divided into 13 parts. They are:

1. Establishment of the Court
2. Jurisdiction, Admissibility and Applicable Law
3. General Principles of Criminal Law
4. Composition and Administration of the Court
5. Investigation and Prosecution
6. The Trial
7. Penalties
8. Appeal and Revision
9. International Cooperation and Judicial Assistance
10. Enforcement
11. Assembly of States
12. Financing
13. Final Clauses

B. Subject Matter Jurisdiction Under the Rome Statute

At present the Statute gives the Court subject matter jurisdiction in cases of genocide, crimes against humanity, and war crimes. If and when an acceptable definition of aggression is arrived at, the Court will add this to its jurisdiction. There have been suggestions that terrorism and trafficking in illegal drugs be added. The elements of the three included crimes are identified on the section dealing with the ICTFY.

1. Territorial and Nationality Bases for Jurisdiction

Almost from the outset of the Rome Conference it became clear that States held different views on the tribunal's jurisdiction. One group sponsored "universal jurisdiction." The proposal that "the acceptance of the state of nationality should be *the* indispensable requirement for the Court to exercise jurisdiction . . . [was] clearly unacceptable to an overwhelming majority of delegations."[5] The United States was opposed to this approach.

Middle ground led to a formula which "requires the acceptance of *either* the state of nationality of the accused *or* the state in whose territory the crime was committed."[6] Thus, Article 12, entitled "Preconditions to the exercise of jurisdiction," prescribes that "the Court may exercise its jurisdiction if one or more of the following States are Parties to this Statute or have accepted the jurisdiction of the Court in accordance with paragraph 3: (a) The State on the territory of which the conduct in question occurred or, if the crime was committed on board a vessel or aircraft, the State of registration of that vessel or aircraft; (b) the State of which the person accused of the crime is a national."

A former president of the American Society of International Law has commented on the foregoing provisions. In his view the Statute "is drafted so as to fit within the classic international law jurisdictional framework: (1) a nation has jurisdiction over criminal acts occurring within its sovereign territory regardless of the nationality of the offender; and (2) a nation has jurisdiction over its nationals regardless of the place where they commit an offense against its law. Often the two bases of jurisdiction overlap and are concurrent."[7] The language of Article 12 may be confusing. As between States the first right to prosecute belongs to the State which has possession of the suspected criminal, i.e., the country holding a person charged, for example, with genocide. Of these two possibilities, the territorial basis enjoys the widest support in the practice of States, but both allow the Tribunal to exercise jurisdiction. In short, customary international law gives to the territorial sovereign unrestricted jurisdiction. However, the treaty grants primary jurisdiction to the State of nationality, unless, as will be pointed out below, the State of nationality were "unwilling or unable genuinely" to exercise its primary jurisdiction. If that were the case the new Court would have contingent jurisdiction. Article 12 applies to the prosecution of individuals; not to States. The treaty does not take away from any State in whose territory a crime is committed the right to prosecute.

The United States interpreted the foregoing to mean that its citizens even if it were not a party to the agreement, could be subject to the jurisdiction of the court. This was exactly what the vast majority of the negotiators wished to provide. To allow a non-party to refuse to exercise jurisdiction over a national for a violation of the crimes set forth in the convention would "mean that the most notorious war criminals would continue to be immune from the jurisdiction of the new court."[8]

Article 13 also deals with the exercise of jurisdiction. It allows for prosecution when a matter is referred to the court by a signatory, by the Security Council, and by the Prosecutor. They may name the national or nationals of a non-party State, and the latter must invoke the defenses contained in the Statute.

In commenting on the terms of Article 12, with its reference to the jurisdictional principles of territoriality and nationality, it has been stated that the Statute "effectively lets off future Saddam Husseins or Pol Pots, who kill their own people on their own territory. This provision makes the court largely ineffective in dealing with Rogue Regimes, except when the Security Council exercises its authority to extend jurisdiction to them."[9]

It was, therefore, suggested that the United States give its support to proposals whereby the Court would have jurisdiction over individuals who are massacring their own people within their own country.

Professor Meron observed that if the negotiators were too timid in not allowing for the suggested jurisdiction, they were too bold in imposing the Statute's obligations on "non-parties,"[10] because the Statute does not require a "government's consent . . . before its nationals could be prosecuted."[11]

The U.S. representative at the Rome Conference, Ambassador David J. Scheffer, also expressed concern of the United States regarding the potential of rogue States. On the assumption that such States would not become parties to the Statute he told members of the U.S. Senate that "the United States has long supported the right of the Security Council to refer situations to the Court with mandatory effect, meaning that any rogue State could not deny the Court's jurisdiction under any circumstances."[12] Only under these circumstances was the United States willing to grant to the Court the right to exercise jurisdiction over non-parties.

2. *"Trigger Mechanisms" for Access to the Court*

Article 13 of the Statute establishes "trigger mechanisms" for access to the Court in which it appears that crimes over which it possesses jurisdiction have been committed. A State Party may refer the facts of a crime to the Prosecutor with the request, authorized by Article 14 of the Statute, that the Prosecutor "investigate the situation for the purpose of determining whether one or more specific persons should be charged with the commission of such crimes." The Prosecutor may also, upon his/her own initiative engage in investigations, and on the basis of the findings, may refer a matter to the Court.

Or, the Security Council may refer the situation to the Prosecutor, under the authority granted to it in Chapter VII of the Charter. The Prosecutor may also initiate investigations *proprio moto* on the basis set forth in Article 15, relying on information possessed by the Office of the Prosecutor.

Article 14 also deals with referrals by a State Party. The same limitation is set forth in the first of the three situations identified in Article 13. However, the State Party issue is not made a condition of the Court's exercise of jurisdiction in matters referred to the Prosecutor by the Security Council or in matters in which the Prosecutor, under his or her own initiative has established the facts required to prosecute.

C. The Principle of Complementarity

The balance between the administration of justice by States and by the ICC has been given the term "complementarity." Article 17, under the heading of "Issues of Admissibility," accords to parties to the Statute the first right to prosecute violators of the precepts of international Human Rights' law set forth in the Statute. This approach is based on the proposition that States, as primary actors in the world's legal system, possessing dominant, but not necessarily exclusive, authority within their territories, should be provided with a good faith opportunity to resolve matters affecting them in their own courts before such problems are turned over to an international institution.

Article 17 also refers to situations where a State "is unwilling or unable genuinely to carry out the investigation or prosecution." Two conclusions may be drawn from this language, and from the other terms of Article 17. The most obvious is that jurisdiction is conferred on the Court in the event that the affected State cannot meet the two conditions. Second, the jurisdictional source referred to does not specify, to the exclusion of others, a single foundation upon which the Court is enabled to act. From this it may be concluded that the Court's substantive jurisdiction is derived from both customary international law and the language of the convention.

It is not possible to consider all of the 128 Articles of the Statute. However, to identify the scope of agreement, the following can be mentioned: application to Heads of State, responsibility of commanders for failure to exercise control over subordinates, nonexistence of a statute of limitations, grounds for excluding criminal responsibility, superior orders as not a defense, selection and role of judges, selection and role of Prosecutor, governing authority entitled the Assembly of State Parties, provisions relating to fair trials, limitation on penalties, appeals and revisions of court decisions, incarceration, prohibition against making reservations to the Statute, and the right to withdraw from membership. There is an interesting "Transitional Provision." It allows a party to declare that, for a period of seven years after the agreement enters into force, the signatory does not accept the court's jurisdiction regarding war crimes. The invocation of the seven-year non-application of the Statute would, in many instances prevent making charges. After seven years the non-availability of effective witnesses would affect confidence regarding to the requirement of a fair trial.

The division of prosecutorial authority between a State where a crime has occurred and the ICC, pursuant to the principle of complementarity, has been employed by the United States in a different context. For many years the United States has shared authority for the prosecution of the American citizens with other countries. Examples closest to the jurisdiction of the ICC are the 1951 Status of Forces Agreements (SOFA).

D. Effectiveness of Concurrent Jurisdiction: The SOFA Agreements

The SOFA agreements govern trial procedures for American military personnel serving in friendly foreign countries. The treaties allow the United States to apply the statutory Articles of War to military personnel engaged in official duties. Other crimes are subject to local laws. In such prosecutions the U.S. military forces can send their lawyers to the court room to observe the trial. Included in the agreements are detailed guarantees of fundamental rights available to U.S. citizens.

These procedures have worked well and have received the approval of the U.S. Supreme Court. The sharing of jurisdiction over U.S. nationals has been upheld in *Wilson v. Girard* (1957), in *Reid v. Covert* (1957), in *Kinsella v. Krueger* (1957), and in lesser American courts.

In the application of the SOFA the basic rule is that of a fair trial. The foreign government is not bound by the United States Constitution or the U.S. Articles of War. Under the latter military personnel cannot claim all of the benefits of the Constitution, yet it is generally accepted that they enjoy the basic guarantees of a fair trial.

The reluctance of the United States to allow an international criminal tribunal to exercise jurisdiction over U.S. citizens stands in sharp contrast to the sharing of jurisdiction in SOFA situations. If America's experience under SOFA with the exercise by foreign States of jurisdiction over U.S. citizens had been unsatisfactory, it would be understandable that the U.S. should be cautious in accepting the ICC. But the experience with over twenty SOFA agreements has demonstrated that these agreements serve a useful purpose and that U.S. sovereignty has not been placed in jeopardy.

E. An Appraisal of the ICC

A permanent international criminal tribunal is not a new idea. International lawyers have long favored its creation. The law set forth in the 1998 Statute is well established. The present demand for this court has been influenced by the magnitude of the killings of humans during the past 50 years, particularly in internal wars.

Not only was there a real and pressing need for such a tribunal, supported by a formal body of law at the end of the 21st century, there was also a need for a permanent institution. While the International Military Tribunal (the Nuremberg Court) was hailed for its success, it was an *ad hoc* court. Although important prosecutions took place in Germany for lesser Nazi officials, they lacked the status of a truly international court supported by more countries than simply the victors. While the trials in Germany in Japan at the close of World War II were impressive in their commitments to the concept of "fair trial," they did not provide for permanent procedures. When there are many defendants a consolidated code of law is required, as well as provisions identifying the qualities and qualifications of judges.[13]

As indicated international criminal tribunals can take at least two forms, *ad hoc*, and permanent. The Under-Secretary-General for Legal Affairs for the United Nations has identified arguments for creating a permanent institution, as opposed to a series of *ad hoc* courts. These are: first, the Security Council does not have adjudicating as a primary function and is limited by Chapter VII of the Charter; second, when established a permanent court can act immediately, whereas it takes time to create a new *ad hoc* tribunal; third, the formation of a court via the treaty process is more traditional, and States are "more inclined to feel bound by their common effort;"[14] fourth, the mere existence of such a permanent body would constitute a deterrence to would-be warlords; and fifth, "a coherent practice would develop, in which an experienced team of judges, prosecutors, investigators and court administrators would create a *sui generis* international regime that would be immediately available should the need arise."[15]

Four major problems can be solved by the creation of a permanent tribunal. First, the substantive law would prevent a Head of State, who had violated the law, from claiming sovereign immunity as a defense. Although not a new assertion, such a claim has become increasingly unreal and unpopular. Second, imposing a just sentence on any violator, Head of State and lesser persons, would provide solace to victims, and, it was hoped, serve to some degree as a deterrent to would-be tyrants. Third, such a court would provide an alternative to prosecution under national laws in national tribunals where conditions foreseeably could prevent a fair trial. Fourth, the creation of a criminal tribunal would eliminate a missing link in the world's legal system.

As a matter of policy the United States has accepted the existence of the crimes set forth in the Statute, namely, genocide, crimes against humanity and crimes listed under the laws or customs of war, as violative of international law. There was agreement, that, if and when defined, aggression would also fall within the court's jurisdiction. But, for the time being, terrorism and drug trafficking would not.

The vast majority of States at Rome built their policies on globalism, and, on more than one occasion inquired as to whether the United States would forego its unilateralistic outlook. While globally oriented accommodations are not necessarily founded in moral authority, neither is it the case that being the most powerful country in the world is evidence of a singular moral authority.

Looking at the creation of the new court from a legal perspective it is correct to say that it fills a void in the international legal process. It will have the power to apply the fundamental provisions of international humanitarian law. Individuals must comply with this law, which is set forth in formal international agreements and in the general principles of international law, which is also referred to as customary international law. The Statute recognizes the existence of the right of a State to prosecute for violations occurring within its territory by anyone and for violations on the part of its nationals, whether they occur at home or abroad.

The Statute, through the application of the principle of complementarity, fixes a priority for investigations and prosecutions in the event of violations. The right of States to prosecute on the two overlapping and concurrent bases of jurisdiction depends, according to Article 17 of the Statute on their willingness and ability "genuinely to carry out the investigation or prosecution." If such a State fails to meet these criteria, the matter is then admissible to the Court for its determination. The final decision on a State's capacity to act would be made by way of an interlocutory appeal to the five-judge appellate chamber of the Court. In this manner due regard is given to the sovereign right of a State to exercise original jurisdiction, while at the same time preventing a State, because of unwillingness or inability, from frustrating the work of the court.

The respect to be given to the decisions of the court will depend on the integrity of the judges and the Prosecutor, as well as the court's staff. The Statute sets forth the professional requirements for the judges and the Prosecutor. It provides the manner for their selection, which is based on the terms of the Statute of the International Court of Justice. The membership of the latter is broadly based with due regard for nationality, legal systems employed in the judge's home State, and, even, ideologies. These diverse qualities have enriched the World Court.

Respect for the ICC will also stem from close adherence to the fair trial provisions set out at length in the Statute. In the event that judges or the Prosecutor should stray from the identified standards, the Statute contains a detailed list of sanctions and penalties.

The ICC will have the benefit of the opinions, decisions, and management experience produced at the ICTFY and the ICTR. These should be particularly helpful, because of the common subjects and common experience.

From the practical point of view there is no immediate way of knowing what the caseload of the tribunal will be and how States will respond to their rights to exercise primary jurisdiction. There will be the need to select and train investigators, so that common approaches will be made. If the experience of the ICTFY is repeated with respect to the arrest and transmission to the court of accused persons, there will be a need for the Prosecutor and staff to educate slow-moving States of their duties.

Since the accused may be reluctant prisoners, and since the physical security of all court personnel may be in danger, there will need to be secure areas. All of the court's operations will be budgeted. The Statute identifies means for funding, with money to be the product of a U.N. assessment formula, by gifts, and by charges for court services and documents.

The optimum value of the court will depend on a wide-spread dissemination of the court's decisions and opinions. This may take several forms including web-sites and printed materials. The easy dissemination of such information will improve the court's chances for success.

Since it is anticipated that defendants will range all the way from a lowly military person to an existing Head of State, the court will have a broad duty of educating such persons on the unacceptable criminal aspects of their conduct. Since deterrence has been an announced purpose of all criminal tribunals, this will have to be brought to the constant attention of convicted persons, and those who have the inclination to put themselves at risk.

The Statute of the court is a sound document. The court can be expected to play an increasingly important role in the stabilization of international relations over time.

F. Rejection of the Court by the United States

Attacks have been mounted against the Tribunal. One is that a politically motivated Prosecutor would allow the office to be used for ideological purposes or with general harassment in mind. This point was considered by the drafters, and a number of checkpoints were introduced into the treaty. Further, any country which is a party to the agreement, even the U.S. in the future if the value of the court is finally perceived, will play an active role in the selection of the Prosecutor. It has also been alleged that an accused will not receive a fair trial because the "bill of rights" listed at length in the statute do not conform entirely to those enjoyed by U.S. residents under the American Constitution.

In fact the treaty provides that an accused shall have the right not to incriminate himself and is also entitled to the right of cross-examination. The Statute does not provide for a jury. The court will be the finder-of-fact and will determine what law is applied. This was also the case at Nuremberg. The same rule applies to U.S. military service personnel in court martial proceedings.

The treaty has been attacked by important political figures who have been active in managing foreign policy. Coming from such backgrounds with their well-known biases against legal restraints, the criticism has been directed at the rule of law, particularly to the role of international courts. The managers of foreign policy see international tribunals as adversaries empowered to restrain, on legal grounds, their claims to power.

Thus, former Secretary of State Henry A. Kissinger has mounted several criticisms of the ICC. He began by noting that only recently had judicial processes developed to rule on international politics. In his view this could risk "substituting the tyranny of judges for that of governments."[16] But, one of the fundamental purposes of the proposed court is to inhibit the tyranny of governments that have fallen into the hands of political tyrants.

Mr. Kissinger made references to "an indiscriminate court,"[17]and "a dangerous precedent," where he criticized the ruling of the judiciary committee of the House of Lords when it held that Augusto Pinochet, as a Head of State, was subject to international law.[18]

The Kissinger position has received support from some U.S. senators, political figures, and even some international lawyers. In hearings before the U.S. Senate, one critic of the proposed tribunal urged that the role of law in world affairs was subordinate to "politico-military power in international affairs."[19]

This outlook, derived from a view of the meaning and application of national sovereignty, has its supporters. It is the foundation for the unilateral approach to a nation's involvement in world affairs. It has, as believed by many, been overcome by the forces of globalization. As such, with respect to the need to bring terrorists and violators of basic Human Rights to justice, the wiser approach is to return the unilateral approach to the annals of an earlier era.[20]

Although there are a large number of persons in the United States who see for the United States important benefits from a full-fledged participation in the Court, including America's leading international lawyers, the decision to become a party to the Statute will not be made by them. The decision will be made by the President on the basis of the advice given him by his political advisors and by those who occupy positions of leadership in the U.S. Senate. The descriptive term "flawed" has been addressed to the Statute.

In mid-Summer, 2000, some members of Congress, who observed the momentum driving the finalization of the treaty began consultations with officials of the Departments of State and Defense, former cabinet members, and other influential Americans. Wisely, they concluded that they could not persuade the leaders of America's traditional allies, who were very supportive of the Statute, to modify their positions. They adopted the strategy of claiming that American membership in the Court would seriously imperil U.S. security.

The principal allegation put forward by the treaty's opponents is that States unfriendly to the United States will bring specious charges against American military personnel, without any factual basis, for political purposes. These purposes would be to harass and seek to embarrass them, as well as to bring them to trial so that they could be demeaned. The judicial process it is claimed would be used to paint the U.S. as a bully in its world-wide peacekeeping activities. Opponents to the treaty have urged that the Court would be an unacceptable threat to America's sovereignty.

Based on these allegations in June, 2000, Congressman Tom DeLay introduced HR 4654, referred to as the "American Service Members Protection Act of 2000," into the House of Representatives. It is designed to isolate the United States from the proposed tribunal. The bill would require a position of non-cooperation with the court. For example, under the bill the United States could not provide assistance to the Court with respect to finding and turning over to it prospective defendants who were located in the U.S. American officials could not locate properties owned by accused persons, could not participate in search and seizure matters, could not assist in the service of process or in the gathering of evidence, and could not participate in requests for extradition. The proposed law deals with the sharing of classified security information with U.S. treaty partners. They were to be denied access if the treaty partner had expressed an intent to make such information available in courts. One of the bill's more unusual provisions would authorize the President to invade The Hague to release U.S. citizens and allies from the custody of the Court.

In the Senate several efforts were made to gain approval, where Senator Jesse Helms, former chairman of the Senate Committee on Foreign Relations, had expressed forceful opposition to the Court and vigorous support for HR 4654. In January 2001, after learning that President Clinton had authorized the signing of the Rome Statute on December 31, 2000 Senator Helms stated that it constituted an "unprecedented attack on American sovereignty." He vowed to protect American military personnel "from the jurisdiction of this kangaroo court."[21] Illustrative of the same point of view is the title of a book by Michael Boos. It is "The Proposed U.N. Criminal Court: A Grave Threat to American Freedom, Liberty and Sovereignty." An opposing characterization is that of a former U.S. diplomat, Alvin P. Adams, who sees the debate as a "struggle between the forces of ignorance, isolation and the petty self-interest and those who have declared themselves for enlightened internationalism. . . ."

After concluding that the Rome treaty "is consistent with the security interests of the United States and the due process interests of U.S. citizens" in February 2001, Monroe Leigh, on behalf of nine former presidents and an Honorary President of the American Society of International Law, wrote to Congressman Henry Hyde, Chairman, House Committee on International Relations. In the letter to Congressman Hyde emphasis was placed on the "faulty assumptions as to the relevant provisions of customary international law" made by the eminent Americans who had expressed their disapproval of the Rome Statute. These included four former Secretaries of State, two former Secretaries of Defense, three former directors of the CIA, three former National Security Advisors, and a former Ambassador to the U.N. In 2001 the president of the American Society of International Law in a review of HR 4654 assessed the courts that could possibly deal with the prosecution of a U.S. citizen for violations of international Human Rights law. One could be the ICC; the other a foreign national court. He rejected the view that an American defendant would be more likely to receive a fairer trial in a foreign tribunal than before the ICC. He observed that "an assumption so obviously wrong should not become a foundation of our policy toward the new court."[22] He noted that the fair trial procedures in some countries in which an American citizen is held as a prisoner are far below those of the United States. And the Americans should not be subjected to those lower standards.

In his letter to Congressman Hyde, Mr. Leigh emphasized the fact that the Statute of the ICC would allow for the trial of an American citizen in an American court. He stated: "The Rome Statute will create a treaty-based alternate to the unrestricted jurisdiction which customary international law accords to the territorial sovereign. It will create vis-à-vis the new court, a primacy of jurisdiction in the state of nationality of the accused. This means that the United States will have the first right to exercise jurisdiction over its nationals for offenses occurring abroad but within the nominal jurisdiction of the new court. In the case of U.S. military personnel this means court martial jurisdiction under the Uniform Code of Military Justice."[23]

One response to the opponents of the tribunal is: "Seeking exceptions for U.S. nationals demeans our nation and the rule of law. Our current posture of superpower sulking silently is unworthy of our great traditions."[24] With its recourse to unilateralism the United States progressively has become a lesser figure in international affairs. Unilateralism is also referred to as a "new Sovereigntism," meaning that the U.S. "has the power to opt out of international norms, even those universally accepted by other nations."[25] It is evident that the supporters of the Rome Treaty, as well as States in many other current forums, have rebuffed this approach and rejected the premises upon which it rests.

G. Continuing Involvement by the United States

Following the adoption of the Statute in June, 1998, the Preparatory Commission considered new proposals made by the United States. In its March 2000 session the United States endeavored to obtain a "relationship agreement," accompanied by a rule, which would "allow the Court to enter into agreements with States to limit surrender of individuals to the Court."[26] Such an agreement was viewed by the United States as a commitment between the United States and the court. It was the hope of the United States that these parties would grant an exemption from surrender to the Court "of officials and military personnel of the United States and of other non-State parties to the Court."[27] Although the United States continued to press for the acceptance of this proposal it was so far out of step with the thinking of States dedicated to the creation of a meaningful tribunal that they disregarded a plea made by Secretary of State Albright.[28]

When the Preparatory Commission met in June, 2000, in a truly remarkable effort and with dogged intensity, the United States again sought approval of the proposed rule. Again, it could not obtain the approval from the Commission. This did not result in a modification of the 1998 Statute.

The Preparatory Commission met again at the end of November. The United States, seeking to rely on its leverage in the Security Council, urged that the United Nations should be interposed between the court and non-party States regarding "documentation about admissibility of specific cases."[29] This proposal would apply to United Nations "peacekeepers," who as military personnel would fall within the jurisdiction of the Court. This did not result in a modification of the 1998 Statute.

The United States took the position that "One cannot, through this treaty, create or impose the jurisdiction of an international court on states which do not join. If states wish—through the treaty's provisions—to create an international criminal court to prosecute offenders, they can do that, but only for the parties. The Vienna Convention on the Law of Treaties articulates the elementary rule that treaties cannot create obligations for states that are not parties."[30] Diplomats from other countries were not able to give much credence to possible concessions by the United States to further its goal. As a result "they were increasingly irritated by U.S. demands for concessions to which it was now clear there would never be any return."[31]

Diplomacy has been enlisted by the Bush administration to reduce the possibility of the prosecution of American military personnel. The United States, after threatening to withhold funds for UN peacekeeping forces, was able to secure a Security Council resolution delaying for twelve months the exercise of jurisdiction over investigations and prosecutions. It was premised on the exercises by non-Party States of their responsibilities within their jurisdictions regarding international crimes.

The United States also negotiated with the European Union seeking exemptions from prosecution in member countries of war crimes committed by American servicemen and women. Agreement was reached on September 30, 2002. The United States also embarked on bilateral negotiations seeking the same result. By 2004, it was reported that over thirty-five countries including India and Israel had exempted U.S. military personnel from the Court's jurisdiction.

Representative of the agreements preventing delivery of persons to the Court is the one negotiated between the United States and Uzbekistan dated September 18, 2002. It applies to "former Government officials, employees (including contractors), or military personnel or nationals of one Party." It recites that Americans in the territory of Uzbekistan are not to be "surrendered or transferred by any means to the International Criminal Court for any purpose." Further, Uzbekistan agreed not to transfer Americans to "any other entity or third country . . ." as way points en route to the Court. Normal requirements to prosecute or extradite are modified by a provision that such processes may not be implemented without the express consent of the United States. Reliance for this approach is based on Article 98 of the Statute.

These efforts were consistent with the notice given on May 6, 2002 by the United States to the U.N. that it did not intend to become a party to the Rome Statute. The deep-seated opposition to an international criminal tribunal is reflected in the Bush Executive Order of November 13, 2001 dealing with terroristic acts. By that Order terrorists held by the U.S. were to have no access to "international tribunals."

H. Conclusion

Critical aspects of the ICC can be summed up under three headings: policy matters, legal matters, and practical matters.

As a policy issue the world's legal superstructure, in order for it to be complete, requires a permanent international legal tribunal. A gap has existed. That vacancy has been filled. It is difficult for most American lawyers to understand why the citizens of a country which is not a party to the agreement should be exempt from the court's jurisdiction over violent conduct and behavior that has been prohibited by international law.

Four major problems can be solved by the creation of this tribunal. First, the substantive law would prevent a Head of State, who had violated the law, from claiming sovereign immunity as a defense. Although not a new assertion, such a claim was becoming increasingly unreal and unpopular. Second, imposing a just sentence on any violator, Head of State and lesser persons, would provide solace to victims, and, as has been hoped, would serve to some degree as a deterrent to would-be tyrants. Third, such a court would provide an alternative to prosecution under national laws and in national tribunals where conditions foreseeably could prevent a fair trial. Fourth, the creation of a criminal tribunal would eliminate a missing link in the world's legal system.

The United States during the Rome conference made every effort to obtain a "weak" Statute and to "control" the functioning of the court by referring matters to the Security Council, where it has a veto. Unlike its traditional democratic allies, the United States asserted that it has to exercise its national sovereignty to the end that Americans, since individuals are subject to the jurisdiction of the court—not States—would not become the targets of countries which had become displeased with U.S. foreign policy. The expressed concern was fear over political harassment by instituting unsupportable cases in the Court. U.S. allies considered this to be a flimsy excuse, but the U.S. was not persuaded. In this posture the United States received support from countries generally regarded as having little or no interest in or support for Human Rights.

The wisdom of the concerted effort of the United States, as a non-party to the terms of the Statute, has been challenged, particularly on the part of those who have approached the creation of the tribunal from a global or multilateral perspective.

With regard to effort of the United States to exempt nationals of non-party States from the jurisdiction of the Court it has been urged that such an exemption "would mean that the most notorious war criminals would continue to be immune from the jurisdiction of the new court."[32]

Unfortunately, the treaty has no applicability to present-day terrorists. They are excluded from its application. It is applicable to those unlawful conduct occurs after the agreement has entered into force.

Legal systems, both national and international, cannot exist without a judicial process. It is hard to imagine, particularly in reasonably democratic societies, how governments can function in the absence of courts. For the resolution of disputes by peaceful means it is generally accepted that courts provide the best answer. There are alternatives, but courts have not been displaced, and there is a small likelihood that they will be.

2. THE INTERNATIONAL CRIMINAL TRIBUNAL FOR THE FORMER YUGOSLAVIA (ICTFY)

When leaders of the free world saw the extreme and barbarous behavior of Yugoslavian, Bosnian, Croatian, and Serb leaders beginning in the early 1990s, they determined to create an *ad hoc* court for the prosecution of individuals who had engaged in this conduct. Acting through the Security Council of the United Nations they concluded that such behavior constituted a threat to the peace and security of nations, pursuant to Article 51 of the U.N. Charter. In only the most serious situations does the Security Council invoke Article 51.

On February 22, 1993, by Resolution 808, the Security Council with the support of the United States decided that an international tribunal should be established. On May 25, the Security Council adopted the draft Statute and thus established the International Tribunal.[33]

Functioning since 1994 the ICTFY presents several foreign policy problems to the United States including the prosecution of grave breaches of the 1949 Geneva Conventions, the laws or customs of war, crimes against humanity, and genocide. Its jurisdiction applies to crimes committed in Yugoslavia. Non-citizens of Yugoslavia are not defendants. The court will go out of existence when it has prosecuted all of the chargeable persons that can be found or it runs out of funds. Its budget in 2003 was $223,170,000.

NATO provided military personnel in order to terminate the hostilities in the area. Nation-building efforts have been promoted. Under such circumstances it seemed reasonable to create a judicial institution, operating under established international law, to bring a measure of stability back into the area.

The ICTFY at the end of December 2003 had indicted 76 persons. The cases of 68 were under consideration. 50 were in detention with 8 having been provisionally released. 22 remain at large. Convictions resulted under the established procedures of the tribunal. In this way a body of case law, allowing for reliance on precedent, has enriched international criminal law.

Also, reflecting the unsettled conditions in the area was the litigation of Bosnia and Herzegovina against Yugoslavia entitled "Case Concerning Application of the Convention on the Prevention and Punishment of the Crime of Genocide," before the International Court of Justice.[34] The court held that those who engage in genocide owe obligations to the world community as a whole. When the creation of the ICTFY is compared with the creation of other international courts, the comparative ease in the formation of this court came as a pleasant surprise.[35]

If the United States continues to engage in the role of the world's policeman, it will have to decide if it will continue to support international humanitarian law. If it does it will have to give careful thought to its position on the utility of international regional judicial institutions able to implement this area of law. In doing so it will have to consider a policy under which both Americans and aliens may fall within the jurisdiction of international and national courts.

Of foremost importance for any tribunal is its competence. The ICTFY has competence going back to January 1, 1991, over serious violations of international humanitarian law committed in the territory of the former Yugoslavia. This law encompasses both treaty law and customary international law and provides the basis for the subject-matter jurisdiction of the court. The court may exercise jurisdiction over natural persons who are individually responsible for their conduct.

Article 6 of the Tribunal's Statute, entitled "Personal Jurisdiction," states that "a plea of head of State immunity or that an act was committed in the official capacity of the accused will not constitute a defense, nor will it mitigate punishment."[36]

The Statute also allowed for concurrent jurisdiction between the tribunal and national courts, with the tribunal having primacy of jurisdiction over national courts. Individuals who are tried by the tribunal may not be tried subsequently in a national court. However, a conviction in a national tribunal does not preclude a subsequent trial before the tribunal when the charge at the national level was characterized as "an ordinary crime," or where the national proceedings "were designed to shield the accused from international criminal responsibility, or the case was not diligently prosecuted."[37]Article 8 of the Statute fixes the territorial and temporal jurisdiction of the Court. Included are the land, airspace, and territorial waters of the former Yugoslavia as of January 1, 1991.

The tribunal is composed of two trial chambers and an appeals chamber. Each trial chamber consists of three judges, and each appeals chamber consists of five judges. The court began with 11 independent judges. An accused is entitled to having his case heard "without undue delay." With arrest and delivery to The Hague of numerous defendants, and with some cases taking much time, the need for new judges has had to be addressed.

The court cannot impose death penalties, but an accused may be obliged to return to an aggrieved party property belonging to such person. The penalty may be for an indeterminate number of years up to life imprisonment with account being taken of the "gravity of the offense and individual circumstances of the convicted person."[38] Further, in arriving at the sentence the Trial Chamber is authorized "to have recourse to the general practice regarding prison sentences in the courts of the former Yugoslavia."[39] Members of the trial court shall be both finders of fact and appliers of law.

A critically important element of the tribunal is the Prosecutor, whose status is such that he/she "should act independently as a separate organ . . ." of the court.[40] The Prosecutor is to be assisted by a prosecutorial and an investigative staff. Further, in order to insure the independence of this office, the Statute provides that "He or she shall not seek or receive instructions from any government or from any other source."[41] The term of office is 4 years, with the right to be reappointed. The appointment is made by the UN Security Council upon the recommendation of the Secretary-General.

The first Chief Prosecutor was Richard J. Goldstone, a South African jurist. He was appointed on July 8, 1994, and served from August 15, 1994 until his resignation on September 30, 1996. He was followed on October 1, 1996 by Louise Arbour of Canada. She was appointed as Chief Prosecutor for the ICTFY and for the International Criminal Tribunal for Rwanda (ICTR). She resigned upon her appointment to the Supreme Court of Canada. Her successor is Carla del Ponte, who had been Attorney General of Switzerland.

Following investigations a number of detainees have been released. Further, the Appeals Chamber has overturned convictions and has reduced sentences of others. Convictions have been reversed when a trial panel relied on unreliable witnesses.

The ICTFY has heard cases charging Bosnian Serbs and Croatian Serbs with causing harms to Muslims, and in the case of the latter to ethnic Albanian minorities in Kosovo. The most notorious of the defendants is President Slobadan Milosevic.

A. The Court's First Case, 1994–2002

Dusko Tadic, a Bosnian Serb, became the first defendant to come before the ICTFY. The competence of the Court was based on Article 1 of the Court's Statute:

"The International Tribunal shall have the power to prosecute persons responsible for serious violations of international humanitarian law committed in the territory of the former Yugoslavia since 1991 in accordance with the provisions of the present Statute."[42]

He was indicted on February 13, 1995 for crimes committed in Bosnia-Herzegovina. While serving with Bosnian troops Tadic was assigned to command a military prison in which Muslims and Croats were being held. He was charged with violation of Article 2 of the Court's Statute dealing with grave breaches of the Geneva Conventions of 1949, of Article 3 on violations of the laws or customs of war (often referred to as war crimes), and of Article 5 on crimes against humanity. Article 4 of the Statute gives the court jurisdiction over the crime of genocide.

Article 2 crimes, include willful killing, torture or inhuman treatment, willfully causing great suffering or serious injury to body or health, and the unlawful deportation or transfer or unlawful confinement of civilians.

Article 3 crimes include but are not limited to destruction of property, attacks on undefended towns, villages, dwellings, or buildings, destruction of religious, charitable, educational and similar institutions, and the plunder of public or private property.

Article 5 crimes, when committed in armed conflict, whether international or internal in character, and directed against civilian populations, included murder, extermination, enslavement, deportation, imprisonment, torture, rape, persecutions on political, racial, and religious grounds, and other inhumane acts.

Until the Security Council had identified rape as a crime against humanity, it had been considered to be only a violation of domestic law and not within range of international law. This innovation has been hailed almost unanimously as a desirable and progressive step. In the Tadic case, the charge became academic when the alleged victims refused to testify.

On June 23, 1995, Tadic's counsel filed a preliminary motion alleging that the court did not have jurisdiction, and asked for a dismissal of all charges.[43] In his challenge to the power of the court he raised three points. First, he claimed that the court had been improperly established by the Security Council. Second, he urged that the Security Council did not have the power to give the court primary jurisdiction, thereby excluding Yugoslavia from dealing with the charges. Third, his motion asserted that the court did not have the subject matter jurisdiction identified in Articles 2–5 of the Statute.[44]

On August 10, 1995, Tadic's jurisdictional motion was rejected. First, the court held that it did not have the legal authority to pass judgment on the lawfulness of the actions of the Security Council. It was held, in effect, that Tadic should address this question to the Security Council.

The primacy contention was also rejected, since it was also a challenge to the legality of the Security Council's establishing the court. The opinion also questioned the standing of the accused to raise this issue, which was addressed to the violation of the sovereignty of a State. Tadic was not allowed to represent Yugoslavia. In this manner opportunities on the part of the accused persons to engage in forum shopping were prevented. The tribunal addressed the allegations dealing with subject-matter jurisdiction. The defense contended that for Article 2 to have any application there must exist a state of international conflict and that none in fact existed at any time and place. The Tribunal in its ruling of August 10, 1995 stated that "the requirement of international conflict does not appear on the face of Article 2. Certainly, nothing in the words of the Article expressly requires its existence . . ."[45] The court concluded that the trial court had jurisdiction over the events identified as a grave breach when committed upon a protected person, provided the spatial and temporal requirements of Article 1 were met.

The accused also urged that he could not be prosecuted for violations of the laws or customs of war under Article 3 of the Statute because the Article was based on Hague Convention (IV) of October 18, 1907 and the 1997 Protocol I, which apply only to an international conflict, and this condition did not exist at any time or place. The Prosecutor contended that "laws or customs of war" as set forth in Article 3 apply to both international and internal armed conflicts. The court ruled that Article 3 had made no mention of the above treaties, and stated that "nothing in the words of Article 3 expressly requires the existence of an international conflict."[46] The court then found that the "character of the conflict, whether international or internal, does not affect the subject-matter jurisdiction of the International Tribunal under Article 3 to try persons who are charged with violations of law or customs of war."[47] The Tribunal also observed that it could exercise jurisdiction over the obligations identified in Article 3 because they constitute a part of customary international law. Tadic also challenged the court's jurisdiction to deal with crimes against humanity under Article 5 of the Statute, if the identified crimes had been committed in the execution of or in connection with an international armed conflict. It was also argued that broadening the scope of Article 5 crimes when committed in armed conflicts of an internal character violate the *nullum crimen* principle.[48]

It its analysis, the tribunal inquired into the need for there to be a state of belligerency before a charge of a crime against humanity could be sustained. Since it was evident that an armed conflict existed, the court could determine Tadic's guilt of innocence under this charge.

The defense took the position that the Tribunal did not have jurisdiction unless the Prosecutor were able to demonstrate that there was a nexus between crimes against humanity and war crimes. In rejecting this argument the Tribunal concluded that crimes against humanity were separate and autonomous.[49] In support it stated that crimes against humanity "are now generally regarded as a self-contained category, without the need for any formal link with war crimes . . . citing R. Jennings and A. Watts. 1 *Oppenheim's International Law* 966 (1992)." Thus, the Tribunal reaffirmed the provision in Article 5 that gave it jurisdiction in situations where the alleged crime was committed in armed conflict, whether international or internal in character, and directed against any civilian population.

Tadic appealed from the adverse rulings of the trial court. After considering the issues, the 5 person appeal's chamber rendered its holding on October

2, 1995.[50] It rejected the position taken by the trial court and reviewed the power of the Security Council to establish the Tribunal. It reasoned that the Tribunal could not review the exercise of jurisdiction by it until it was determined that the Security Council had the appropriate authority.

The appellate court also disagreed with the trial court on the primacy issue finding that Tadic did have standing to claim a violation of Yugoslav sovereignty. It concluded that the Security Council did have the power to create primary jurisdiction.

With regard to the right of the Tribunal to exercise subject-matter jurisdiction, it concluded that the basis for the application of international humanitarian law was the presence of a resort to armed force between States or protracted armed violence between governmental authorities and organized armed groups or between such groups within a State. This condition existed in Yugoslavia, with combat taking place on both an international and internal level. It added that with regard to Article 2 grave breaches that its jurisdiction was limited to international armed conflict involving harm to persons and property. These holdings constituted a response to the contention of the accused that the Tribunal did not have subject-matter jurisdiction because Articles 2, 3, and 5 "are applicable only to international armed conflicts, and that the alleged crimes, if proven, were committed in an international armed conflict."[51]

In addressing the application of Article 3, it was concluded that the crimes listed applied to any conflict, international or internal. The appeals chamber also held that the enumerated instances dealt with serious offences, that conviction depended on individual criminal responsibility, and that the enumerated crimes had to be and were violations of customary international law. If, on the other hand, it were determined that their validity were based on a treaty, the trials would have to be binding on the parties at the time of the alleged offence.

This meant that crimes identified as grave breaches in the Geneva Conventions could not be prosecuted, per se, but could be prosecuted if they constituted violations of the laws or customs of war. This caused the prosecutor to withdraw the charges under Article 2 of the Statute and to refile them under Article 3. The appellate chamber upheld the prosecution under Article 5 since it was evident that there was an armed conflict and that the crimes against humanity were recognized by international law.

In sum, the manner in which the jurisdictional issues were resolved stands as an "important judicial affirmation that serious violations of international humanitarian law committed in non-international armed conflicts are international crimes."[52]

The tribunal also dealt with fair trial issues. It noted that Tadic had been arrested and indicted in Germany for crimes committed in Yugoslavia before he was turned-over to the ICTFY. Since he had not been prosecuted prior to his release, the condition of double jeopardy was not present. Concern was expressed concerning the Prosecutor's wish to grant anonymity to some witnesses on the ground that they could be subject to harms in Yugoslavia if their identity were known. The court, while reluctant to allow this to occur in light of the accused's right to confront his accusers, decided that this would be allowed, subject to the right to strike such testimony from the record at the end of the trial if the Prosecutor were not able to provide supportive evidence.

Also, considered was the proposed practice of examining witnesses via video links. This would avoid travel hazards. The Prosecutor urged the tribunal to make arrangements for the safe conduct of witnesses. The court declined to enter into such procedures, but indicated in exceptional instances it would accept testimony in this form.

The tribunal also issued a ruling dealing with the admissibility of hearsay (out of court statements not made in the presence of the accused) identified in Article 21 of the Statute. At the trial court's discretion, such statements would be admissible provided they were relevant and had probative value.

The prosecutor asked for a ruling on his right to examine prior statements made by defense witnesses, followed by the right to question such witnesses on such statements. The defense urged that these were privileged communications. The tribunal denied access by the Prosecutor.

The defense asked for a ruling respecting a motion to dismiss charges following the Prosecutor's presentation of its case in chief. Such a motion was to be denied if as a matter of law, as determined by the trial court, there were charges in the indictment which would lawfully support the conviction. Following the clarification of the foregoing issues, the Prosecution filed 31 charges against Tadic. After hearing 125 witnesses and receiving 400 exhibits presented as evidence, he was convicted under 11 counts. The verdict was announced on May 7, 1997. He was convicted on charges of crimes, such as beatings, murder, torture, and other inhumane acts. The court also found that the facts supported convictions for crimes against humanity, namely, systematic and large-scale killings. The concept of "fair trial" played an important role. Article 21 of the Statute sets out the rights of the accused. With respect to the burden of proof, it states: "3. The accused shall be presumed innocent until proved guilty according to the provisions of the present statute."

Article 21 enumerates conditions designed to achieve a fair trial. The terms of Article 21 are remarkably close to U.S. constitutional guarantees; they unquestionably provide all of the guarantees required to obtain a fair trial for an accused person. When enforced they will prevent egocentric defendants from seeking to turn the tribunal's judicial forum into political theater. Defendants enjoy wide-ranging rights in presenting defenses.[53]

In order to control judicial proceedings the Tribunal has issued its Rules of Procedure and Evidence. According to the rule entitled "Closed Sessions" a trial chamber may exclude the press and the public from all or part of the proceedings. This may occur to protect public order or morality, to secure the safety, security or non-disclosure of the identity of a victim or witness, to protect "the interest of justice."[54] The guiding consideration throughout is to ensure a fair trial and a fair determination of the matter before the court. To this end a chamber may exclude evidence if its probative value is substantially outweighed by the need to ensure a fair trial. Further, the chamber is not to be bound by "national rules" of evidence.[55]

Following a finding of guilt on July 14, 1997, Tadic was sentenced to a 20 year imprisonment. A series of appeals were instituted concerning the fairness of the penalty and whether he should be credited for the time that he had been in custody in Germany. On January 26, 2000 he was re-sentenced to a 20 year term not ending earlier than July 14, 2007. He was given credit for the detention period in Germany and incarceration in Holland during the trial resulting in a credit of 5 years, 11 months, and 14 days on the 20 year sentence. In 2002 his case was reopened on the ground that he had not received competent legal advice during the trial. With a ruling against him the case was finally closed on July 30.

The outcome of the case, in which basic constitutive challenges had been addressed on the competence and jurisdiction of the court, has been received generally in the world's international legal community as being fair and reasonable. A major contribution to the scope of international law was the confirmation that such law has direct application to individuals. They have unique rights which they may claim. Individuals owe specific duties to human beings. Penalties, when applicable, can be imposed.

The court ruled that an international tribunal can be assigned primacy over national tribunals in Human Rights matters. Soundly based international decisions should, on the basis of fairness and consistency, be used by national tribunals when a relevancy exists.

B. Getting Serbian Defendants to the Hague; Representative Prosecutions.

The Statute of the tribunal in Article 29 specifies that States "shall cooperate with the international tribunal in the investigation and prosecution of persons accused of committing serious violations of international humanitarian law."[56] Such States have the specific duty to identify, locate, arrest, or detain such persons. This duty has become the responsibility of the members of NATO, having military forces in the former Yugoslavia.

The Security Council has made it clear that all States are obliged to cooperate fully with the tribunal, including orders issued by a Trial Chamber, and with the organs of the tribunal, which include the office of the Prosecutor. The extent of the required cooperation imposes on all States the duty to take "any measures necessary under their domestic law to implement the provisions of the present resolution and the Statute."[57] Unfortunately, considerable variance exists between the foregoing obligations and the performance of some of the States directly responsible for and engaged in military operations in the former Yugoslavia.

International political considerations have made it difficult for the government of Yugoslavia to apprehend and send its war criminals to The Hague. Since 2001, however, more Serbs have been apprehended or have voluntarily agreed to go to The Hague for prosecution. In December 2002 former President Biljana Plavsic of the Serb portion of Bosnia-Herzegovina during the war, and who later served as president of Republika Srpska, pleaded guilty to persecution of non-Serbs on racial and religious grounds and forced removal from their homes in Bosnia. She is the highest-ranking ethnic Serb to enter a plea of guilty. Since Yugoslavia has not been able to apprehend some of the principal defendants there have been increasing demands for outside action.

Some of the members of NATO have found pretexts for not taking action to facilitate the court's function. Early possession resulted from the voluntary surrender of two Bosnian nationals, Milan Simic and Miloslav Tadic, to U.S. armed forces in mid-February 1998. NATO-led troops escorted them to The Hague. At the end of August 1999, the head of the Bosnian Serb Army, General Momir Talic, while attending a conference in Vienna, was arrested by Austrian authorities, who escorted him to The Hague.

The first capture effected by the United States occurred with the detention of a Bosnian prison camp commander, Goran Jelisic. He was the fourth suspect taken into custody following the December 1995 Dayton accords, which had ended the war in Bosnia-Herzegovina.[58]

In an article entitled "Why Doesn't the US Arrest War Criminals?" it was concluded that the daily avoidance by US troops "of their legal and moral duty to take suspects into custody seriously undermines all we have invested in helping the tribunal succeed."[59]

The United States verbal commitment to basic Human Rights as implemented in Yugoslavia shows important inconsistencies. In 1993 the United States, as a member of the Security Council, called for the creation of a court for the prosecution of major atrocities.[60]

The second prosecutor of the ICTFY, Louise Arbour, in 1999 sought international assistance in securing the arrest of Radovan Karadzic and General Ratko Mladic. Her successor, Carla del Ponte of Switzerland, in November

2002 accused Yugoslavia of shielding General Mladic from apprehension. She also stated that the Republicka Srpska was providing sanctuary to Radovan Karadzic. Speaking on behalf of the victims and successors of the Bosnian conflict, she told the Security Council that the freedom of the two "is an affront to the authority of this council and mocks the entire process of international criminal justice."[61]

The role of the United States has been ambiguous. Its leaders have used words of positive intent. The United States announced a reward of $5 million for the capture and delivery of President Slobodan Milosevic, General Ratko Mladic, and political leader Radovan Karadzic. From 1999 onward the hands-off policy of the United States in capturing indicted persons received scathing reports from on-the-scene journalists and from editorial commentary. Until 2002 U.S. military personnel were in the immediate presence of the three leaders and lesser wanted persons. Capable United States military personnel, apparently acting on strict orders from higher authority, made no effort to apprehend such persons. One of the consequences of such inaction was the initiation of an all-out offensive action by President Milosevic against Albanian minorities in Kosovo.

On the other hand the United States did not try to control the terms of the Statute of the court with the purpose of creating a weak or ineffective tribunal. It has indicated that *ad hoc* judicial bodies should not be expected in the long run to replace national courts. It has not manifested the vigorous opposition that has been directed at the broader jurisdiction over persons set forth in the Statute of the ICC.

Apparently stung by world opinion, NATO's peacekeeping force in Bosnia, which is known as SFOR, for Stabilization Force, made an attempt at the end of February 2002, to capture Radovan Karadzic. With some 40 military personnel from several countries, using helicopters and using explosives they engaged in a show of force in the southern mountain village of Celebici, in Bosnia.[62] Continued efforts were made early in March, 2002, but with the support of sympathizers, he was not found.

At the end of November, 2001, he had been living in Belgrade, where the Yugoslav army was providing him with security. In March, 2002, his family members regarded the effort to capture him as a "betrayal", since in their view high American political officials had entered into a gentlemen's agreement with him whereby he would not become the subject of a capture if he withdrew from political life.[63] Despite the fact that Karadzic and General Ratko Mladic were the object of a $5 million bounty for their capture and delivery, this has not proven to be an inducement for cooperation with international authorities. There was not a similar effort to capture Mladic in March, 2002, who was reported to be living in Serbia. Both have been charged with genocide and crimes against humanity.

Nevertheless, the number of prisoners at The Hague began to swell. In August, 1999, German and French troops captured a former Bosnian police commander, Radomar Kovac, and sent him to The Hague. In January, 1999, French military personnel killed another suspect, Dragan Gagovic, who had been accused of raping and torturing Muslim women. He was killed after he had tried to run down the French soldiers in his automobile.

In December of 1999, Bosnian General Stanislav Galic was seized by NATO troops. NATO authorities declined to identify their nationality for fear of repercussions. This did not prevent Galic's being taken to The Hague.[64]

In April, 2000, French troops captured Momcilo Krajisnik, president of the Bosnian Serb Assembly between 1990 and 1995. As a political figure he had engaged in the planning of the military action which allegedly resulted in the wholesale death via ethnic cleansing of Muslims in Bosnia-Herzegovina. During this time he was a close ally of the Bosnian Serb leader Radovan Karadzic. Karjisnik at the time of his arrest was under secret indictment for genocide, crimes against humanity, and grave breaches of the Geneva Conventions.

In April of 2002, after a five-year search, Dargan Nikolic, a Serbian detention camp commander, was detained by NATO forces. He was found within the zone assigned to the United States in northern Bosnia. This was the first capture in the U.S. zone since the apprehension of General Radislav Krstic in December, 1998. With Nickolic's transfer to The Hague the number of detainees reached 41 of the 76 publicly indicted during the period from the tribunal's creation in 1993.[65] In March, 2001, a Bosnian Serb official, Blagoje Dimiv, surrendered voluntarily to the tribunal while stating his innocence and his wish to clear his name. And in July of 2001 a Croatian army general surrendered voluntarily. He had been charged with allowing his troops to kill civilians.

In August, 2001, Vidoje Blagojrvic, a Bosnian Serb army colonel, was arrested by British military authorities. He was under indictment for crimes against humanity, genocide, and violations of the laws or customs of war stemming from the killing and expulsion of non-Serbian inhabitants in northern Bosnia. In September, 2001, at the request of the tribunal, Croatia arrested and delivered to the court two generals accused of wartime atrocities.

In recent years armed forces of England, France, Germany, and The Netherlands, as well as the government of Austria, have taken possession of Bosnian Serbs, and have turned them over to tribunal authorities in The Hague. Bosnia Serbs, who were in the immediate presence of U.S. military personnel, identified by the Tribunal as probably guilty, have not been apprehended.

Despite the intransigence of U.S. policy relating to the capture of highly placed leaders, the United States has supported the tribunal in several ways. Americans participated in the drafting of the Statute of the Court. The United States cast its Security Council vote in favor of the creation of the tribunal.[66]

Americans share in the staffing of the several elements of the tribunal, including serving as judges, the office of the prosecutor, and the registry. Others have served privately as counsel for defendants. The Court, as an instrumentality of the United Nations, is funded from official national assessments.

Questions based on far-reaching political considerations, have been posed in connection with the American policy. This is to put to one side the obvious risks and uncertainties involved in using force to capture the wanted persons. It is hard to conclude that the individuals found within the American zone would be more difficult to capture, as major prospects for punishment, because they have surrounded themselves with better defenses. American intelligence capabilities have generally been praised. As has been noted, frequently, the United States has provided more material resources to the tribunal than any other country, including the $5 million reward mentioned above.

One suggestion, going back to 2000, and before, has been that the United States' inaction, which resulted from its hope that the 1995 Dayton Accords which produced an armistice in the hostilities between Croats, Muslims, and Serbs, would, in fact, stabilize relationships. The United States in brokering the Accords in effect gave President Milosevic a new "lease on life." In a sense the Accords can be viewed as confirming his prior conduct, and, unfortunately, at the same time providing him with an opportunity to inflict upon the ethnic Albanians in Kosovo the same treatment that had been accorded to Muslims in Bosnia and Croatia.

Another excuse, made at the outset of the Bush-Gore campaign, was that the Clinton administration should not preempt options open to the two presidential candidates.

Another approach, and perhaps of greater substance, was the effort to get the Yugoslav government, under the presidency of Vojislav Kostunica, who assumed his office in October, 2000, to turn Slobodan Milosevic over to the authorities in The Hague. The new president had indicated his distrust for the ICTFY, and had voiced the view that it was engaged in a selective application of the law.

Further, Milosevic was protected by an existing law prohibiting the extradition of Yugoslav nationals. In Kostunica's view a proposed new law, if it could obtain parliamentary approval, would create so much contention that his shaky command of a majority would result in his loss of office. Consequently, he urged that the place for the trial of Milosevic ought to be in Yugoslavia, with the charges being corruption, electoral fraud, and even war crimes during the Bosnian war.

This approach took into account a commonly held view that a trial before a court whose charter granted it primacy of jurisdiction, would be seen as a prosecution of the Serb people, as a whole, rather than the former president.

Since a very large number of Serbs held this view it was dangerous for president Kostunica to allow the international tribunal to exercise jurisdiction over Milosevic. Some Yugoslavs suggested that the best way to make Milosevic a martyr would be to allow him to be prosecuted in The Hague. In August of 2002, the Serb Socialist party was collecting 10,000 signatures on a petition to put him on September's ballot as its presidential nominee. In December 2003 he was elected to the Parliament of Serbia and Montenegro.

President Kostunica was an expert on constitutional law. He interpreted the Yugoslav constitution as limiting his powers, and that he could not, in the context of Yugoslav law, honor the very exacting demands of the tribunal's Prosecutor. In this situation the United States again became a decisive player in the politics of international justice. This was coupled with the fact that a majority of the members of the Yugoslav cabinet, who were reformists, and who did not owe allegiance to President Kostunica, determined that they must act. Failure to do so would imperil promises of immediate foreign aid to Yugoslavia of about $1.2 million, of which roughly one-half was being provided by the United States. A donor's conference had fixed a deadline for the gift of funds for humanitarian relief.

Despite the evident need of such help in Yugoslavia, President Kostunica at that time expressed a hope for cooperation with the ICTFY, but asserted that Yugoslav dignity should not be tainted by the receipt of a "handful" of dollars. With a deadline of March 31, 2001, Yugoslav authorities, with much trepidation, considered Milosevic expendable. On June 28, 2001 he was surrendered to The Hague tribunal by Serbian authorities.

The effective spokesman for the Yugoslav government had become Interior Minister Zoran Zivkovic. At this time Milosevic was being held in a Belgrade prison on domestic charges of corruption and abuse of power. In April, 2001, Milosevic had admitted diverting federal funds to Bosnian and Croat Serb armies during the campaigns against ethnic minorities.

Leading cabinet ministers, including Zoran Djinjic of Serbia, held the view that Mr. Milosevic's presence in Yugoslavia posed an internal danger. Djinjic's efforts to rebuild democracy while Prime Minister of Serbia led to his assassination in 2003.The ministers were successful in adopting a new law calling for extradition, but allowing for internal legal review.

Opposing the decision to send him to The Hague was the Yugoslav Socialist party (formerly communist party) urging a domestic prosecution. It was their view that a trial at The Hague would destroy the pride of the nation, and that the tribunal was a tool of the West. Opposition to the prosecution of Mr. Milosevic at The Hague was advanced by some well-informed Americans. In their view if Yugoslavia were to advance toward a condition of democracy, it should be encouraged to use its own tribunals to purge "its own demons."[67]

No longer able to delay and possible defeat the jurisdiction of the ICTFY Milosevic was obliged to decide what kinds of defense he would address to a tribunal whose function was to advance the cause of international justice. As might be expected, in light of the tactics he practiced in a tempestuous political career, he "came out swinging."

By mid-March, 2002 it had become evident that the government of Serbia, a province of Yugoslavia, had become increasingly opposed to the policies of President Kostunica. At stake was the loss of about $40 million which the United States had agreed to pay to Yugoslavia if it would assure delivery of suspects to The Hague and release from imprisonment ethnic Albanians who lived in Kosovo. The deadline for compliance was March 31, 2002.

On March 27, 2002, the government of Serbia indicated that it would reaffirm the 2001 decree whereby President Milosevic had been turned over to The Hague. This was intended to forestall the possibility that the constitutional court of Yugoslavia, dominated by Serbian nationalists, would revoke the decree.

The parliamentary leader of the ruling Democratic Opposition of Serbia reform alliance, Cedomir Jovanovic, called upon persons who had been indicted by the ICTFY to surrender to the Court. This would include General Ratko Mladic and Bosnian Serb leader Radovan Karadzic. At that time Mr. Jovanovic stated that these Serbs "should not expect us to put their interests before those of the State."[68]

C. The Trial of Slobodan Milosevic

When the final history of international law is written there will certainly be a significant reference to the trial of Slobodan Milosevic, the Yugoslavian Head of State between 1989 and October, 2001, when he was ousted. He was the first Head of State to be arrested by his own government to be tried by an international tribunal. He had been elected president of Serbia in 1989, and re-elected in 1990 and 1992. It will be interesting to observe whether emphasis is placed on the powers vested by the U.N. Security Council in the Court, or, whether the central focus is given to Milosevic's claim that his official status conferred upon him the right to be above the law.

Over the space of history Heads of State when they get into trouble have often asserted that they are above the law. Such claims have been variously supported such as the royal family tree, or the possession of enough power to keep them in office, and even by invoking divine authority. In the case of President Milosevic it was based more on the autocratic nature of his office and the fact that he had, for a long time, the support of powerful military figures in command of troops loyal to them.

If Adolph Hitler had been tried at Nuremberg he, undoubtedly, would have invoked the same or similar arguments. Although Augusto Pinochet, the Chilean Head of State, had raised such arguments, they were disavowed by the British House of Lords.[69] But, only President Milosevic remained in power after the commission of basic violations of the new international law of Human Rights. In all of these situations none of the accused fired a weapon in anger nor personally caused direct physical harm to human beings. Thus, culpability will have to depend on decisions taken by a person acting in an official capacity which produced grievous harms to individuals and to specifically identifiable groups of individuals.

At the time when President Milosevic came into power in 1989 applicable international agreements were in force. Included were the U.N. Charter, the 1949 Geneva Conventions, and the 1948 Universal Declaration of Human Rights. Principles of the law of warfare were reconfirmed in the Nuremberg Tribunal decision at the end of World War II, and in the prosecutions of Japanese World War II criminals. In 1948 the Genocide Convention was adopted and it entered into force in 1951. The indictments of Milosevic were based on these sources of international law.

1. Indictments

The prosecutor issued three indictments. The first, which was issued in May of 1999, referred to crimes committed in Kosovo.[70] Count 1, based on Article 5 (d) of the Statute, which identified crimes against humanity, focused on the deportation of Muslims. Count 2, based on Article 5 (a), charged murder. Count 3, based on Article 3, dealing with violations of the laws or customs of war, also dealt with murder as identified in Article 3 (1) (a) of the 1949 Geneva Convention. Count 4, based on Article 5 (h) dealing with crimes against humanity, referred to persecutions.

In all of the indictments Milosevic was charged with both individual criminal responsibility as set forth in Article 7(1) and with superior criminal responsibility set forth in Article 7(3) of the Statute. Individual criminal responsibility applies to a "person who planned, instigated, ordered, committed, or otherwise aided or abetted in the planning, preparation or execution of a crime"[71] identified in Articles 2–5 of the Statute. These are grave breaches of the Geneva Convention of 1949, violations of the laws or customs of war, genocide, and crimes against humanity. Attached were schedules with the places and dates of the atrocities and the names and ages of the victims. They ranged from two to 95.[72]

Superior criminal responsibility is the product of failure of a superior to take necessary and reasonable measures to prevent subordinates from violating Articles 2–5, if he knew or had reason to know that the subordinate was about to commit such acts, or, if he had done so, the failure to punish the perpetrator.

Amended charges were filed on June 29, 2001, identifying atrocities that occurred up to June 20, 2001. More detail was furnished respecting the charge on the exercise of superior authority.[73]

A second amended statement of charges was filed on October 29, 2001. It dealt with individual criminal responsibility. It made specific references to times and places when the atrocities occurred to the victims. Several general allegations were made. One was that at all times "a state of armed conflict existed in Kosovov in the Federal Republic of Yugoslavia".[74] It was also charged that the accused had engaged in "acts or omissions against humanity and systematic attacks on civilians of Kosovov and the Federal Republic of Yugoslavia."[75]

The second indictment, issued in October of 2001, dealt with conduct in Croatia between August 1, 1991 and June, 1992. At the heart of this charge was Milosevic's joint criminal enterprise seeking the "forcible removal of the majority of the Croat and other non-Serb population from approximately one-third of the territory of Croatia, an area he planned to become part of a new Serb-dominated State."[76] This indictment repeated the charges of grave breaches of the 1949 Geneva Conventions and violations of the laws or customs of war.

The third indictment dealt with military conduct in Bosnia between 1992–1995, with the charge being genocide. The principal event under this heading occurred in the Bosnia-Herzegovina town of Srebrenica in which Serbian forces over three days massacred an estimated 7,000 Muslim men and boys. In August, 2002, new grave sites were discovered containing several hundred new victims.

The indictments were consolidated for trial with evidence of the conduct in Kosovo to be heard first. His trial started on February 20, 2002.

Following his jailing, and during a period in which his conduct was given much attention by the press, he maintained that the trial was a farce and that the court, as a political "circus," had been constituted for political rather than legal reasons. He claimed to be a victim of anti-Serbian enemies with an eye on creating support for his defense at home. Initially he refused to consult with counsel, while indicating that if there were true defendants that it should be NATO and its personnel, since civilians had been killed during the bombing of Serbians in Kosovo. Having been allowed to address the trial court he asked that he be discharged from custody so that he could prepare for trial. He stated he would not attempt to escape. He announced his intent to call as witnesses distinguished world figures. He was cautioned by the presiding judge for his repetitiveness.

Although Milosevic initially had proclaimed that he was not the subject to the court's jurisdiction, and that he would represent himself, he sought the advice of a former U.S. Attorney General, Ramsey Clark, and British barrister, John Livingston. They met with the accused both privately and in the presence of ICTFY personnel. Milosevic soon declined outside assistance.

In February 2002, the accused gave notice, pursuant to Article 21 of the Statute, that he would call upon former U.S. President Jimmy Carter and other democratic leaders to corroborate his testimony.[77] In his view their testimony would be relevant since they were "direct actors in all events."[78] Others named include former U.S. Secretary of State Madeleine Albright, Secretary-General Kofi Annan, British Prime Minister Anthony Blair, and leaders from Italy. The procedure for accomplishing this would be for the Court to issue subpoenas, following its own investigation, to determine if the proposed testimony were relevant.[79]

Although Milosevic is being prosecuted in The Hague, the courtroom, as a result of his strategy, is Yugoslavia and beyond. Despite his disdain for the Statute of the Court, he has demonstrated an awareness of Article 21 dealing with the rights of an accused and Article 22 with witnesses.

In normal trials counsel stipulate that written documents, when the statement is beyond dispute, can be used without having to present witnesses to verify that fact. Milosevic has refused to accept this practice. This is an obvious maneuver to try the patience of the court and engage in delay. At the present rate the trial will last for at least three years.

But, in less mundane matters, a witness confronted with a public court appearance and the need to return to his/her home in Yugoslavia, may have legitimate concerns about his/her personal safety and his/her family, if he/she is forced to testify. This has presented the Tribunal with the need to balance the right of the accused to a "fair and public hearing," under Article 22 and the "protection of victims and witnesses."

This issue was raised in the Milosevic case in November of 2001 when the Prosecutor asked that 29 witnesses might testify under a pseudonym. In its opinion of January 4, 2002, the Tribunal granted the Prosecutor the liberty to "apply for specific protective measures for individual witnesses when testifying, including the use of pseudonyms, image distortion, and closed sessions, prior to the date on which each witness is to testify." Further, it ordered that the names and addresses of such persons were not to be disclosed to the public or to the media, and that the names of such potential witnesses were to be sealed and not made a part of the public record.

Aside from fears over retribution, delays favor an accused. Witnesses have dimmer recollections; they disappear; they long for more tranquility.

Milosevic is not an experienced trial lawyer, but has rejected the suggestion of the Tribunal that it appoint counsel to defend him. He has categorically rejected this proposal, viewing it as a trap. Article 21 allows for the assignment of counsel "in any case where the interests of justice so require." The court's interest in justice includes the right to bring the case to closure. This may result in the designation of public counsel for the accused.

Included in the Article 21 rights of an accused is the provision that they are "presumed innocent until proved guilty according to the present Statute." This issue was addressed in the first amended complaint against Milosevic[80] under the heading of a prima facie case.

When first examined it was concluded that this meant "that the material facts pleaded in the indictment in relation to any particular charge constitute a credible case which would (if not contradicted by the accused) be sufficient to convict him on that charge."[81]

After a review of the above formula the court adopted a different standard. Under it a prima facie case exists where there is evidence (if accepted) "upon which a reasonable trier of fact could be satisfied beyond reasonable doubt of the guilt of the accused" on the particular charge in question.[82]

This formulation with its express reference to "beyond reasonable doubt" is more closely aligned with the practice in the criminal courts in the United States. It is also more beneficial to Milosevic and the other defendants who have come within the jurisdiction of the ICTFY.

The Statute of the Tribunal set the tone respecting the rights of an accused by providing that it is "axiomatic that the International Tribunal must fully respect internationally recognized standards regarding the rights of the accused at all stages of its proceedings."[83]

These rights for an accused were 9 in number: (1) a fair and public hearing; (2) presumption of innocence until proved guilty "according to the provisions of the present Statute;" (3) entitlement in full equality to be informed promptly and in full detail of the nature and cause of the charges; (4) time and facilities for the preparation of a defense with the assistance of a counsel of his/her own choice; (5) to be tried without undue delay; (6) to be present at his/her trial with the right to counsel or to engage in self-defense with "legal assistance assigned to him in any case where the interests of justice require," without having to pay for such legal assistance if the accused does not have sufficient means to pay for such assistance; (7) the right to examine witnesses testifying both in his/her favor and against him/her plus the right to "obtain the attendance and examination" of all such witnesses; (8) to have the free assistance of an interpreter if the accused does not understand or speak the language used by the Tribunal; and (9) "not to be compelled to testify against himself or to confess guilt." In the numerous cases heard by the Court before the Milosevic trial, these guarantees have been employed. They are available to him if he calls upon the court for their application.

In furtherance of his argument that a future prosecution of him would be against the "wrong man," he filed an action in a Dutch court seeking an order of release from jail. His argument was that he had been "kidnapped" by Yugoslavian authorities before his delivery to the ICTFY. In August of 2001 the Dutch court held that it did not have jurisdiction to rule on the matter and that the ICTFY was not under the domination of NATO. In December, 2001, he asked the European Court of Human Rights to order his release, arguing that Holland had acted wrongfully in allowing him to be held in that country. The Human Rights tribunal did not agree with Milosevic.

2. *Results of Milosevic Trial*

The fair and disinterested application of the foregoing standards should produce a fair trial for this accused. Their use should also be determinative in assessments by critics of the tribunal that the final verdict is supported by application of fair and objective standards. In this manner the court's decision should serve several purposes. First, an individual's guilt or innocence will have been determined. Second, a record will have been established upon which the accused's guaranteed rights of appeal can be based. Third, Heads of State will come to realize that they are not above the law in the areas in which convictions have been obtained. Fourth, to the extent that criminal convictions can be cited as precedents with respect to future and like misconduct, the cases will serve as a full-fledged warning. Fifth, confidence in the operation of this international criminal court may make it easier for States, and, in particular the United States, to understand the merits of a permanent international criminal tribunal. Sixth, with reasoned opinions on the part of the judges serving on the ICTFY it may be possible for the many innocent and blameless nationals of Yugoslavia to understand the work of Milosevic and thus be spared the pain and anguish flowing from a sense of collective guilt. This feeling can be reinforced from the successful prosecutions of Bosnian and Croatian officials occasioned by their wrongdoing. National courts can be encouraged to prosecute lesser offenders. Programs of truth and reconciliation may serve a healthy purpose. Regional peace may come closer to realization.

D. Growth of International Jurisprudence

Several small, but important rulings have been made by the ICTFY. Its appellate chamber in July, 2001, examined decisions of the trial chambers.

Goran Jelisic, a Bosnian Serb, was charged with genocide and with violations of the laws or customs of war. He was convicted of the last, but was acquitted of genocide. On appeal, which involved a number of technical issues, he was sentenced to a 40-year term of imprisonment.[84] A reason given for not remanding the matter to the trial court was the limited resources of the trial chambers.

In October, 2001, an appellate chamber reversed the convictions of three Bosnian Croats who had been charged with the slaughter of Muslim civilians in 1992. Finding the trial court's decision to be critically flawed, it was decided that the indictment had been too general and vague and that the testimony of witnesses had not been reliable.

In the week following the start of the trial of Slobodan Milosevic, testimony offered to the trial court by the Prosecutor's chief investigator for war crimes for Kosovo was rejected. The senior investigator endeavored to present a summary of statements made by his subordinates, but not directly to him. The summaries were held to be inadmissible hearsay.

Although the prosecution of Slobodan Milosevic has captured much attention, the prosecutions of Bosnian and Croatian political and military figures may also be of precedential value respecting international crimes. The following case brought into the field of human rights the unacceptability of rape as an instrument of war.

E. The Establishment of "Rape Camps": Sexual Enslavement

As noted above the Tribunal's jurisdiction for crimes against humanity included both "enslavement" and "rape." The conduct of three Yugoslavian Serb soldiers toward Muslim women in Bosnia during the 1992–1995 war resulted in their prosecution. Over 30 counts of war crimes, crimes against humanity, including rape, torture, enslavement, and outrages upon personal dignity were filed. Following an extended trial, between April 2000 and February 23, 2001, each of the defendants was convicted. Dragoljub Kunaract was sentenced to 28 years in prison; Radomir Kovac to 20 years; Zoran Vukocic to 12 years. The findings were unique, since in past wars it has been necessary to show a linkage between rape and murder in order to obtain a conviction. In the instant case the charge was singularly that of sexual enslavement.

The dehumanization of the Muslim women, who testified behind blindfolds, and whose voices were electronically modified so as to avoid identification, recited instances of sexual assault, detention in the military quarters of the rapists, denial of food, requirement of cooking and room cleaning, exclusive control by the accused over particular women, the requirement that the prisoners engage in sexual acts with others, who then paid the captors, and physical abuse, such as beatings, all resulted in the denial to the captives of control over their own lives. At the sentencing the presiding judge stated: "You abused and ravaged Muslim women because of their ethnicity, and from among their number whomsoever you fancied."[85] The tribunal examined the entire context of the war. It concluded that the described conduct on the part of Serb soldiers was an official use of terror in order to intimidate a civilian population.

Unfortunately rape was a common occurrence by all sides in the Bosnian conflict. In a study completed by the European Union it was reported in 1992 that 20,000 rapes had occurred with Muslim women being the principal victims. The commission concluded that the Bosnian Serb government was, as a matter of policy, encouraging such conduct.

F. Croatians Charged with Crimes

Croatian Serbs played a heavy role in the destruction of Muslims, frequently under the auspices of the Bosnian Croatian militia known as the HVO. Among those prosecuted at The Hague were Vladimir Santic, Drago Josipovic, Zoran Kupreskic, Mirjan Kupreskic, and Vlatko Kupreskic. These individuals, members of military police units, in the spring of 1993 attacked the Muslim residents of Ahmici in central Bosnia. There were 116 Muslim fatalities with 172 Muslim homes and two mosques destroyed. Not a single Croatian Serb home was harmed.

The accused were charged with "ethnic cleansing," a term sued to describe one aspect of genocide, namely, "deliberately" inflicting on the group conditions of life calculated to bring about its physical destruction. This crime results from the intentional killing and terrorizing of persons in order to induce them to flee their homes and to give up their worldly possessions. In this case, which was the first to refer to "ethnic cleansing," the accused received jail sentences ranging from 10 to 25 years. One person charged in the case was acquitted for lack of evidence.

In the case of the Bosnian Croatian General Tihomir Blaskic, whose trial lasted more than two years, a conviction in March of 2002 resulted in a sentence to prison for 45 years. He was convicted on 20 counts of crimes against humanity, war crimes, and violation of the 1949 Geneva Conventions. This prosecution was directed against a general who had not fired a weapon in anger against Muslims, but who had personally issued orders requiring systematic attacks. The orders were given by him as the commander of the HVO Bosnian Croatian forces between 1992 and 1994. Hundreds were killed and thousands fled their homes.

The presiding judge in sentencing the accused stated: "The acts of war carried out with disregard for international humanitarian law and in hatred of other people, the villages reduced to rubble, the houses and stables set on fire and destroyed, the people forced to abandon their homes, the lost and broken lives are unacceptable."[86]

G. Effectiveness of the ICTFY

The supporters of the international law of Human Rights have been pleased with the manner in which the ICTFY has succeeded in achieving the mandate given to it by the Security Council. It was no small task to assemble highly qualified judges,[87] prosecutors, defense counsel, and the staff required for the court to operate efficiently. Language barriers had to be overcome with heavy demands being placed on interpreters and translators.

Perhaps the brightest spot, with the prospect of enduring consequence, has been the positive and creative role created by the chief prosecutors. Their unflagging efforts to require national governments to send major suspects to The Hague, as well as to take them into custody, has become a hallmark of this new system of international criminal justice.

The work of the court, with its focus on the trial of cases stands in contrast to the more politically oriented role of NATO's peacekeepers. The commitments of some of its member States, with some exceptions, as previously indicated, have been marked by a reluctance to effect the early arrests of readily identifiable suspects.

With the general acceptance that individuals charged with causing grievous harms to humankind should be prosecuted in appropriate courts, and because of the relative novelty of criminal prosecutions in international tribunals, the question has arisen as to the fairness of the decisions. The universal question, for both national and international tribunals, is: What is the balance between maximum procedural and substantive protections and the practical importance of punishing those who have caused so much grief to so many innocent and hapless persons? Such new tribunals as the one for Yugoslavian defendants must continually demonstrate on a case by case basis that they merit approval. A satisfactory basis for humanitarian involvement must have been demonstrated prior to the existence of judicial procedures. Courts will be able to apply law to those who have violated humanitarian norms.[88]

To the present the procedural and substantive protections employed by the ICTFY have resulted in fair trials. The high qualifications of the judges and the availability for review should lead fair-minded critics to conclude that justice under law is taking place. The jurisprudence of the court at The Hague may also provide guidance to those who see merit in the establishment of a permanent international criminal tribunal.

3. OTHER ILLUSTRATIONS

A. Civil Suits in the United States: Jurisdictional Issues

Human rights violations of the kind associated with Chile, Yugoslavia, Bosnia-Herzegovina, Croatia, Rwanda, Cambodia, Sierre Leone, and elsewhere have increased interest in the international law principle of universal jurisdiction. Originally developed as a means to prosecute those engaged in slave trading and maritime piracy, in more recent times it has been employed against persons charged with aerial hijacking, piracy, sabotage, and terrorism.

Even more recently the principle of universal jurisdiction has been employed in civil actions in the United States by relatives of individuals harmed as a result of unlawful orders on the part of political and military leaders in the former Yugoslavia.[89]

In those instances in which a State allows trials in absentia against foreign defendants for harms caused by them to resident citizens, it is impossible for international criminals to hide from justice. When the facts became known relating to the conduct of the Bosnian Serb military leader Radovan Karadzic involving the ethnic cleansing of Muslims and war crimes in Bosnia in the early 1990s, survivors and relatives instituted civil actions in U.S. Federal District Courts. Access to such courts is facilitated because of a line of cases in which such courts can hear matters involving violations of international law and U.S. treaties. Such suits have been authorized by the U.S. Alien Tort Claims statute.

In the case against Mr. Karazic a New York jury awarded the 12 plaintiffs the sum of $745 million dollars. Recovery will depend on discovering assets being held by him in the United States, which is not likely. The suit, which was financed by organizations that had provided humanitarian aid to war victims living in Bosnia-Herzegovina and Croatia, carries symbolic meaning. It reinforces the wide demands that Mr. Karadzic be apprehended by Yugoslav or NATO officials and delivered to the tribunal at The Hague.

The concept of universal jurisdiction is being reviewed by States having firm commitments to the protection of universal Human Rights. The principle also can be taken into account when courts, such as The Hague tribunal, are needed in countries where Human Rights violations are rampant and where, up to the present, such courts have not been instituted.

A second universal jurisdiction case, also being heard in the United States, resulted from the 1996 terrorist attack against an American citizen in Jerusalem.

Defendants are Syrian officials and the head of the Syrian military unit in Lebanon. They are charged with aiding and abetting Hamas, a Palestinian terrorist organization, in staging the attack. Jurisdiction is based on a federal anti-terrorism statute. The practical and symbolic ramifications of this case are similar to those involving Mr. Karadzic.

In May 2003 a Federal District Court held Iran responsible for the bombing in 1983 of the Marine Corps barracks in Beirut in which 241 American servicemen were killed. Counsel for plaintiffs have expressed the hope that Iranian assets in the United States would be available to make payments to the families of the deceased. The United States has been reluctant to engage in such practices for fear that foreign courts would seize American assets in foreign countries. Alternatively, the Treasury Department has funded some claimants.

The American debate over the wisdom of applying the principle of universal jurisdiction in the United States finds division between the proponents of multilateralism and unilateralism. The latter are fearful that courts in States unfriendly to the United States, or later identified as "rogue States," will allow politically inspired suits designed to cause embarrassment to the U.S. If the action were a civil one, there could be a monetary judgment against the American citizen or company doing business in the plaintiff State.

At present U.S. law allows only the filing of civil actions. A question deserving further debate in the United States is whether U.S. courts should be allowed to hear criminal in absentia cases against foreign defendants. If this policy were adopted it would be difficult to object to the same policy on the part of foreign States.

Although the recent cases in Federal District courts constitute strong demands for symbolic justice, this approach should not be allowed to impede the constructive work of the ICTFY.[90] Its practical day-to-day dedication to the highest ideals of criminal justice is a landmark some would say, almost a modern miracle—in light of the prejudices of super-sovereignty oriented, national political figures. Such figures, it is sad to say, may be obliged to consider that the ICTFY may, because of the progressive development of the international law of Human Rights, plus the stabilizing influence of the 1949 Geneva Conventions, put them in a defendants' dock. Through such international criminal tribunals the frequently dormant, community-oriented conscience of mankind has found effective representation.

Nonetheless, tantalizing questions remain.

B. The International Criminal Tribunal for Rwanda (ICTR)

Rwanda became a State on July 1, 1962. Prior to that date it had been supervised by Belgium as a U.N. trusteeship. Its population at the beginning of 1991 was about 7 and a half million persons. Of these about 14 per cent were Tutsi, while Hutus made up the balance. Despite this ratio the Tutsi, being more proactive, frequently ruled the country. Neighbors are Uganda, Zaire, Burundi, and Tanzania. Political unrest has been a hallmark of the area.[91]

In 1994 the world witnessed an awful slaughter in Rwanda. Induced by a former prime minister, Jean Kambanda, of the extremist Hutu government, killings which led to the charge of genocide, resulted in the deaths of more than half-a-million ethnic Tutsis and moderate Hutus. Also a leader in this extended rampage was Jean-Paul Akayeshu, a municipal official. Kambanda is the first head of a government to be convicted of genocide by an international criminal tribunal.

The world community was appalled by the gravity of the situation in Rwanda. On November 8, 1994 the Security Council adopted a resolution entitled "International Tribunal for the Prosecution of Persons Responsible for such Violations Committed in the Territory of Rwanda and Neighboring States."[92] Reference was made to the fact that the tribunal was being created at the request of the government of Rwanda. The Security Council limited prosecutions to the time when acts of genocide and other serious violations of international humanitarian law had occurred, i.e., from January 1, 1994 through December 31, 1994.

The Statute of this court closely parallels that of the ICTFY. Thus, for example, all States are obliged to cooperate with the court and its organs, and must adopt national legislation to implement the Statute, as well as to comply with orders issued by a Trial Chamber.

The jurisdiction of the Court was limited to two of the four subjects given to the ICTFY, namely, genocide and crimes against humanity. The ICTR was given jurisdiction respecting common Article 3 of the Geneva Conventions relating to War Victims and the 1977 Additional Protocol, which had not been given to the court at The Hague. The ICTR was not given jurisdiction respecting violations of the laws or customs of war.

Although there are substantial special differences between the roles and performance of the ICTFY and the ICTR, such as the areas, the ethnicity, the detailed fashion in which the situations were covered by the press, administrative skills, and the manner in which the recruiting of staff was carried out, there were basic similarities. These include the obligation to apprehend accused persons, a factual inquiry into the details of the person's conduct, a prosecutorial decision that there was evidence of that person's guilt, and a trial before a competent court.

However, underlying all of these issues was the basic question of whether the criminal judicial process is able to cope with so much criminal conduct carried on within a fairly short time span with such devastating effects. More basic was the question of the purpose of the trial.

Is it a finding a guilt with attendant sentences designed to punish the identified criminal conduct? In light of the enormity of the prospective list of defendants, should only the graver cases be prosecuted? How is one to determine who are the more "serious" defendants? What of the contention that "selective" prosecutions are inherently unfair to the person who is actually prosecuted? What is the role of domestic courts?

These are common quandaries. For the time being, at least, the agreed policies are clear. These prosecutions will proceed. And with the coming into existence of a permanent international criminal court, perhaps even more mature processes will be available. In any event the grant of amnesty or the use of selective prosecutions may be approaches to be considered.

C. Proposals for New Regional International Criminal Tribunals

1. Special Court for Sierra Leone

A civil war erupted in normally peaceful Sierra Leone on March 23, 1991. It resulted in atrocities until a peace accord was signed in Lome, Togo, in July 1999. Under the leadership of Foday Sankoh, the commander of the Revolutionary United Front, it flared again in early 2000. The unusual brutality, often against children, was resumed.

The United States government in July, 2000, was a leader in trying to bring the situation under control. In late July, 2000, it asked the Security Council to address a proposal for a special mixed *ad hoc* court having jurisdiction over Human Rights violations by the rebel forces. On August 14, 2000, the Security Council adopted Resolution 1315, in which the Secretary-General was requested to negotiate an agreement with Sierra Leone to create such a court and also to submit a report to it on the implementation of the resolution.[93]

On March 10, 2003 seven persons, including Foday Sankoh, were indicted by the Prosecutor. The crimes alleged included murder, rape, extermination, acts of terror, enslavement, looting and burning, sexual slavery, conscription of children into an armed force, and attacks on United Nations peacekeepers and humanitarian assistance workers.

The tribunal is to comply strictly with all procedural requirements for a fair trial. It may impose imprisonment, and may refer to the sentencing practices of the country, but may also take into account the practice of the ICTR. It may order forfeiture of property acquired unlawfully by criminal conduct.

2. Proposal for Cambodia

As repressive States, depending on the means favored by dictators, accelerate their prosecutions of ethnic and religious minorities, and violate international humanitarian law, demands have been made that special courts cope with the situation. This has been the case for Cambodia, Burundi, Congo, East Timor, Kosovo, and Sudan in all of which there have been savaging civil conflicts.

In the case of Cambodia the three-year terror reign of Pol Pot, who was instrumental in the formation of the Khmer Rouge movement, engaged in genocide. A 1979 U.N. report identified the extent of the killings, saying it was the worst since the Nazi experience of World War II. As in the more recent violations of Human Rights, proposals were made that the matter should be referred to a court of law, either Cambodian, or international, for adjudication. As in the foregoing situation the idea of referring such matters to a mixed court seemed the natural thing to do, and received very substantial support. However, Cambodia has called for a national court supported by foreign judges and prosecutors.

The draft statute of the court contains provisions for individual criminal responsibility which are consistent with international law, criminal law norms, and rights of an accused pursuant to international Human Rights standards.[94]

Although the court will depend on the assistance and support of the U.N., it will come into existence upon the adoption of the required national legislation. Again, the internal unrest in Cambodia has prevented the implementation of the foregoing provisions. The internal condition was serious enough for the General Assembly in 2001 to declare it to be a threat to international peace and security. With the matter stalled the General Assembly in January 2003 instructed the Secretary-General to resume talks with Cambodian officials.

3. The Proposal for Kosovo

The ICTFY and the ITCR have been presented by the prosecutor with critical cases, involving major violations of international humanitarian law. These two courts, faced with the requirement of undelayed prosecutions are in need of help. One such possibility is the quasi-international court now sitting in Kosovo. It is a part of the International Judicial Support special program authorized by the U.N. upon the recommendation of the Secretary-General.[95] As a result nationals of other countries are participating in the work of the local tribunals. They are engaged in cases involving war crimes committed in Kosovo.

D. National Tribunals: The Trial at Lockerbie

Pan Am flight 103 took off from London's Heathrow airport with New York as its destination on December 21, 1998. Explosives on board detonated when the plane was above Lockerbie, Scotland, killing its 259 passengers and crew and eleven more on the ground.

Investigations led to the conclusion that responsible for this tragedy were two citizens of the Libyan Arab Jamahiriya. Named as defendants in the case were Abselbasset al Megrahi, a Libyan intelligence agent, who had been educated in the United States, and al Am Khalifa Fhimah, an airline employee.

A grand jury inquiry in the United States concluded that prosecutions should be based on a conspiracy to destroy a U.S. aircraft, to destroy a vehicle used in foreign commerce by means of an explosive to kill U.S. nationals, the destroying of a civil aircraft, and aiding and abetting in the foregoing acts.[96]

When the matter finally came to the Lockerbie court the charge was murder for acts in Scottish air space.

The court was created as the result of an agreement between Scotland, Libya, the United Kingdom, and the United States. It was stipulated that the trial should take place at Camp Zeist, the Netherlands, that Scottish law was to apply, that there was to be a three-judge tribunal drawn from the Scottish High Court of Justiciary, that a majority vote would prevail, that proof would have to be "beyond reasonable doubt," and that the court's findings could be either guilty, not guilty, or non-proven, meaning an acquittal. If convicted, an accused would serve his period of imprisonment in a Scottish prison. The court rendered its decision on January 31, 2001. Megrahi was convicted and sentenced to life imprisonment. Fhimah was found not guilty.

Both defendants were represented by counsel. Aside from the typical arguments presented in murder cases, the defendants urged that there was an absence of international legal standards, and that this inherent defect should result in a dismissal. The tribunal, with the charge of murder before it, examined in great detail an extraordinary set of facts tracing the activities of the defendants. It concluded that a fair trial had taken place and that the proof of guilt was beyond a reasonable doubt.[97]

The United Nations played an instrumental role in getting this case before a court. It had long been interested in the safety of international civil air travel, and in 1970 and in 1989 the Security Council had adopted resolutions furthering this objective. On December 30, 1988, two days after the plane was lost the president of the Council condemned the act and called on all States to assist in the apprehension and prosecution of those responsible for the act.

As facts began to develop, which implicated officials of the Libyan government, the Security Council, with its concern for terrorism as a threat to international peace and security, made demands on Libya to respond to requests for information.[98] This was followed in March, 1992, by a resolution calling on all States to impose restrictions on flights to and from Libya, to stop providing military assistance to Libya, to reduce the staffs of foreign relations representatives, and to expel Libyan terrorists from their countries.[99]

The foregoing resolution, not having produced the required information, caused the Security Council on November 11, 1993, to impose more restrictive sanctions on Libya. The new approach was to freeze funds or other financial resources belonging to Libya, to institute embargoes against the delivery of critical items by States to Libya, and to obtain the closure of all Libyan Arab Airlines offices in the territories of U.N. members. Further, persons who had entered into contracts with Libya were to be excused from noncompliance, if the contracts related to the above subjects.

Even though the above were intended to limit Libyan assets the resolution took a hard-line position respecting the payment by Libya of its debts. They were expected to be paid and on time. The U.N. asserted that it expected nonmembers and international organizations to conform their conduct to the terms of the resolution.[100]

Economic sanctions were notoriously slow in taking effect. Not having resulted in the expected action on the part of Libya the Security Council in 1998 restated its demand for Libya to comply with the Security Council's demands. By this time it had become clear that the accused would be the two persons identified above. So that a fair trial could occur the Security Council decided that Libya was to "ensure that any evidence or witnesses in Libya are, upon request of the court, promptly made available at the court in the Netherlands for the purpose of the trial."[101] Further, Libya was directed to deliver the accused to the government of the Netherlands for detention pending trial. Once Libya had complied with this directive, the sanctions identified above were to be immediately suspended.[102]

It was not until March 2003 that Libya agreed to accept a measure of responsibility for the Lockerbie disaster. Libya agreed to pay as much as $2.7 billion to compensate the victims' families. Libya continued to reject criminal liability. It also expressed the hope that UN financial sanctions would be lifted. This would require the approval of the Security Council. In May 2003 the United States expressed the view that Libya would have to take responsibility, pay the indicated compensation, and renounce terrorism.

The borders of most European countries are open in the sense that these States have minimized the need for passport control when transit is by land. Terrorists, either foreign born or local products, have found it possible to develop their cells, improve their weapons and other destructive capabilities, and to communicate with foreign and native terrorists. These conditions have existed for a long time, but were not so clearly evident before September 11, 2001.

When the Scottish High Court in the Lockerbie trial proceeded only on the charge of murder, and declined to proceed on the basis of national and international aviation laws, States began to recognize that there was not a pressing need to make terrorism a crime. The terrorist could be prosecuted under standard felony charges. This has now been appreciated in European countries. These countries, in moving against members of Al Qaeda, in an increasing number of active cases, have been relying on felony charges.

4. THE LONG-TERM EFFECT OF JUDICIAL PROCEEDINGS INVOLVING INTERNATIONAL CRIME

There has not been much evidence until recently that either international tribunals, or those of a mixed variety now in operation in Kosovo, would be created to deal with international humanitarian law, and if created, would have much of an impact. The one hope was based on the general approval given to the Nuremberg court at the end of World War II and in 2001 to the Lockerbie tribunal. There is now new hope. The responsible manner in which the ICTFY, in particular, has addressed its legal responsibilities should be a convincing argument in favor of the world judicial process. The need will be for momentum to continue.

Support for the use of criminal courts to deal with the kinds of cases identified above, it seems, is based on the proposition that a civilized society requires that such matters be referred to a non-political institution which requires a factual support for conclusions reached by it. Since courts, world wide, and over history have established the reputation, although sometimes flawed, of comporting with the criteria of "fair trial," the association of such institutions with such problems, has been, almost without exception, readily accepted.

Alternate procedures have not made an appearance. Nonetheless, it would be foolish, despite the principles enunciated in Nuremberg, and supported at Lockerbie and the general confidence reposed in the judicial process, to suppose that tyrants committed to the violation of international humanitarian law will disappear in the midrange or even longer time frames.[103]

A more plausible scenario might be one in which States, observing the successes of international criminal tribunals, would be more inclined to make use of their own domestic laws in order to prosecute their own citizens or foreign terrorists. Excluded from such a process, unfortunately, might be national political figures who, especially through the use of the power available to them, could demonstrate that they are still above the law. This is an old refrain by tyrants. Even so, the world community, able to prove that such personages were threats to international peace and security, might have the last word. The availability of a permanent international criminal tribunal established by treaty can address such matters.

Much would depend on the backgrounds of the persons who are to serve as judges in future cases. It may be questioned if a court composed only of knowledgeable lawyers would suffice. Perhaps a larger world-wide panel drawn from persons eminent in their understanding of the course of history could be added to the present pool of judges, or could serve as consultants.

DISCUSSION QUESTIONS

1. The ICC was described as a "missing link" in an evolving international legal system. Is there really a need for the so-called "missing link"?
2. The United States has long been opposed to the establishment of the ICC. America's most powerful and long-term allies have scoffed at the concerns relating to jurisdiction advanced by the U.S. Are the American concerns justified relating to the exercise of jurisdiction by the Court over nationals of non-party States?
3. It has been suggested that a permanent international criminal tribunal would undoubtedly engage in judicial tyranny. What is the evidence to support the allegation?
4. Assume that an American military pilot is in custody in country X, which is a party to the Rome Statute, and wishes to prosecute him for a violation of the laws or customs of war. What peaceful and legal avenues are open to the United States to prevent such a prosecution?
5. The Rome Statute sets forth a large number of rules designed to insure that an accused receive a "fair trial." Compare these guarantees with those available to an accused being prosecuted on a criminal charge in the U.S. Federal District Court.
6. How do you account for the comparative ease in establishing the ICTFY and the major difficulties encountered in the acceptance of the ICC?
7. Are you satisfied that an accused charged with violating the crimes identified in the Statute of the ICTFY can receive a fair trial?
8. Former president Slobodan Milosevic appears to have developed a trial strategy. What are the principal elements? How can the court arrive at a decision based on the terms of the several indictments?
9. Assuming that only the major defendants can be prosecuted before the ICTFY, how would you structure the judicial process so that the lesser figures will also be subject to prosecution.

10. Where on a scale of 1 to 10 would you place the principles and practices identified in this Chapter in American foreign policy?

NOTES

1. A/COND.183/9, July 17, 1998. The web site is http://www.un.org.law/icc/index.html., L.N. SADAT, THE INTERNATIONAL CRIMINAL COURT AND THE TRANSFORMATION OF INTERNATIONAL LAW (2001).

2. The Statute and testimony supporting the U.S. position is in: "Is a U.N. International Criminal Court in the U.S. National Interest?" Hearings before the Sub-committee on International Operations of the Committee on Foreign Relations, United States Senate, 105 Cong., 2d Sess., July 23, 1998, 131–140. http://www.gpo.gov/congress/senate. For the Statute see 37 *ILM* 999, September 1998.

3. M. Leigh, "The United States and the Statute of Rome," 95 *AJIL,* 127, No. 1, January 2001.

4. *Ibid.*

5. P. Kirsch, "The Rome Conference on the International Criminal Court: A Comment," *ASIL Newsletter* 8 (November-December 1998). As a Canadian delegate to the Conference he served as Chairman of the Committee of the Whole.

6. *Ibid.*

7. M. Leigh, *Supra*, Note 3 at 125.

8. *Ibid.*

9. T. Meron, "The Court We Want," *ASIL Newsletter* 9, November–December 1998. Professor Meron was a member of the U.S. delegation to the Rome Conference.

10. *Ibid*. See Article 13.

11. *Ibid.*

12. *Supra.*, Note 2, at 13.

13. JEFFREY S. MORTON, THE INTERNATIONAL LAW COMMISSION OF THE UNITED NATIONS (2000). When the Commission's draft statute was released in 1979 it came under the review of the American Bar Association's Law and Practice. Under the chairmanship of Lucinda A. Low it submitted a recommendation favoring such a tribunal. Brian J. Newquist, "The International Criminal Court," 34 *The Int'l Law* 691 (Summer 2000); L.N. Sadat and S.R. Carden, "The New International Criminal Court: An Uneasy Revolution," 88 *Geo.L.J.* 381 (March 2000); Jennifer Schense and J.L. Washburn, "The United States and the International Criminal Court," 35 *The Int'l Law* 614 (Summer 2001).

14. H. Corell, "International Judicial Responses to International Crimes," *International Practitioner's Notebook* 12–13, Issues 60 and 61 October 1995, 12–13.

15. *Ibid.*

16. Henry A. Kissinger, "The Pitfalls of the Universal Jurisdiction," 80 *Foreign Affairs*, No. 4, 86 (July/August 2001). For a legal appraisal of "jurisdiction," see D.D. Bowett, "Jurisdiction: Changing Patterns of Authority over Activities and Resources," in R. ST. J. MACDONALD AND D.M. JOHNSTON, eds., THE STRUCTURE AND PROCESS OF INTERNATIONAL LAW, 557 (1983).

17. Id. at 92

18. *Ibid.*

19. John R. Bolton, "Is a U.N. International Criminal Court in the U.S. National Interest?" *Supra,* note 2 at 48. Additional criticisms were identified in his remarks to The Aspen Institute, Berlin, Sept. 16, 2002. www.state/gov/t/us/rm/13538.htm. See also Marc Grossman, Under Secretary for Political Affairs, "American Foreign Policy and the International Criminal Court." May 6, 2002. http://www.state.gov/p/99491."

20. For a commentary on the Kissinger-Bolton perspective, see Kenneth Roth, "The Case for Universal Jurisdiction," 80 *Foreign Affairs*, No. 5, 150, September/October 2001. Mr. Roth is Executive Director of Human Rights Watch. See also Richard Falk who states that Mr. Bolton's approach is to treat "the obligation of international law as subordinate to the geopolitical whims of government." "Letters to the Editor," 78 *Foreign Affairs*, No. 3, 159, May/June 1999.

21. http://pdq.state.gov/scripts/cqcgi.exe/@pdqtest1.env?. In authorizing signing President Clinton said: "We do so to reaffirm our strong support for international accountability and for bringing to justice perpetrators of genocide, war crimes, and crimes against humanity." *Los Angeles Times*, A1, January 1, 2001.

22. A. Rovine, "Notes from the President," *ASIL Newsletter 5*, January–February 2001.

23. Letter dated Feb. 13, 2001, p. 7.

24. B. Ferencz, 95 *AJIL*, No. 2, 386 (2001).

25. Peter J. Spiro, "The New Sovereigntists," 79 *Foreign Affairs*, No. 6, p. 9, November/December (2000).

26. Schense and Washburn, *Supra*, Note 13 at 616.

27. *Ibid.*

28. *Ibid.*

29. *Id.* at 619.

30. D.J. Scheffer, 29 *Courier* 2, Fall 1998.

31. Schense and Washburn, *Supra*, Note 13 at 615. For later developments, see D.A. Mundis, "The Assembly of States Parties and the Institutional Framework of the ICC," 97 *AJIL* 132, No. 1, Jan. 2003.

32. M. Leigh, *Supra*, Note 3 at 126.

33. U.N. Doc. S/RES/827 (1993).

34. 1996 I.C.J. 616 (Preliminary Objections) (Order of July 11, 1996).

35. On the recent proliferation of international dispute resolving processes, see *Implications of the Proliferation of International Adjudicatory Bodies for Dispute Resolution*, Proceedings of the American Society of International Law Forum Co-Sponsored with the Graduate Institute of International Studies, L. Boisson de Chazournes ed., 1995; C.P. R. Ramano, "The Proliferation of International Law Judicial Bodies: The Pieces of the Puzzle," 31 *N.Y.U.J. Int'l l & Pol* 709 (1999).

36. "Report of the Secretary-General Pursuant to Paragraph 2 of Security Council Resolution 808 (1993), U.N. Doc S/25704, 14, 3 May 1993.

37. *Id.* at p. 18.

38. *Id.* Art. 24.

39. *Ibid.*

40. *Supra*, note 1 at 22.

41. *Id.* at 23.

42. *Supra*, note 1 at 9.

43. ICTFY Doc. (Case IT-94-1-T) For assessments of the Tadic case see C. Greenwood, "International Humanitarian Law and the Tadic Case," 7 EJIL 265 (1996); F. Patel-King and A-M. la Rosa, "The Jurisdiction of the Yugoslavia Tribunal: 1994–1996," 8 EJIL 123–180 (1997).

44. ICTFY Doc. (Case IT-94-1-T).

45. *Id.* At 12.

46. *Id.* at 14.

47. *Ibid.*

48. *Nullum crimen sine lege* means that no one is to be held guilty of any criminal offence on account of an act or omission which did not constitute a criminal offense, under national or international law, at the time the act was committed.

49. *Supra*, note 44 at 19.

50. ICTFY Doc. (IT-94-1-AR72.)

51. George H. Aldrich, "Jurisdiction of the International Criminal Tribunal for the Former Yugoslavia," 90 AJIL, No. 1, 64 (1996).

52. *Id.*, at 69. Aldrich also stated: "Surely the Bosnian Serb forces are recognized as a belligerent, and it is only realistic that the Serbian civilians in the areas those forces control should equally by recognized as protected persons under the Geneva Convention." *Id.* at 67.

53. G.G.J. Knoops, *Defenses in Contemporary International Criminal Law* (2001).

54. ICTFY Doc. IT32/Rev.16, 62, July 22, 1999.

55. *Supra*, note 2 at 68.

56. UND OC S/25704 at 32.

57. U.N. Doc. S/RES/827 (1993), 25 May 1993.

58. "Symposium: The Dayton Agreements: A Breakthrough for Peace and Justice," 7 EJIL 147 (1996).

59. *The Christian Science Monitor* 19, January 6, 1998. Attention was called to an article in the Washington Post dated December 9, 1997, which identified the embarrassing U.S. position as an example of Orwellian doublespeak. P.L. Hicks, "Painful Lesson on Peacekeeping," *ABA Journal*, 103, July 1999.

60. For example, Secretary of State Albright stated in May 2000, referring to the court for Yugoslavia and the court for Rwanda, that the "war crime agenda is more than the pursuit of abstract U.S. goals and interests. . . . There is now no turning back from the judicial process [for the two courts]. . . . The United States continues its significant support . . . [so that justice will be brought to] the perpetrators of genocide, crimes against humanity, and war crimes in our time" (http://secretary.state.gov/www/statements/2000/000505.html).

61. *Los Angeles Times*, A14, November 28, 2001.

62. *Los Angeles Times*, A3, March 1, 2002.

63. *The Christian Science Monitor*, p. 7, March 6, 2002.

64. The more positive approach taken by NATO forces can be attributed in part to a follow-up in November, 1999, of the 1995 Dayton peace accords. The meeting between American and Bosnian leaders focused on means to alleviate corruption in Bosnia, where the collection of taxes had been reduced so much that the government was almost at a standstill. Dayton had produced a commitment on the part of the Western States of $5.1 million for reconstruction. This was coupled with a promise on the part of NATO to be more effective in capturing persons indicted at The Hague.

65. *Los Angeles Times*, A3, April 23, 2000.

66. U.N. Doc. S/Res 808 (1998).

67. A. Frye and P.R. Rosenblatt, Los Angeles Times, B11, July 2, 2001. They favored a policy of jurisdictional "complementarily," and suggested that danger existed that American military personnel might be prosecuted in the future International Criminal Tribunal.

68. *Los Angeles Times*, A15, March 28, 2002.

69. General Pinochet was found to be subject to prosecution for Human Right's violation, but was allowed to return to Chile because of failing health, which has been disputed. Having been granted amnesty by Chile's legislature, this was set aside by the Chilean Supreme Court, thereby rendering him triable under Chilean law. This has not happened.

70. ICTFY Doc. IT-02-54.

71. U.N. Doc.S/25704 (3 May 1999)

72. Indicted at the same time were Milan Milutinovic, president of Serbia, Nikola Sainovic, former deputy prime minister of Yugoslavia; General Dragoljob Ojdanic, former chief of staff of the Yugoslav army; and Vlajo Stojijkovic, former Serbia minister of the interior. For editorial comments on NATO's Kosovo intervention, see 93 *AJIL*, No. 3, 824, October, 1999.

73. ICTFY Doc. IT-99-37-1.

74. ICTFY Doc. IT-99-37-PT at par. 69.

75. *Id.*, at par. 70.

76. ICTFY Doc. IT-02-54.

77. *Los Angeles Times*, A5, February 16, 2002.

78. *Ibid.*

79. *Ibid.*

80. ICTFY Doc. 99-37-PT, June 29, 2001.

81. *Id.* at par. 3.

82. *Ibid.*

83. U.N. Doc. S/25704, p.27

84. ICTFY Appeals Chamber: *Prosecutor v. Jelisic*, 40 *ILM* 1295 (2001).

85. *Los Angeles Times*, A10, February 23, 2001.

86. *Los Angeles Times*, A10, March 4, 2000.

87. The U.N. General Assembly appointed the first panel of 19 judges on April 8, 1997. U.N. Doc. S/RES/1104, April 8, 1997.

88. "Editorial Comments: NATO's Kosovo Intervention," 93 *AJIL* 824 (October 1999).

89. Among the scholars who have written on the subject of universal jurisdiction are D.W. Bowett, "Jurisdiction: Changing Patterns of Authority Over Activities and

Resources," in R. St. J. Macdonald and D.M. Johnston, Ed., *The Structure and Process of International Law* 555 (1983); W. Michael Reisman, Ed., *Jurisdiction and International Law* (2000); Carl Q. Christol, "Jurisdiction and Control; Permissible Unilateral Reponses to Dangerous Space Debris," in M. Benko and W. Kroll, eds., *Liber Amicorum Karl-Heinz Bockstiegel* 303 (2001). See also *Restatement (Third) of the Law of Foreign Relations of the United States* (1986).

90. In 2000, the United States adopted legislation allowing U.S. citizens to have broader rights in suits against Iran and Cuba for human rights' violations. 95 *AJIL* 134, January 2001.

91. For a detailed history study of the crisis with recommendations see the Organization of African Unity's "International Panel of Eminent Personalities (IPEP): Report on the 1994 Genocides in Rwanda and Surrounding Events (Selected Selections)," 40 *ILM* 141 (2001).

92. U.N. Doc S/RES/955 (1994).

93. U.N.Doc. S/RES/1315 (2002), 1, August 14, 2002.

94. D.A. Mundis, "The Creation of New *Ad Hoc* International Criminal Tribunals and Other International Efforts to Prosecute Violations of International Humanitarian Law," 35 *The Int'l Law,* No. 2, 635, Summer 2001.

95. *Id.* at 636.

96. U.S.C. ## 271, 32, 34, 844(i), 233 and 232.

97. "Opinion of the Court," 40 *ILM* 582 (2001).

98. U.N. Doc. Security Council Resolution 731, January 21, 1992.

99. U.N. Doc. Security Council Resolution 748, March 31, 1992.

100. S/RES/883, November 11, 1993.

101. S/RES/1192 August 27, 1998.

102. *Ibid.*

103. P. Akhavan, "Beyond Impunity: Can International Criminal Justice Prevent Future Atrocities?" 95 *AJIL*, No. 1, 7 (January 2001).

Chapter V

The Human Environment and Climate Change

1. INTRODUCTION

Scientific and technological innovations for almost 100 years have placed very heavy demands on many energy sources. Environmental problems have resulted. Policy makers with varying degrees of commitment to the human environment have been forced to address an increasingly critical issue. Simply stated: If ongoing greenhouse trends are not soon arrested, will the condition of humans on planet Earth be very gravely impaired?

There is evidence that emissions from automobiles are causing destructions of rain forests, species extinction, and atmospheric changes. Sea levels have risen. Receiving less attention, but equally in need of international regulation, has been the atmospheric pollution caused by the fuels, consisting in part of chlorine and aluminum particulates, used for the launching of space objects. When satellites use nuclear power sources there is a radiation problem.

The need for a healthy living environment has always enjoyed commanding popular support. A poll conducted by *The New York Times* in 1997 disclosed that 65% of those polled wanted the United States to cut emissions regardless of what other countries do and that 57% wanted environmental improvements regardless of cost. Writing in *The New York Times*, Russell Baker observed recently that the greenhouse effect of automobile emissions had caused each of the 260,000,000 residents of the United States to be "hemmed in by 175,999,999 motorized exhaust fume spewers."

In December 2002 NASA scientists revealed that Earth's average temperature during the 2002 meteorological year was 58.35 degrees Fahrenheit, more than one degree warmer than the long-range average of 57.2 degrees.[1]

It was concluded that greenhouse gases were warming the planet faster than had been predicted earlier.

Since the deterioration of the climate is a common concern it is a subject ideally qualified for international negotiations and international agreements. Reasonable corrective and protective measures can serve human interests. Unfortunately there has been a notorious failure of political will on the part of the national leaders of the principal polluters to embark on such measures. Strong leadership on the part of the Heads of State in China, India, Russia, and the United States will be required. Even if American foreign policy were successful in all of its critical manifestations, it would still be a failure if a viable accord cannot be adopted and implemented on this subject.

2. THE STOCKHOLM, RIO DE JANEIRO, AND JOHANNESBURG CONFERENCES

The United Nations convened a Conference on the Human Environment in Stockholm in 1972. The delegates agreed to important principles. Pursuant to Principle 1 humankind has a fundamental right to live in "an environment of quality" with the "solemn responsibility to protect and improve the environment for present and future generations."

Possibly the most important declaration, opposed vigorously by China until the conference was winding down, is found in Principle 21:

> States have in accordance with the Charter of the United Nations and the principles of international law the sovereign right to exploit their own resources pursuant to their own environmental policies, and the responsibility to ensure that activities within their own jurisdiction and control do not cause damage to the environment of other States or of areas beyond the limits of national jurisdiction.

This statement was summed up at the conference with the observation: "Let the polluter pay."

The Rio de Janeiro Conference in June, 1992 was attended by 118 countries. It had a broader mission than the Stockholm meeting. In addition to the protection of the human environment there were demands to further the sustainable development of the world's resources. Thus, the Conference was titled a "Global Program for Environmental Restoration, Preservation and Social Development." On June 14 the delegates adopted a Declaration of Environment and Development consisting of 27 principles. The second Principle restated Stockholm's Principle 21. Principle 3 called upon States to act in such ways as to protect the needs of present and future generations.

Principle 4 identified the concern for sustainable development, which had been made a critical element of the Conference by the developing countries. It stated: "In order to achieve sustainable development, environmental protection shall constitute an integral part of the development process and cannot be considered in isolation from it." Listed as subjects of particular concern were the destruction of rain forests, species extinction, and atmospheric change.

The World Summit on Sustainable Development, with delegations from more than 190 countries, produced a report including a political declaration and a 65-page Johannesburg Implementation Plan on September 2002.[2] It called for increases in the sources of clean water and for a greater availability in poor countries of prescription drugs. It favored the phase out of lead-based toxic chemicals, the prevention of global warming, the elimination of destructive fishing practices, coping with problems of poverty and hunger, and measures to cut significantly the rate at which rare animals and plants are becoming extinct. These goals were to be realized through a series of partnerships in which affected parties are to select areas of concern.

The United States proposed partnerships with governments and private entities to protect the Congo's rain forest, to battle AIDS, and to provide cleaner water and energy to underdeveloped areas. At the same time the United States was successful in weakening the summit's implementation plan. It prevented a decision that multinational corporations should be more accountable for the environmental consequences of their actions and it defeated a European effort to obtain a plan to increase the world's reliance on non-pollution energy sources, such as solar and wind energy.

America's negativism relating to the elimination of greenhouse gases hampered its effectiveness at the conference. President Bush did not attend. High-ranking American diplomats experienced indignities of the kind that had occurred at the 1998 Rome Conference on the ICC.

All conferences were attended by private individuals from non-governmental organizations recognized by the United Nations. They drew world-wide attention to the seriousness of their concerns. Their vigorous involvement has continued to serve notice on public officials, both national and international, of the need to preserve and protect mankind from the ever-increasing harms caused by pollutants attributable to the more highly industrialized countries. Developing States, while demanding higher standards of control for advanced countries, also have campaigned for allowances to themselves because of the past non-pollutional activities on their part. Their argument is based on considerations of fairness and equity. The inhabitants of developing countries wish to enjoy the same material benefits which are commonly available in advanced countries.

3. SPECIAL SUBJECT MATTER TREATIES

Several international agreements have been designed to protect against quite specific, and limited, concerns. In 1977 agreement was reached on a Convention on the Prohibition of Military or Any Other Hostile Use of Environmental Modification Techniques. Four subjects were identified. The parties promised not to modify atmospheric conditions, for example, by increasing or decreasing precipitation; second, not to change the long-term atmospheric conditions over any part of the Earth's surface; third, not to engage in activity that would precipitate earthquakes; and, fourth, not to cause any ocean modification activity, such as producing tidal waves. The agreement entered into force in 1978. The United States became a party in 1980.

In 1979 a Convention on Long-Range Transboundary Air Pollution sponsored by the Economic Commission for Europe was signed in a Geneva Protocol dealing with nitrogen oxides and their transboundary fluxes. The United States is a party, with the agreement coming into force in 1991.

In 1985 a Convention for the Protection of the Ozone Layer, with annexes, was signed in Vienna. The United States is a party, with the agreement entering into force in 1988.[3] This was followed in 1987 with the Montreal Protocol on Substances that Deplete the Ozone Layer. The United States is a party, with the Protocol coming into force in 1989.[4] It focused on greenhouse gases including anthropogenic emissions by sources and removals by sinks and the anthropogenic emissions of carbon dioxide.

On March 30, 1992, the Council of the OECD adopted a plan for the Control of Transfrontier Movements of Wastes Destined for Recovery Operations. It entered into force for the United States on the same day.

The foregoing special illustrations, only one of which was signed in the past ten years, identify a willingness on the part of many States, with varying degrees of enthusiasm, to formalize international policies and programs for the protection of the human environment.

4. THE 1992 UNITED NATIONS FRAMEWORK CONVENTION ON CLIMATE CHANGE

On May 7, 1992 a major international agreement was reached in New York on environmental problems. Entitled United Nations Framework Convention on Climate Change, it was supported by 177 countries. It entered into force for the United States on March 21, 1994.[5]

Indicative of the progress being made in this area it referred to some of the principles set forth in the 1992 Rio Conference and to provisions of the 1985

Vienna Convention and the 1987 Montreal Protocol. The agreement in Article 1 provided definitions of key terms.[6] For example, "sink" means any "process, activity or mechanism which removes a greenhouse gas, an aerosol or a precursor of a greenhouse gas from the atmosphere." Article 2 sets forth the objective of the agreement. It is to "ensure that food production is not threatened and to enable economic development to proceed in a sustainable manner." Article 3 assigns to developed countries the lead in combating climate change with the admonition that action is required even though there may not be "full scientific certainty" as to the nature of the problem. The Bush administration has argued that the agreement is fatally flawed because in its view there is not adequate scientific evidence of the causes of adverse effects on the climate.

In 1992 the delegates stressed that "economic development is essential for adopting measures to address climate change." Advanced States were expected to reduce their overall emission of specified gases by at least 5 percent below 1990 levels for the 2008 to 2012 commitment period.

Article 4, entitled commitments, specifies in detail the respective rights and duties of the two kinds of States, advanced and developing, which are named in Annexes I and II. Such States are to adopt national policies intended to further the provisions of the agreement. Cooperative sharing of relevant research data is called for, including the standardization of computations.

Article 4 contains a commitment on the part of developed States to "take all practicable steps to promote, facilitate and finance, as appropriate, the transfer of, or access to, environmentally sound technologies and know-how to Parties, particularly developing country Parties, to enable them to implement the provisions of the Convention."

The treaty consists of 26 articles plus Annexes I and II. Annex I identified States with advanced economies. Annex II referred to the developing countries. In order to facilitate compliance with the agreement, and to work out problems encountered in its implementation, the Parties provided in Article 7 for a Conference of the Parties. This allows for annual meetings, or more often as necessary, to resolve problems.[7]

The First Meeting of the Conference of the Parties occurred in Berlin in 1995. The participants reviewed the adequacy of their 1992 Framework Convention, and particularly Article 4.2(a) which applied to developed countries. They concluded that the 1992 commitment of these States was inadequate. The 1992 provision reads "Each of these Parties shall adopt national policies and take corresponding measures on the mitigation of climate change, by limiting its anthropomogenic emissions of greenhouse gases and protecting and enhancing its greenhouse gas sinks and reservoirs."[8] The means to meet this need was to be a new Protocol, which was completed in Kyoto in 1997.

Prior to Kyoto the Second Conference of the Parties occurred in Geneva in 1996. The participants focused particularly on Annex I parties, and those whose economies were in transition. They were to clarify their policies and measures in such areas as energy, transport, industry, agriculture, forestry, waste management, economic instruments, institutions, and mechanisms. They were to move toward significant emission limitations within time frames of 2005, 2010, and 2020.

5. THE KYOTO PROTOCOL TO THE U.N. FRAMEWORK CONVENTION ON CLIMATE CHANGE, DECEMBER 1997

The parties to the 1992 New York Climate Change Convention met in Kyoto in 1997 in order to identify legally binding obligations and to further the goals outlined in 1992. Agreement was reached on limiting the emissions attributable to greenhouse gases, approaches open to developed States, and a procedure for cooperation between the two sets of States.[9] Agreement was also reached on emission targets and timetables.

Pursuant to Article 3 of the Kyoto Convention advanced States were to meet quantified emission limitation and reduction levels. This was to be accomplished during the years of 2008-2012. At the end of 2012 overall emissions were to be at least 5% below the 1990 levels. Reductions were to occur for carbon dioxide, methane, nitrous oxide and for HFCs, PFCs, and SF6 (aerosols). Consideration was given to the fact that some countries, depending on the status of science and technology, were more able and better economically positioned, to reduce emissions. States were authorized to trade emission rights.

In order to determine the existence of "emission rights," a quantitative figure, a methodological scheme was devised. Pursuant to Article 5, this figure was to be an estimation based on a "national system" with respect to anthropogenic emissions by sources and removals by sinks of all greenhouse gases not controlled by the Montreal Protocol. A process for making "appropriate adjustments" to such estimates was identified. These figures were to be on hand no later than one year prior to the start of the first commitment period. When such figures, to be referred to as units, were known a trading of such units was to occur. Thus, according to Article 6 any "Party included in Annex I may transfer to, or acquire from, any other Party emission reduction units resulting from projects aimed at reducing anthropogenic emissions by sources or enhancing anthropogenic removals by sinks or greenhouse gases in any sector of the economy."

This broad authority was made subject to four conditions: first, the project had to meet with the approval of the Parties; second, any project had to provide a reduction in emissions by sources, or an enhancement of removal by sinks "that is additional to any that would otherwise occur;" third, no emission reduction units would be available if the parties were not in compliance with Articles 5 and 7; and, fourth, for the purpose of meeting Article 3 commitments, the "acquisition of emission reduction units shall be supplemental to domestic actions."

The purpose of this complicated formula was to ascertain whether developing States, by reason of non-pollutional activities, would achieve credits or units which could be transferred to States which had exceeded their quotas. Such trading would let countries sell credits if they produced less of a pollutant than under a cap set by agreement. The buyers are countries which exceed the cap.

In calling for trading it was expected that a price could be established for units. This would provide an immediate benefit to the developing country and also would be beneficial to the advanced country.

On the other hand, if a developing country in the course of its economic activity were to increase its output of pollutants, arguing that in doing so it was trying to catch up with the production of manufactured goods and, thus, emulating the historic practices of the presently advanced countries, it might exercise its right to purchase emission rights. They would be available from an advanced country, where thorough-going efficiency measures were in place, and which had emission rights for sale. As a further inducement under Article 6 credits were to be granted to States where change reduced emissions. Such bonus points were to be granted for reforestation and those activities which create carbon "sinks" able to absorb greenhouse gases.

The negotiations reflected disparate outlooks on the part of the industrialized States and developing States. Accommodation was attempted by a "Clean Development Mechanism," set out in Article 12 of the Convention. It took into account the two basic demands of the developing countries, namely, to make progress in development while cooperating in preventing climate change.

Over time there were to be additional limits on pollutional activities, with a net reduction in pollution. Looking into the future there was always the possibility that the worldwide limitation on pollutants would be reduced by agreement at periodic intervals. It was expected that trading in emission rights would occur since the advanced States were to reduce emission of greenhouse gases by at least 5%, based on 1990 emission levels, for the 2008-2012 period. This formula called for a reduction in Europe of 8%, for the United States 7%, for Japan and Canada 6%.

In 1997 the United States was responsible for 25% of the world's total carbon dioxide production, with China rating at 14%, Russia and Japan at 6%, and Germany at 4%.[10] A study made in 1998 by the White House Council of

Economic Advisors indicated that the goals established at the 1997 Kyoto conference would cost the average American household $70 to $110 a year more for energy.[11] The 1997 *New York Times* poll also indicated that only 15% wanted the U.S. to delay acting until an international agreement was reached. Only 16% expressed the view that global warming resulted from normal climatic fluctuations rather than from the burning of hydrocarbons. A 1998 poll conducted by the World Life Fund disclosed that nearly eight out of 10 U.S. voters supported the Kyoto accord and that the majority wanted the U.S. to reduce emissions even if other States do not.[12]

If greenhouse gases are viewed from an economic rather than a public health perspective it is easy to see that a move away from present manufacturing procedures and lifestyles would result in enormous competitive economic advantages or disadvantages.

For example, lobbying efforts conducted by such organizations as the Global Climate Coalition, supported by energy companies and automobile manufacturers, oppose the Kyoto Protocol. On the other hand, the Environmental Defense Fund and the Pew Center on Global Climate Change have publicized environmental facts and have obtained commitments from many industrial polluters to alter their ways. Major American energy companies have left the Global Climate Coalition. In 1997 the president of Sun Oil Company stated that "there is sufficient concern over man-made climate impacts to justify initiation of prudent mitigation measures now."[13]

Japanese automobile manufactures have stated that they could live with the Kyoto convention's reduction in emission requirements.

Other major firms have focused on limiting the amount of energy employed in the manufacturing process. Hybrid vehicles using gas and electricity, or only electricity, have been engineered and are in use. Cleaner fuel, using alcohol, has been favored, especially in the "corn belt," which is a major source of industrial alcohol.

The Clinton approach to climate change included a proposal for a "carbon tax" on fuels that contribute to global warming. Congress expressed no interest in this proposal.

The negotiations in Kyoto in 1997 found the United States confronted by a European formula for reduction of greenhouse gases that was more demanding than it favored.

Other countries were not so concerned over extending the list of gases to be identified in the agreement. Major developing countries such as China and India are in line to become the world's greatest polluters, and indicated an unwillingness to be bound by limitations. On the whole there were major differences on reduction targets, policies and measures, sinks, emissions trading, joint implementation treatment of developing countries, and compliance.[14]

Two viewpoints arose relating to allowing caps on emissions trading. The United States, joined by Canada, Japan, and New Zealand argued that no caps should be placed on emissions trading. They claimed that it would produce a cost-effective and market-based foundation for the Treaty. Members of the European Union and others opposed them arguing that the presence of emission limitations would ensure the implementation of carbon reduction projects in industrialized countries.[15] It was understood at Kyoto in 1997 that the Convention was not in final form, and that there would be periodic meetings before it was open to signature.

6. THE BUENOS AIRES SESSION, NOVEMBER 1998

In November of 1998 the interested States met in Buenos Aires to resolve details on emissions trading and to achieve a necessary accommodation of the views of the advanced and the developing countries.[16]

This follow-up on Kyoto made it evident that a market for emissions trading constituted a key element of the goal to reduce greenhouse gases. European Union countries urged that a limit should be imposed on such agreements. This was based on the view that every country must do all that it could to reduce its own emissions. Argentina offered a "voluntary commitment" to set up targets and timetables to reduce emissions and some developing countries indicated they would discuss this proposal. Although regarded as constructive interventions, it was noted that effective procedures were absent. This evoked public criticisms by American observers. Nonetheless, the U.S. agreed to cut energy use by more than 30 percent over the next 12 years.

In an effort to obtain political support for a cleaner environment the Clinton administration proposed making monetary credits available to American producers for reductions of emissions before the treaty would become operational. The U.S. chief delegate to the Buenos Aires meeting signed the new protocol. In doing so he stated: "We are guided by the firm belief that signing will serve our environmental, economic and national security goals."[17]

7. THE BEIJING SESSION, NOVEMBER-DECEMBER, 1999

In a five-day session in Beijing efforts were made to reduce, via a long-term phase out, the production of certain chemicals known to be harmful to the environment. These included chemicals produced in advanced countries, including CFC, halons, and hydrofluorocarbons. For the HCFCs, known to deplete the ozone layer, the advanced States were given a deadline of 2030, while the developing countries were assigned the date of 2040. Freezes on the production of HCFCs were also promulgated

When these decisions became known to major American producers of such materials, which had commercial and industrial use as refrigerants, they began searches for alternatives. This was anticipated in 1999 and the delegates requested the Conference's Scientific Assessment Panel and the Economic Assessment Panel to provide recommendations. It was also decided that there should be a huge payment to the less-developed countries in order for them to phase out their manufacture of CFC. This figure was $475,700,000. It would be deposited with the Protocol's Multilateral Fund, which since 1991 had expended about one billion dollars to secure the end of manufacture of CFCs in 110 developing countries.[18] Their net greenhouse emissions at the present are in excess of those of the developed countries.

8. THE BUSH ADMINISTRATION AND THE HUMAN ENVIRONMENT

The change in administrations placed in President Bush's hands the opportunity to lead in the protection of the Earth environment against the dangers of excessive warming. At the outset he convened a Cabinet-level task force. It conferred with the National Academy of Sciences to obtain its views on the science of climate change. On the basis of reports received by him the president on June 11, 2001 announced his decision to reject the Kyoto premises and determinations. In his words, the protocol "was fatally flawed in fundamental ways."[19]

The "flaws" were of two types. First, the unknowns or uncertainties relating to global warming were said to be substantial, although admittedly a natural greenhouse effect contributes to warming. Secondly, the proposed terms were characterized as unfair. While the United States accounts for around 20 percent of man-made greenhouse emissions, such States as China and India are principal emitters. The Protocol offered special conditions to developing countries, yet both China and India were excluded from the Kyoto requirements. Further, the coverage of the agreement was not complete, namely, it did not deal with black soot and tropospheric ozone.[20] In economic terms the Protocol would have adverse effects for Americans, since it would cause "layoffs of workers and price increases for consumers."[21] In his remarks the President made specific reference to a number of international initiatives that the U.S. would support.

On July 13, 2001 President Bush, seemingly to provide evidence of a good faith effort to uphold the policy outlined on June 11, identified scientific projects to reduce the buildup of greenhouse gases in the atmosphere. The Department of Commerce was charged with the development of a federal research plan. Further studies were authorized for land use and forestry practices for storing carbon. Major international oil companies, from several countries, were charged with finding a new set of technologies "for reducing the cost of capturing carbon dioxide from fossil fuel combustion plants."[22] International scientific conferences were scheduled to examine regional aspects of climate change. The United States stated it would continue to participate in the Framework Convention on Climate Change, with representatives to attend the Bonn Session later in July 2001.[23]

9. THE BONN SESSION, JULY 2001

The Kyoto Protocol, following a final review, was signed on July 23, 2001 at Bonn. In doing so the delegates rejected rear-guard efforts on the part of the United States to obtain concessions that would have allowed the United States to continue to produce greenhouse gases. At the last minute Secretary of State Powell indicated that the United States was going to unveil "some new ideas" on the subject. When the top American official at Bonn expressed the same view, her remarks were "loudly booed."[24]

Note was taken that the United States would not block the formation of consensus of the Kyoto Protocol rules. The proposed rules were considered not to be sound policy. Objected to by the United States were: "An institution to assess compliance with emission targets that is dominated by developing country members without targets, more favorable treatment for Parties operating within a regional economic integration organization relative to other Parties, and rules that purport to change treaty commitments through decisions of the Parties rather than through the proper amendment procedure."[25] These particulars mirror those proclaimed by the United States in the decade-long negotiations for a Law of the Sea Convention. They reflect the fear that a forum dominated by developing countries, voting on a State by State basis, would not take into account the interests of the economically more advanced countries. Further, there was a concern that the proposed process for changing rules would not be seen as a treaty process, in which the United States is bound only by its own constitutional provisions. Aside from maintaining a policy in this instance consistent with that followed regarding the Law of the Sea Convention, the United States should not be obliged to make an election between breaching the treaty or acting contrary to its Constitution.

At the Bonn session the United States referred to global goals shared with other counties, namely: "developing and promoting use of innovative energy technologies, advancing climate science and modeling, promoting carbon sequestration, and developing market-friendly approaches to environmental protection."[26]

The participants reconfirmed the rule for the entry into force of the Protocol. It would require approval by 55 States. These States were to include industrialized States producing at least 55% of the total 1990 greenhouse emissions from this group. With the United States being a declared non-signer, in order to reach the 55% requirement, it will be necessary for Russia and Japan to become parties. They, as well as the United States, with its record of producing one-third of the world's pollution, promised to reduce the emission of greenhouse gases.

By November, 2003, the Kyoto Protocol had been signed by 84 countries, with a total of 120 either ratifying or acceding to it, including Japan and the 15-nation European Union. However it has not entered into force since these countries account for 44.2% of the emissions. Russian officials stated it would be approved "as soon as possible." When the Russian Federation ratifies the 55% requirement for countries producing greenhouse emissions will have been exceeded, and the agreement will enter into force.

While believed to be economically feasible, a trading approach will require world-wide cooperation between public and private bodies engaged in the control of pollution.

When one considers the turmoil visited on the World Trade Organization in recent times, one can only express the hope that market influences will be enough to obtain the desired result. The Bush plan for increased modeling would facilitate an understanding of the practicality of this approach.

At the Marrakesh meeting in October, 2001 the announced goal would be to reduce emissions by an average of 5% from 1990 levels by 2012. To further that end agreement was reached on the extent to which carbon dioxide absorbed by carbon sinks could be counted towards meeting the Kyoto targets; on how the joint implementation of an emissions' trading system would work; and on rules for ensuring compliance with commitments. Agreement was also reached on the role of the Clean Development Commission, consisting of 15 members. It was assigned the mandate to promote sustainable development by encouraging investments in developing countries, with the expectation that this would produce a reduction or avoidance of emissions.

If such a procedure could be brought to fruition, it would enable advanced States to receive credit against their Kyoto targets. Advanced States renewed their commitments to reduce the emission of greenhouse gases. The United States sent representatives to the conference who assumed the role of observers.

The negotiators, aware of the positions advanced by the United States, reached agreement on a number of key provisions. It was agreed that sanctions would be imposed on countries that failed to meet established emission targets. The sanctioned country would be obliged to make up its shortfall at a penalty rate of 130 per cent. It would have to provide an action plan showing how it proposed to cut emissions. It would not be allowed to engage in emissions trading. After a State had been assigned emission numbers, they could be enlarged, provided the State installed pollution reducing carbon sinks. Annual reports were to be made on the effectiveness of carbon sinks.

Unresolved, and left for consideration at the October Marrakesh meeting, was whether the Kyoto rules were to be legally binding. Opposed to this result were Russia and Japan. An ambiguous compromise left the matter open. The final decision on this was reserved for the future, but it was concluded that States would have to accept the rules as legally binding if they were to engage in the trading of emission credits.

10. THE MARRAKESH SESSION, OCTOBER 2001

In looking toward the meeting in Marrakesh, in October 2001, the United States was faced with certain strategies, all of which would have domestic consequences. At the worst it could do nothing and let the rate of pollution from emissions grow, which, for comparative purposes was about 13 per cent greater than it had been in 1990. This, of course would be self-defeating. A second approach, also quite passive, would be to encourage polluters, but without legal sanctions, to become more efficient, with governmental subventions payable to reach a desirable result. A more aggressive approach would be to back a market, both domestic and international, in which emission credits could be traded.[27]

11. THE UNITED STATES: SCIENCE, ECONOMICS, AND FOREIGN POLICY

President Bush's often quoted view that the Kyoto Protocol is fatally flawed has produced a number of consequences. Among them is the willingness of the United States to continue on a policy of unilateralism in an area of gathering importance. By following a go-it-alone policy in this area there is the risk of loss of political capital, although important attempts to redress this situation have been made in concessions to obtain support against terrorism. Countries and people have refused to believe that the Bush administration is correctly interpreting scientific and technological findings, even when they are the product of America's most highly respected authorities. There is the belief that the Bush economic approach will produce greater losses than gains. Dissatisfaction with low standards for emission of pollutants has led cities and states to adopt more stringent legislation.

Several American examples identify what other countries are giving credence to. On November 20, 2001, a report was published by President Bush's Commission on the Science of Climate Change. Headed by Ralph J. Cicerone, and composed of eleven top climate scientists, it concluded that the Earth's surface temperatures had raised about one degree Fahrenheit during the 20th Century, with warming trends having intensified in the past 20 years.

On the basis of computer modeling it was predicted there would be a rise in average global surface temperatures of between 2.5 and 10.4 degrees Fahrenheit by the end of the 21st Century. The Cicerone Commission also recommended additional research to reduce uncertainties in climate-change science.

A 2002 report dealing with greenhouse gases was prepared by the Environmental Protection Agency with the support of the White House Council on Environmental Quality, the Department of State, and other agencies and was submitted to the United Nations. It stated that such man-made gases in the U.S. would increase 43% between 2000 and 2020. President Bush is reported to have said that the EPA document was "a report put out by the bureaucracy."[28]

In the area of economic gains reports have been issued indicating that under the Kyoto Protocol sulfur dioxide, when recovered, could be used for emissions trading. Another example is the prospect for the sale by American manufacturers of energy-efficient technology to developing countries. This fits in with the "clean development mechanism" identified in the treaty.

A legal issue regarding the procedure to be employed in modifying the agreed terms of the Protocol has caused some debate. It is doubtful that the proposal with respect to voting procedures, and in particular those designed to modify previously identified changes in the provisions of the agreement, should be treated as a flaw. In order to avoid the challenges to the U.S. constitutional system, relating to the formation and termination of treaties, the United States could adopt a familiar practice. In agreeing to the Protocol all it would have to do is to make a statement, reservation, or interpretation preserving its right to accept changes only pursuant to its unique constitutional requirements.

12. CONCLUSION

As has been suggested intelligent programs and policies can be based on established facts. In recent years this has been augmented by modeling procedures.

Experience with this approach suggests that it can be helpful. In the United States, following such approaches to the environment and climate change, Presidents Clinton and Bush have referred to "uncertainties" as to their status.

Such "uncertainties," if substantiated would constitute a flaw, as President Bush has indicated, to the Kyoto Protocol. Yet, a preponderance of scientific findings has produced a general acceptance that greenhouse emissions and chemical pollutants in the atmosphere were detrimental to the health of humans and the world's ecosystems. This was the thrust of the Cicerone Commission Report.

On July 13, 2001 President Bush made a statement on climate change.[29] He identified specific initiatives that had been taken by the Cabinet-level climate change working group. It is an impressive report dealing with the "science of climate," "technological innovation," and references to bilateral discussions on environmental problems.

Under the heading of climate change the president referred to a federal research plan. It includes an investment by NASA over three years of $120 million for research "on the natural carbon cycle, climate modeling, and the link between atmospheric chemistry and climate to help reduce *uncertainties* in the science highlighted by the recent National Academy of Science's report requested by my Cabinet-level working group."[30]

The issue of "uncertainties" was referred to on July 23, 2001, at Bonn by the U.S. representative at the conference. In arguing that the Protocol was "not sound policy," she stated that "among other things, the emissions targets are not scientifically based or environmentally effective, given the global nature of greenhouse gas emissions. . . ."[31]

If it were concluded that the foregoing cannot be supported empirically by scientific data now in hand, the flaw or flaws must be discovered on other than scientific reasons. The principal flaw, it seems is based on economic considerations, namely the fairness to the parties in sharing the costs of environmental protections. On this issue the U.S. representative at Bonn referred to the "exclusion of developing countries from . . . the Protocol's emissions limitation requirement. . . ."[32] To this was added the American objection to "an institution to assess compliance with emissions targets that is dominated by developing country members without targets, [and] more favorable treatment for Parties operating within a regional economic integration organization relative to other Parties. . . ."[33]

Americans love to refer to sporting, and other engagements, where there is a level playing field. This automatically produces a sense of fundamental fairness. Yet, at the same time it is not deemed unfair for competitors in golf matches to be given handicaps, or for swifter horses to be assigned heavier weights than those that have not been so successful.

This approach applies to the Kyoto Protocol where the playing field in the past has been tilted, and where handicaps have been acknowledged. The very characterization of States as advanced, on the one hand, and as being developing, or in the mode of development, on the other, suggests the difference.

The Conference, particularly with its antecedent at Rio in 1992, and the decade-long negotiations leading to the Law of the Sea Convention, as well as the agenda put forward by developing States at the annual meetings of the United Nations General Assembly Committee on the Peaceful Uses of Outer Space, have highlighted the hope that in the long term there would be more equal relationships between all States. It was in this context, both economic and political, that decisions had to be made regarding the apportionment between advanced and developing countries of the assignment of emission credits. This included the prospect that developing countries would be excused at the beginning from conforming to environmental standards imposed on advanced countries.

The over 175 countries which gave their support to the Kyoto Protocol understood that they had a choice to advance the economic needs of the developing countries now while at the same time affording a greater environmental protection to all countries over a longer term. To achieve this they agreed to the Kyoto Protocol knowing that among its provisions were those allowing for a fine tuning over time.

The United States also understood that this was the issue. But, it decided to take the other road.

This was based on two major considerations. In the first case it became necessary for the United States to determine if there were a sufficient balance between the concessions it was willing to grant to the developing States and those received by the United States from them. In the second case the United States was obliged to decide if there were sufficient grounds for it to adopt a policy different from those acceptable to the other advanced States. The answer in both situations was the same. Under the then present circumstances the American economy was geared to those processes antecedent to and involved in the manufacture of products where if restrictions were to be imposed on such processes they would cause excessive harm to the American economy. The American economy is engaged in the supply to Americans of the goods and services allowing for their preferred style of living. This required a unilateral rather than a global approach to the world's environmental problems.

Happily, the story does not end here. President Bush in February 2002 issued four reports. Entitled "Clear Skies Policy Book," "President Announces Clear Skies and Global Climate Change Initiatives,"[34] "Fact Sheet," and "Global Climate Change Policy Book."[35] They identify the immediate and unquestioned need for the United States to embark on environmental policies designed to protect both American and world needs. The approach is long-term, but there are exceptions. For example, although much had been made of the uncertainties respecting the degree of climate change, the Policy Book states: "In the near term, we will vigorously pursue emissions reductions even in the absence of complete knowledge."[36] These measures for action are grounded in the recognition that "sustained economic growth is the solution, not the problem."[37]

Although many of the identified policies are proposals for future federal action, they also take into account international considerations. In the latter category are numerous references to bilateral commitments, including agreements with separate developing countries.

Enhanced science and technology are expected to give direction to improvements in the environment. Examples given are investments in modeling, obtaining reliable information on long-term climate changes, adequate recording of data, maintenance of records, and the funding of university research, including joint research with foreign countries, and an ear-marking of funds for promising environmentally-oriented programs.

These limited prescriptions, since they do not call on the United States to take the lead in the drafting of new multilateral agreements, are reminiscent of U.S. policies for anti-personnel land mines or the new International Criminal Court. While rejecting a landmine convention, the U.S. has endeavored to ease the pain of those who have suffered. While rejecting the ICC the United States has formulated policies for the domestic prosecution of terrorists.

With regard to the environment and climate change in the pre-Kyoto era there were a goodly number of environmentally focused treaties, and the United States was a willing participant. They have served the needs of their constituents. They were designed to deal with scientific problems, such as pollution of international rivers or the transboundary movement of hazardous materials. They did not, as in the case of the Kyoto Protocol, seek to effect an adjustment to the larger threats to humankind resulting from the manufacture and use of toxic substances easily disseminated into the atmosphere thereby causing them to be worldwide threats.

Out of this have come policy issues of a new order of magnitude. One has been the decision of smog-ridden states, such as California, to adopt its own standards.

In December, 2002, the Bush administration proposed a slight increase in fuel economy rating for SUVs, mini vans and pick up trucks, the first modification since 1996. If implemented by 2007 it would increase fuel economy standards by 1.5 MPG. This would result in a saving of 2.5 billions of gallons of gasoline a year.[38]

This proposal, if implemented, would prevent California from pursuing its own environmental policy. California grants credits to automobile companies who built hybrid vehicles, powered by electricity and gasoline. The federal government has asserted that such action unlawfully preempts its regulatory powers. Californians have charged the Bush administration with being more concerned for car makers than clean air. Over 100 cities in the United States, including some of California's largest, have adopted ordinances setting emission standards which are more protective of the public than those of the Federal government. Some are even more favorable than the Kyoto convention formula.[39] If courts were to rule against California's approach it follows that they would also have to rule against the municipalities.

While the policy issues have become more important because of enhanced dangers, the physical sources, e.g. manufacture and use of substances or finished products, remain the same. To take the case of the much-maligned, heavy duty, recreational vehicle which is a heavy consumer of gasoline, this has become a part of the lifestyle of fiscally favored individuals. Although over time there has been a reduction in pollutants produced by a motor vehicle, the popularity of the recreational sports vehicle has increased pollution.

How to reduce emissions without wrecking preferred lifestyles in the manufacture, sale, and use of all gasoline burning vehicles, that is the question.

DISCUSSION QUESTIONS

1. In 1972 at Stockholm the expression "Let the Polluter Pay" summed up the international effort to protect the human environment. What are the means to make that view more relevant today?
2. Although the advanced countries and the developing countries favor improvements in the human environment, they have substantial disagreement as to their respective responsibilities. How can they be brought to the point of making fair and equitable accommodations?
3. Assess the influence exercisable by the United States when it sends official delegates to human environment conferences and when it refuses to send such delegates but sends observers.
4. Is it fair and correct to assert that the United States is so much in need of protecting its automobile industry, which is obliged to meet the preferences of customers for large vehicles, that the U.S. cannot satisfy international standards on emissions? Consider the fact that a number of American states have adopted legislation imposing stricter emission standards than the national government.

5. How do you respond to the policy question of whether there are or are not sufficient uncertainties concerning the causes of long-term climate change?

NOTES

1. *Los Angeles Times*, A22, Dec. 12, 2002.

2. U.N. Doc. A/CONF 199/20, www.johannesburgsummit.org.html

3. 26 *I.L.M.* 1516 (1987).

4. 26 *I.L.M.* 1541 (1987).

5. United Nations 1992 Framework Convention on Climate Change. 31 *I.L.M.* 849 (1992) http://unfccc.int., It has entered into force for over 177 countries. The United States is a party. See generally P. BIRNIE AND A. BOYLE, INTERNATIONAL LAW AND THE ENVIRONMENT, 2nd ed. (2002).

6. 26 I.L.M 1550 (1987).

7. 31 *I.L.M.* 849 (1992).

8. *Ibid.* at 853.

9. 37 I.L. M. 22 (1998), http://unfcc.int.

10. *The Christian Science Monitor*, 7, November 13, 2000. The quoted figures were supplied by the International Energy Agency using 1997 data.

11. *The Los Angeles Times*, A22, August 1, 1998.

12. *The Los Angeles Times*, A6, November 13, 1998.

13. *The Christian Science Monitor*, 3, May 11, 1998.

14. B.P. McGivern, "Introductory Note," 37 *I.L.M.* 29 (January 1998). For an analysis of short-term and longer-term prospects, taking economic prospects into account, see T.C. Schelling, "What Makes Greenhouse Sense?" 91 *Foreign Affairs*, No. 3, 2 (May/June 2002).

15. S. Safrin and others, "Environmental Law," 34 *The Int'l Law.*, No. 2, 713 (Summer 2000).

16. S.E. Eizenstat, "Combating Global Warming," *The Christian Science Monitor*, 19, November 10, 1998. He noted that the negotiations would be based on the consensus arrived at in Kyoto, namely, the "ambitious emissions target was premised on the availability of market measures to cut costs." *Ibid.*

17. *The Los Angeles Times*, A6, November 13, 1998.

18. Safrin and others, *Supra*, Note 15 at 716-717.

19. "Remarks by the President on Global Climatic Change," p. 1, June 11, 2001. http://www.whitehouse.gov/news/releases/2001/06/200020611-2.2.html, 1.

20. *Id.* at 3.

21. *Ibid.*

22. http://www.state.gov/g/oes/climate/index.cfm?ocid=4105, p. 1, July 13, 2001.

23. www.state.gov/g/oes/climate/inoet.cfm?docid=4191, p.1 July 23, 2001.

24. *The Los Angeles Times*, B. 12, July 25, 2001

25. http://www.state.gov/oes/climate/index.cfm?docid=4191, p. 1, July 23, 2001.

26. *Id.* at p. 2.

27. *The Los Angeles Times*, A14, June 9, 2001. See generally D.A. Wirth, "The Sixth Session (Part Two) and Seventh Session of the Conference of the Parties to the Framework Convention on Climate Change," 96 *AJIL,* No. 3, 648 (2002). A.D. Ellerman, P.L. Jockow, and D. Harrison, Jr., "Emissions Trading in the United States: Experience, Lessons, and Considerations for Greenhouse Gases," Pew Center on Global Climate Change (2003).

28. *The Christian Science Monitor*, 2, June 7, 2002.

29. *Supra.*, note 22.

30. President Bush, *Statement on Climate Change*, Department of State, 1. (Italics added.)

31. Paula J. Dobriansky, Under Secretary of State for Global Affairs, U.S. Department of State, 1, 2001.

32. *Ibid.*

33. *Ibid.*

34. www.whitehouse.gov/news/releases/2002/02/2002012, Feb. 14, 2002

35. www.whitehouse.gov/news/releases/2002/02/climatechange, Feb. 2002

36. *Ibid.*

37. *Ibid.*

38. *Los Angeles Times*, A32, December 13, 2002.

39. *The Christian Science Monitor*, p. 3, June 7, 2002.

Chapter VI

Anti-Personnel Land Mines: Unilateralism Prevails

1. INTRODUCTION

The land mine problem is toward the top of the international humanitarian agenda. More than 100,000 military personnel have been killed or wounded by land mines since 1942. Many thousands of civilians have suffered the same fate. It has been estimated that as many as 26,000 have been killed or maimed annually in recent years.

Mines are indiscriminate in their devastation. Hidden and dormant they do not discriminate between military and civilians. In recent years they have been used to target and to demoralize civilians. The latter have the right to be immune from such devices in the fields, forests, and parks where they work and play and the roads and roadsides where they travel.

Those who are casualties suffer from loss of limbs and are often disabled for life. Where, as in Afghanistan or Kosovo, maps do not disclose their location, whole communities can be imperiled. Anti-personnel land mines, once in place, are often forgotten by those responsible for their emplacement. In the heat of battle records of mine fields either are not made or themselves become casualties. In many instances the demining process becomes a hit-or-miss exercise. Efforts by the United States to demine are very costly and can interrupt reconstruction and humanitarian relief.

The eradication of these weapons requires a high level of international cooperation. Treaties are the best way to formalize international commitments. The United States has agreed to some treaties; others have been rejected. Popular demands relating to land mines have made their disposition a matter of U.S. foreign policy. America's choice to cooperate with others or not to cooperate had been to go-it-alone.

Military commanders the world over are reluctant to give up weapons that may be useful in gaining victory against an adversary.

National security requires the right mix of weapons. This is a foreign policy concern for those having military assignments and responsibilities. It is equally a concern for those who are guided by humanitarian considerations.

With the increase in armed conflict during the past 50 years, land mines especially in internal disputes, have become a weapon of preference. They are small, easily concealed, easily transported, inexpensive, and effective.

Anti-personnel land mines did not become a major weapon of war until late in World War I. During World War II these weapons were used in large quantities. With civil strife breaking out in more recent years land mines have been laid in Africa, Asia, Central America, the Middle East, and in the former Yugoslavia. Afghanistan was littered with such weapons during the conflict with the Soviet Union. The United States has employed such weapons in that area in its present war against terrorism. Both sides used them in Iraq in 2003.

In recent years distinctions have been drawn between "dumb" and "smart" land mines. The former are those which remain inert but alive, and explode upon contact. They do not self-destruct or deactivate. The latter are configured so that they automatically explode or become inactive after a period determined by built-in timing devices. They are "smart" up to 120 days.

It is unknown how many land mines are emplaced in the 64 countries where they are on the ground, but in 1996 the number of active mines was estimated to be 110 million.[1] By June, 1998, the United States had completed the destruction of 3.3 million of its non-self-destructing mines. Although active demining operations are going on in many countries, the number of active mines has increased. It has been estimated that in 1996 there were about 110 million mines in national stockpiles.

2. A. SHORT REVIEW OF EARLIER EFFORTS TO DEAL WITH LAND MINES

In 1907 when States met at The Hague to draft the annex to Hague Convention No. IV, embodying the Regulations Respecting the Laws and Customs of War, attention was given to the employment of arms, projectiles, or materiel calculated to cause unnecessary suffering. It was determined that mines did not fall within this classification.[2]

When the laws of war were revised in Geneva in 1949 protections were given to civilians. Thus in Article 13 of Additional Protocol II it is stated that: "The civilian population and individual civilians shall enjoy general protection against the dangers arising from military operations." Article 14 refers to objects which are indispensable to the survivability of civilian populations such as water and areas for farming.

Treaties serve as the basis for civilian rights during times of armed conflict. General principles of international law, often referred to as customary international law, also contain humanitarian provisions which place limitations on the means and methods of warfare. Among these are the duty to carry on warfare without causing excessive suffering or unnecessary losses. Civilians enjoy immunity from military attack; only military objectives can be attacked.

Under U.N. leadership a new civilian-oriented treaty was negotiated in 1980. It is the Convention on Prohibitions or Restrictions on the Use of Certain Conventional Weapons Which May Be Deemed to Be Excessively Injurious or to Have Indiscriminate Effects.[3] Adopted on October 10, 1980, it contains provisions regulating the use of anti-personnel and anti-vehicle land mines. Protocol II, referred to as the "Amended Mines Protocol," addressed the use of landmines, booby traps, and other delayed-action devices.[4] Protocol II was amended on May 3, 1996.[5]

The Protocol applied to land mines placed on the ground manually or delivered by artillery, rockets, mortars, or launched from aircraft. The State activating mines by these means is obliged to record their location. Their targets may not be civilians; they may be emplaced on or directed at military objectives, only.[6]

By 1996 it had become evident that the terms of Protocol II of 1980 were only a preliminary approach to the subject, and that it was in need of amendment. This resulted on May 3, 1996 with the adoption of a "Protocol of Prohibitions or Restriction on the Use of Mines, Booby-Traps and Other Devices."[7] The parties also reached agreement on a Protocol on blinding laser weapons.[8]

The 1996 Landmine Protocol dealt with two basic subjects, first, restriction on the use of anti-personnel land mines, and second, international cooperation in the removal of mines, mine areas, and mine fields. The parties agreed to implement the Protocol through legislative and other measures, and agreed to resolve disputes through consultations. The Protocol was made applicable to internal armed conflicts and international armed conflicts. Restrictions were placed on the use of both remotely-delivered and non-remotely delivered mines. The conference was considered a failure by many participants because it did not create a total ban on the use of anti-personnel land mines.

The Protocol did, however, mark a shift regarding a willingness to take a practical and operational approach to the subject. This was reflected in the assignment of clearance responsibilities on those who deploy mines. States were requires to adopt criminal laws to suppress serious violations of the agreement, including willfully killing or causing serious injury to civilians. The jurisdiction of a State to prosecute persons who violated the agreement extended to both persons or territory under the signatory's jurisdiction and control.

The United States ratified the agreement in 1999, which had received enough ratifications in 1998 to enter into force in that year.

The status of the 1996 Protocol, because it did not prohibit the use of landmines, was on the agenda of the 1996 Review Conference of the U.N. Inhumane Weapons Convention. When the participants found it impossible to deal with the widely perceived demand to draft an international agreement totally banning the use of anti-personnel land mines, the government of Canada proposed that States should deal with this subject outside of the U.N. Conference on Disarmament system. This led to meetings in Cambodia, Canada, and Mozambique in 1996 and in Belgium and Norway in 1997. Important Declarations were made in Ottawa and in Brussels.[9]

3. RESPONSES IN THE UNITED STATES TO THE BANNING OF LAND MINES: THE PRESIDENT AND CONGRESS

Agreement and disagreement has marked the relationship between the President and Congress on a policy for the use of anti-personnel land mines. The congressional leader who first expressed an interest in banning such weapons was Senator Patrick Leahy of Vermont. President Clinton when he first came to office spoke in favor of limiting the use of land mines. As time went by his position became ambiguous. By 1997 he was influenced by Secretary of Defense William Cohen, who listened to the view of the Pentagon and high-ranking retired military personnel. All were aware of the presence of the active and extensive mine fields at the DMZ in Korea.[10]

Senator Leahy began his campaign in 1992 when he sponsored legislation calling for a moratorium on the export from the United States of land mines. President Clinton in his 1994 address to the U.N. General Assembly stated that the United States would strive for the elimination of anti-personnel land mines. In 1995 Senator Leahy's legislation required a moratorium on the use by the United States of such weapons. When President Clinton spoke to the General Assembly in 1997 he indicated that a ban on use by the United States would take place "as soon as possible." The Secretary of Defense at that time, William J. Perry, in echoing the views of the president, stated that the question was one of "timing and developing the proper transition plan so that we can get rid of them."[11] Secretary of State Madeline Albright in September, 1966, also indicated her opposition to such weapons.

In 1996 President Clinton signed the Leahy sponsored moratorium legislation whereby the United States was prohibited, beginning on February 12,

1996 and lasting for one year, from using new land mines. On June 12, 1997 Senators Leahy and Charles Hagel of Nebraska introduced legislation creating a new moratorium period beginning on January 1, 2000. The bill entitled "Land Mine Elimination Act" did not apply to existing minefields. Further, it was not applicable to anti-tank or command detonated mines. Sponsors of the House bill were Representatives Lane Evans of Illinois and Jack Quinn of New York.

At that time President Clinton favored an international agreement rather than national legislation. The matter was undergoing consideration at the U.N. Conference on Disarmament. This is a notoriously slow-moving body, but, in retrospect it did contribute to the negotiations taking place in Oslo, which were completed on September 18, 1997. The scope of the American 1997 ban extended to production, transfer, stockpiling, and use.

However, at about the same time Secretary of Defense William Cohen in June, 1997, in a letter to the Chairman of the Senate Armed Services Committee indicated there should be no ban on anti-personnel land mines. This was also the position of Senator Thurmond, the committee chairman. In July of 1997, 24 retired four-star generals, including Alexander M. Haig, Jr., former Secretary of State, wrote to President Clinton. They stated their opposition to a bill being introduced by Senators Leahy and Hagel. Under their new proposal effective on January 1, 2000, no new anti-personnel mines could be deployed. The military leaders stated that the deployment of such mines "is not only consistent with the nation's humanitarian responsibilities, it is indispensable to the safety of our troops in many combat and peacekeeping situations."[12]

The outlooks of the humanists and the military are clearly drawn. The former wish to outlaw or limit the use of anti-personnel land mines and to embark on demining operations. The military wish to have the right mix of weapons available, and point to their utility, particularly at the DMZ in Korea. This is based on the proposition that an offensive launched by the North Koreans could be a direct "straight-forward attack," and that mines in position would constitute either a deterrent or as a means to slow the offensive.

The United States Army, however, believes that a high degree of mobility serves its tactical operations. Enemy land mines would impose limitations on such desired mobility. Thus, the United States, in analyzing international proposals limiting the availability of land mines, has characterized the DMZ as a special situation. Their utility in this situation has been an essential reason for American opposition to the 1997 Ottawa Convention on the Prohibition of the Use, Stockpiling, Production and Transfer of Anti-Personnel Mines and Their Destruction.

In 1997 the DMZ in Korea was the only place where U.S. military forces were using the non-self-destructing type of anti-personnel land mines. It was argued that if mines were not emplaced a very substantial increase in personnel and costly equipment would have to be deployed in order to provide an equivalent security on the Korean Peninsula.

In examining the risk to American troops if the DMZ mines were removed the Pentagon has tried to find effective alternatives. One suggestion has been to remove the lethal elements for replacement with tear gas, releasing sticky foam, or a broadcast device capable of emitting strong sounds. Devices able to produce very bright illumination might also serve as a warning to friendly forces of the presence of hostile forces. The Pentagon has not perfected equipment as well suited as mines to forestall attacks. However, research is continuing.

In June, 1998, the president's national security advisor, Mr. Samuel R. Berger, approached Senator Leahy to explore a policy that would serve both the humanitarian concerns of the senator and the mixed concerns of the president. The president offered to support accession by the United States to the Ottawa treaty by 2006 if the Pentagon were able to devise an effective alternative weapon. Mr. Berger, taking into account the presence of U.S. troops at the DMZ, urged that the moratorium on the use of land mines in that area should be lifted. Secretary of Defense Cohen and the Joint Chiefs of Staff chairman, General Henry Shelton were firm in the view that the DMZ presented a special case. In August, 2001, a representative of the Department of State indicated that his department believed that land mine policy should be "left to our colleagues in the Department of Defense for their determination and judgment."[13]

Following his decision not to sign the Ottawa treaty President Clinton issued a directive in 1998 promising to obey the ban everywhere but the Korean Peninsula by 2003 and in all countries by 2006.[14]

In March, 2001, Senator Leahy, with the support of Congressmen Evans and Quinn, and now by James P. McGovern of Massachusetts, proposed new legislation. Bearing the number Senate 497 it was entitled "The Landmines Elimination and Victim Assistance Act of 2001." This induced President Bush to order a review of U.S. policy. Pending the establishment of a policy by the Bush administration, on December 18, 2001, a letter was addressed to the White House by 124 members of the House of Representatives urging accession to the treaty by 2006.

4. POPULAR INTEREST AND EFFORTS

Influencing public debate to make unlawful the deployment and use of antipersonnel land mines has been a loosely-integrated network of concerned individuals and private organizations. They are world-wide in scope. Undoubtedly, especially in stirring up the interest of voters, they have had a substantial impact on public policy. Their dissatisfaction with earlier international agreements contributed to the negotiation and adoption of the 1997 Ottawa Convention. Their consternation resulting from the refusal of the United States to accept that agreement has resulted in continuing efforts to achieve a global approach to the subject. For them anti-personnel land mines remain indiscriminate and lethal. They favor the treaty.

The Vietnam Veterans of America Foundation (VVAF) with its coalition partner, the International Campaign to Ban Landmines, have been a driving force for change. Under the leadership of Jody Williams, a housewife, and the late Dianna, Princess of Wales, the message was carried to all the corners of the globe. For her contributions Jody Williams received for her efforts on behalf of the International Campaign to Ban Landmines, the Nobel Peace Prize. The Land Mine Survivor's Network, the Mine Action International Center, and the Human Rights Watch[15] have also provided information and assisted in the formation of public policy. Over 200 organizations have combined their efforts to ban land mines.

Military commanders, including the U.S. Commanding General in the Gulf War, Norman Schwarzkopf, commanders of U.S. forces in Korea, and innumerable infantrymen, who were engaged in recent American campaigns, have given their support to the banning of land mines.

5. THE 1997 U.N. CONVENTION

The U.N. Convention on the Prohibition of the Use, Stockpiling, Production and Transfer of Anti-Personnel Mines and Their Destruction was adopted at Oslo on September 18, 1997.[16] It was opened for signature at Ottawa from December 3 until December 4, 1997, and at the U.N. Headquarters in New York from December 5 until its entry into force.

Over 90 States participated in the negotiations, with 30 States sending observers. Interested groups such as the International Committee of the Red Cross, the International Federation of Red Cross and Red Crescent Societies, and the International Campaign to Ban Land Mines also sent observers. Scores of private humanitarian organizations were present. The treaty entered into force in 1999 for 96 countries. The United States has rejected the agreement. It was signed by 136 nations. It has been claimed that it entered into force more rapidly than any other humanitarian-oriented international agreement.

Before the treaty could enter into force it required that 49 States deposit with the Secretary General of the U.N. their ratifications, acceptances, approvals, or accessions. After the required waiting time of six months it entered into force on March 1, 1999. By July of 2003 the agreement was in force for 134 countries. Fourty-seven countries did not sign the agreement. In this group in July, 2003, were China, India, Iran, Iraq, Israel, North and South Korea, Lebanon, Libya, Pakistan, Russia and the members of the Russian Federation, Syria, Turkey, the United States, Vietnam and the former Yugoslavia.

The Preamble to the 1997 Convention referred to three basic principles of international law as having application to armed conflicts, both international and internal. Referring particularly to international humanitarian law, the principles were, first, "the right of parties to an armed conflict to choose methods of warfare is not unlimited," second, "the principle that prohibits the employment in armed conflicts of weapons, projectiles and materials and methods of warfare of a nature to cause superfluous injury or unnecessary suffering," and, third "on the principle that a distinction must be made between civilians and combatants."

The convention contains 22 articles. They can be divided into three general categories: first, substantive provisions outlawing the use, development, complicity involving prohibited activity, and duty to destroy or ensure the destruction of all anti-personnel mines in accordance with the provisions of the Convention, second, measures designed to secure compliance with its terms, and, third, procedures allowing for reviewing or amending the agreement.

The Convention deals comprehensively with the banning and destruction of anti-personnel mines. General obligations are contained in Article 1. Pursuant to its terms:

"1. Each State Party undertakes never under any circumstances:

a) To use anti-personnel mines;
b) To develop, produce, otherwise acquire, stockpile, retain or transfer to anyone, directly or indirectly, anti-personnel mines;
c) To assist, encourage or induce, in any way, anyone to engage any activity prohibited to a State Party under this Convention.

"2. Each State Party undertakes to destroy or ensure the destruction of all anti-personnel mines in accordance with the provisions of this Convention."

Article 2 contains definitions. Article 3 makes provision for exemptions of certain mines from the agreement. Article 4 requires the destruction of stockpiled anti-personnel mines owned or possessed by a party, or that are "under its jurisdiction or control, as soon as possible but not later than four years after the entry into force of this convention for that State Party."

Article 5 deals with the destruction of anti-personnel mines that are located in mined areas under the State's jurisdiction and control. This is to occur "as soon as possible but not later than ten years after the entry into force of this Convention for that State Party." Article 6 calls for cooperation and assistance among the Parties to secure the fullest implementation of the agreement.

Article 7 of the agreement is entitled "Transparency Measures." This term refers to the duty to report on steps taken by the parties in order to comply with its terms. Article 11 calls for the regular meeting of the parties.[17]

The treaty is an important effort to ban the use and to prevent the future emplacement of anti-personnel mines. It imposes the duty on the parties to remove and to destroy land mines that have been emplaced and those that are held in stock-piles. The probability that parties will conform to it are good, since its existence is based on widespread humanitarian concerns and serves the common interests of countries and their peoples. Non-party States, however, in recent military operations have used large quantities of anti-personnel land mines. With the close of hostilities they will have to use their best efforts to destroy them.

In assessing the elimination of land mines it has been suggested there is a parallel between the terrorism caused by terrorists and the terrorism caused by land mines, and that global efforts now being directed against terrorists should become a global effort to destroy mines and to mitigate their affects.[18]

6. OFFICIAL U.S. RESPONSES TO THE CONVENTION

Responses to the Convention have been mixed. In terms of its potential impact on the conduct of armed conflict it has been noted that the non-signatories include the world's most powerful States. The conclusion has been drawn that countries most likely to engage in military operations are free, unless they are bound by earlier agreements, to make use of anti-personnel land mines. On the other hand, in recent years the smaller countries have been the ones most likely to experience civil wars, and the treaty applies to this kind of warfare.

With the initiation in 2001 of a vigorous war against terrorism, involving military operations in Afghanistan, and with the 2003 attack on Iraq the utility of anti-personnel land mines as weapons of choice in both offensive and defensive situations resulted in support for their deployment.[19] It is to be hoped that there will be record keeping of emplacements, a problem which confronted the negotiators of the 1997 treaty.

7. DEMINING OPERATIONS

A major response to the land mine problem has been the funding of demining operations by governments and by private organizations. The United Nations and NATO have become identified with this goal. In the United States both the Department of State[20] and the Department of Defense have active responsibilities in this area. In 1997 the Office of Global Humanitarian Demining was established in the Department of State. The department also has an Office of Mine Action and Partnerships. Among its functions is the coordination of public-private partnerships and the advancement of promising demining technologies.

During 2002 the program for Humanitarian Demining was supporting initiatives in 38 countries, as well as the Province of Kosovo and Northwest Somalia. The Department of Defense has been researching replacements for mines that do not deactivate automatically within a given time period following emplacement, including mines that provide warning signals rather than causing maiming and killing. Barrier and monitoring devices are being explored.

It has been estimated that more than 200 organizations have become involved in demining operations. These groups employ, train, and pay the wages of deminers operating throughout the globe. Recent developments in aerial reconnaissance have somewhat eased the problem of locating mines. These groups also assist in the rehabilitation of persons injured through contact with mines. These groups include such institutions as the Vietnam Veterans of America Foundation, which carries on an orthotics program for children in Vietnam and prosthetics projects for men, women, and children in Angola and El Salvador. Other organizations, such as the Human Rights Watch provide information to grass roots organizations so that they may engage in humanitarian activities.

The United Nations Association of the United States of America has called for the adoption of a minefield or a community for clearance. Its chapters have responded. Employees of the United Nations and the Department of State have collected funds to be used for demining and rehabilitation. Many church groups and private corporations have made donations.

The generosity of all of these individuals and groups is a demonstration of their concern for the care of individuals who have suffered from these silent and devastating weapons. Unfortunately, generous gifts of money and restorative help cannot overcome the tragedies that the innocent victims have experienced. These consideration led to the finalization of an International Mine Clearance Treaty in 2003 requiring signatories to remove or destroy all unexplored munitions in areas controlled by them after the cessation of hostilities. The United States is a signatory.

8. CONCLUSION

The huge international outcry, which has been especially evident in the United States, for an international agreement banning the use of anti-personnel land mines, produced the 1997 Ottawa Convention on the Prohibition of the Use, Stockpiling, Production and Transfer of Anti-Personnel Mines and on Their Destruction. The outcry has occurred in the time frame of the "here and now."

After large and largely unmarked mine fields were created, and after the fighting had moved on or had become dormant, as is often the case in internal wars, and after an area had achieved a measure of stability, and as the mines began to take their toll on civilians, popular demands to control such weapons reached a new level of intensity.

Individuals began to assert that a central function of international law was to protect them. Just as customers, who have bought goods on a retail basis, are prone to demand quality services, so those endangered by land mines began to assert their own immediate rights, and not on a wholesale basis, but for the direct and personalized protection of international law. They were able to rely on long-standing principles of international law assuring rights to civilians in times of armed conflict. Such principles are derived from the view that with the enforcement of such principles it is possible to arrive at a durable peace, reconciliation, and human development.[21]

These demands began to be heard during the administration of President Clinton. He recognized the humanitarian bases for such concerns. He also was aware that there were varying opinions on the part of his military advisors. At one point he was obliged to conform to a policy of moratorium resulting from legislation. Toward the end of his term he became persuaded that the United States was benefiting from the presence of mines along the DMZ in Korea. He asked the Department of Defense to find alternatives, with the hope that he would be able to maintain the presence of such mines for at least six years. Unable to obtain a satisfactory response, he left the problem to his successor. Under these circumstances he made no effort to sign the 1997 treaty.

This being the case he did not pursue the international political or legal ramifications of the matter. Even if he were persuaded that the treaty contained sound principles, but did not actively support the agreement, this would make it difficult to try to induce other non-signers to become parties. If he thought that the interest of the two Koreas could be resolved within the six year time frame, then negotiations could be encouraged for these two countries.

The treaty, as treaties go, was soundly negotiated and written. It completes what it set out to do. Whether it is good for the United States, depending on different perspectives, will produce different answers. The Bush administration has evidenced no interest in the treaty. One thing is clear, however. In its rejection the United States has contributed to the view that America is committed in this area, as in many others, to a unilaterally based foreign policy.

With respect to this treaty the United States could seek to encourage North and South Korea to reexamine their own medium to long-term perspectives. Depending on any resolution of their differences there could be a determination that the DMZ could be demined. If that were to be the case the United States could then reexamine its own outlook. In the meantime there will continue to be substantial support for demining activities.

DISCUSSION QUESTIONS

1. It appears that the major effort to place limitations on the use of anti-personnel land mines began after World War II. How do you account for this?
2. In present day ground-based military operations how do you rate maneuverability? As a planner of potential military operations how would that condition affect your decisions on anti-personnel land mines?
3. The laws or customs of war are constantly under review by international lawyers serving in departments of defense. To render anti-personnel land mines more humane, what restrictions on their employment, maintenance, and use would you like to see?
4. What if any influence has been derived from public opinion in the United States for changes in the use of such weapons?
5. How would you rate the effectiveness of demining operations? Is this a subject for a formal international agreement, and, if so, who should take the lead?

NOTES

1. G. Boas, "Landmines: The Gap between Law and Humanity," 34 *Law Society Journal*, No. 9, 63 (1996).

2. *The Law of Land Warfare*, Department of Army Field Manual, FM 27-10, 18 (July 1956).

3. 19 *I.L.M.* 1523 (1980).

4. 19 *I.L.M.* 1529 (1980). S. MASLEN, ANTI-PERSONNEL MINES UNDER HUMANITARIAN LAW (2001).

5. Indicative of the interest in 1980 in imposing new restrictions on the conduct of armed warfare were three additional Protocols dealing with non-detectable fragments, incendiary weapons, and blinding laser weapons, with the first two proposed in 1980 and the last in 1995.

6. Protocol, Art. 3.3(a).

7. 35 *I.L.M.* 1206 (1996).

8. *Id.* At 1218.

9. 36 *I.L.M.* 1507 (1997). R. Thakur and W. Maley, "The Ottawa Convention on Land Mines, a Landmark Humanitarian Treaty in Arms Control?" 5 *Global Governance*, No. 3, 273, July-September 1999.

10. For an extended review of U.S. outlooks, see "Chronology of U.S. Policy and International Mine Ban Treaty Events," http://www.fcnl.org/91:ss/Events. An extensive study is "Landmine Monitor Report, 1999" prepared by the International Campaign to Ban Landmines. It contains county by country status reports. http://www.iclb.org. For a detailed program relating to antipersonnel land mines one can consult www.professorlandmine.com.

11. U.S. Department of Defense, *Defense Link, News Articles* 1, April 1996 (updated: 17 June 1998).

12. U.S. Department of Defense, *Defense Link, New Articles*, 1 July 1997 (updated: 17 June 1998).

13. *Los Angeles Times*, A3, August 3, 2001.

14. J.P. Mustoe, "The 1997 Treaty to Ban the Use of Landmines: Was President Clinton's Refusal to Become a Signatory Warranted?" 27 *Georgia J. of Int'l and Comp Law*, No. 3, 54 (1999).

15. The Human Rights Watch prepares each year the "Human Rights Watch World Report" dealing with important weapons, including anti-personnel land mines. www.hrw.org/wr2k1/arms/arms6.html. It is responsible for the "International Campaign to Ban Landmines." www.icbl.org/statements/ccwstat.html.

16. 36 *I.L.M.* 1507 (1997). It is known as the "Ottawa" Treaty since it was signed there and because of the Canadian efforts in securing its approval.

17. The General Assembly monitors national compliance with the agreement. In 1998 it called for the first meeting of the parties. General Assembly Resolution A/RES/53/77N, 20, January 12, 1999. In 1999 the General Assembly Resolution called for the total eradication of anti-personnel land mines and convened the second meeting of the parties. A/RES/54/54B, 3, January 20, 2000. The third meeting was held in September 2001. A/RES/55/33V, 27, January 12, 2001. The vote to hold the 2001 meeting was 143-0-22. The deliberations of the parties at these meetings afford non-parties an opportunity to review their own positions. The UN's Office for the Coordination of Humanitarian Affairs monitors the status of landmine agreements including manufacture and exportation.

18. K.F. Inderfurth, "Unearth the Killing fields," *The Los Angeles Times*, M2, December 23, 2001. That author called attention to Secretary of State Colin L. Powell's underscoring of the need to rid Afghanistan of such weapons.

19. For an analysis see V. Wiebe, "Footprints of Death: Cluster Bombs as Indiscriminate Weapons under International Humanitarian Law", 22 *Michigan J of Int'l Law*, No. 1, 85, Fall 2000.

20. The State Department is responsible for the U.S. Humanitarian Demining Program. See www.state.gov/r/pa/pre/ps/2001/index.cfm?docid-6609.

21. Secretary of State Powell has noted that demining action "is not only critical to public safety, it is a key factor in the process of national reconstruction. Mine action is about healing the wounds of war, reaching out to its victims, and opening economic opportunities for shattered communities." *Supra*, note 18.

Chapter VII

Arms Control and Disarmament

1. INTRODUCTION

National security is of foremost concern in the foreign policies of all States. Such security is the product of many factors, such as the educational level of the inhabitants, the possession of important raw materials or ready accessibility, geography, the scientific and technological structure, well-managed and efficient factories, a stable and responsible system of government, and a strong moral foundation, including respect for Human Rights. Some would claim that above all of these, if a State is to be secure, it must possess unrivaled military personnel superbly equipped and highly qualified in military strategy and tactics.

As in all forms of contest the condition of superiority depends on the assets and capabilities of the opponent. In recent years with adversaries equipped with weapons of mass-destruction, the condition of superiority does not lead necessarily to victory. Undoubtedly the major challenge facing the United States now and in the future is the reduction of the proliferation of weapons of mass destruction.

With an understanding of the destructive capabilities of nuclear weapons those States possessing them have come to rely, for their protection, in large part, on the condition of something called mutually assured destruction (MAD). During the Cold War the manufacture of such weapons and the construction of launching facilities produced more kill-power than a possessor could beneficially use. So, as times have changed, there has increasingly come to be an appreciation of the importance of the international law of arms control and disarmament.

The forum for arms control and disarmament negotiations can be either multilateral or bilateral. Both procedures have been employed. For nuclear weapons and powerful States the bilateral style has been necessary and has been productive of good results. Where the subject has an important impact on many States the multilateral approach has been practical and effective.

Where a number of States address a common problem, including arms control and disarmament, the product of the agreement becomes international law. Where the agreement is bilateral it creates binding obligations for the parties, but the limited number of participants would not produce new international law. In both instances international law provides rules for the interpretation of the agreement. International agreements entered into by the United States are subject to the U.S. Constitution. One American rule is, when a federal statute and a treaty have inconsistent provisions, that the last in time prevails. A statute could rescind a treaty. A treaty could void a statute.

The arms control and disarmament agreements between the United States and the former Soviet Union, and now Russia, have been of paramount significance as they pursue and change their perceptions of the real world, and, most importantly, as they view the policies—threatening or otherwise—of their adversaries or peaceful competitors. In such circumstances both the United States and Russia must demonstrate something, which for lack of a better word, might be called "wisdom," in viewing each other. The term "wise" or "unwise" is frequently employed by commentators in endeavoring to fathom whether a given course of national action best serves the well-being of a State. This applies when a State, in the company of other States, seeks to combine its security interests with all of the others, which must be kept in balance.

National assessments and reassessments are allowed by the rules of the game. It will always be a challenge to determine how dynamic a policy change can be. It will be inevitable, that in the eyes of some, the changes will be wise, or acceptable, and for others they will be unwise, or unacceptable. In a democratic society its leaders and their advisors will have to run the risk of such judgments. This is where the art of persuasion will take place and be helpful.

From the outset the nuclear powers have been engaged in two courses of conduct. They have been manufacturing nuclear weapons and preparing them for launch, as well as placing them in storehouses for launch as needed. At the same time they have entered into international agreements imposing constraints on use, including testing, and also providing for decommissioning and destruction. The agreements are multilateral and bilateral. Additionally, States have entered into multilateral agreements calling for safety-oriented controls for non-nuclear, but lethal, weapons.

2. IMPORTANT MULTILATERAL AGREEMENTS

On August 5, 1963 States entered into the Test Ban Treaty. It banned nuclear weapons testing in the atmosphere, outer space, and under water. It was ratified by the United States and by the Soviet Union and entered into force on October 10, 1973.[1]

On July 1, 1968, the Non-Proliferation of Nuclear Weapons Treaty was signed. It entered into force on March 5, 1970 for the United States, the Soviet Union, and many other countries. They promised in good faith to seek the cessation of the nuclear arms race and to work toward general and complete disarmament, including nuclear disarmament, under strict and effective control. In 2003 the scorecard on nuclear weapons capabilities was:

Acknowledged: China, France, India, North Korea, Pakistan, Russia, United Kingdom, USA.
Unacknowledged: Israel.
Seeking: Iran, Iraq.
Abandoned Nuclear Weapons Development: South Africa, former Soviet States of Belarus, Kazakhstan, and Ukraine.[2]

On January 27, 1967, many States, including the United States and the Soviet Union signed the Treaty on Principles Governing the Activities of States in the Exploration and Use of Outer Space, Including the Moon and Other Celestial Bodies. It entered into force for the United States and the Soviet Union on October 10, 1967. Now almost 100 countries are bound by it.

Pursuant to Article IV the Parties "undertake not to place in orbit around the Earth any objects carrying nuclear weapons or any other kinds of weapons of mass destruction, install such weapons on celestial bodies, or station such weapons in outer space in any other manner." It also provides that the Moon and other celestial bodies shall be used exclusively for peaceful purposes and prohibits the establishment of military bases, installations and fortifications, the testing of any type of weapons, and the conduct of military maneuvers on celestial bodies. It did not say that outer space, per se, should be used exclusively for peaceful purposes.

On May 18, 1977 the Convention on the Prohibition of Military or any Other Hostile Use of Environmental Modification Techniques was signed in Geneva. It entered into force on January 17, 1980 and is binding on the United States and the Soviet Union. The parties undertook not to "engage in any military or other hostile use of environmental modification techniques having widespread, long-lasting or severe effects as the means of destruction, damage or injury to any other State Party."[3]

The agreement provides a means for increasing transparency, verification, mutual understanding, and cooperation among its parties. The treaty had a long history, having been first proposed by President Eisenhower in 1955 and reactivated by former President Bush in 1989. Following its signing in 1992 the signatories agreed to apply its terms provisionally until it was ratified by the requisite number of parties. The provisional application of international agreements has a fairly recent history. Such application has been ordained where the agreement is demonstrably popular and useful and where there may be the likelihood of delayed ratifications on the part of a very limited number of signatories. For example, the United States ratified in 1993, with Russia and Belarus not until 2001.

On September 24, 1996, the Comprehensive Nuclear Test-Ban Treaty was opened for signature at the United Nations. According to its terms each party agreed not to carry out any nuclear weapons test explosion or any other nuclear explosion; to prevent any nuclear explosions at any place under its jurisdiction or control; and to refrain from causing, encouraging, or in any way participating in the carrying out of any nuclear weapon test explosion or any other nuclear explosion. Following his signature President Clinton sent the agreement to the Senate for its review. In his letter to the Senate Mr. Clinton stated that the United States had established a number of measures intended to allow it to resume testing in the event that it were disclosed that a signatory were not conforming to a "zero yield" standard. After unusually careful scrutiny in the Senate the advice and consent motion went to a vote on October 13, 1999.

With Democratic Senators voting for it and Republicans against, and with expressions being quite partisan in nature, the Senators rejected the treaty by a vote of 55 to 45. In light of the vote it has been predicted that the treaty will not enter into force "for an indefinite period of time."[4] The agreement specifies the United States must become a Party before it can enter into force. Nonetheless the treaty was signed by 55 States, including Russia, China, France, and the United Kingdom.

Russia requires the approval of both the Duma and the Federation Council, the Russian upper house in its Parliament, before a treaty can become effective. These approvals were obtained in 2000. At the time of ratification the Russian Ministry of Foreign Affairs observed that "In accordance with the undertakings it made, Russia has not carried out nuclear tests since October 1990 and does not intend to resume such tests provided, of course, that the other nuclear States also follow this plan."[5]

It has been pointed out that this action by Russia, coupled with the Russian ratification of the Strategic Arms Reduction Treaty (START) II[6] may have been an effort to "focus U.S. attention on disarmament, and away from plans for a BMD."[7]

3. BILATERAL AGREEMENTS WITH THE SOVIET UNION-RUSSIA, 1972–1997

On May 26, 1972 the United States and the Soviet Union signed the Strategic Arms Limitations Talks (SALT I) treaty. It is referred to as the 1972 ABM Treaty. It entered into force on October 3, 1972. Each country for defensive nuclear weapons was limited to two sites of 100 antiballistic missile launchers. This was reduced in 1974 to one site per country. A five year freeze was imposed on testing and deployment of intercontinental ballistic missiles (IBMs) and submarine launched ballistic missiles. A short term interim agreement placed a limit on the number of offensive nuclear weapons for each country. In September 1977 the agreement was extended. At the time of its negotiation it was considered that the treaty would help to preserve the credibility of nuclear threats and that it would encourage mutual compliance by example.

On July 3, 1974 the two countries signed a new protocol on antiballistic missile systems, and a treaty and protocol which imposed limits on the underground testing of nuclear weapons.

On June 18, 1979 SALT II was signed. It placed limits on offensive nuclear weapons and on missile launchers. The agreement was not ratified and did not enter into force. President Carter did not seek ratification giving as his reason the Soviet invasion of Afghanistan in December of 1979.

The next major step was the completion of the Intermediate-Range Nuclear Forces Treaty on December 8, 1987. It called for the elimination of all medium and shorter-range nuclear missiles. It entered into force with ratification on May 27, 1988.

By 1991 both countries became more painfully aware than ever that they were burdened by an over-supply of nuclear warheads. On July 1 of that year they signed the first of three Strategic Arms Reduction Treaties (START). After lengthy negotiations the two countries fixed limits for heavy bombers and launchers at 1600, restricted the number of nuclear warheads for each country at 6000, and called for the removal of 3900 nuclear weapons from Minuteman and Poseidon missile sites. This was to be accomplished in three phases over seven years. Having been ratified by both parties, the agreement entered into force on December 5, 1994.

START II was agreed to in January of 1993. It dealt with warheads. It limited each country to between 3000 and 3500 thereby cutting their supplies by about two-thirds. Submarine-launched ballistic missiles were limited to between 1700 and 1750. It was ratified by the United States on January 26, 1996 and by Russia on May 4, 2000.

START III was an attempt to reduce the number of warheads available to each party to between 2000 and 2500 by the end of December 2007. The proposed agreement contained transparency provisions. START III negotiations began in 1997 and continued through 2000, but in the end there was no treaty.

The progress that had been made under both SALT and START was sidetracked in 1999. The United States, citing the presence of "rogue States" with sufficiently real nuclear capabilities as to require a response, decided that, in the interests of its security, it would have to put into operation a National Missile Defense (NMD) system. In January, 1999, the Secretary of Defense, Mr. William Cohen, stated that the Clinton administration had decided to spend $6.6 billion over five years in order to create such a system. The NMD, if and when perfected, would be used as a means to destroy incoming warheads before they reached their destinations. The Clinton administration was aware that such an initiative was contrary to the SALT I agreement of May 26, 1972, and offered unspecified amendments to that agreement, which had contributed so much to stability for about 27 years.[8]

The decision to establish an effective NMD system has produced policy debates in the United States. It has been criticized by Americans who consider it to be politically irresponsible. They have pointed to the conclusions voiced in Russia that the NMD would require it to abandon START II. As summarized by Mason: "Russia's threatened withdrawal from START compliance, if realized, will result in a rule of law vacuum, which would leave no established guidance to total disarmament as previously negotiated, pursuant to the requirements laid out in NPT [Treaty on the Non-Proliferation of Nuclear Weapons, July 1, 1968] Article VI. Adherence to NTP Article VI would thereafter require a new paradigm of arms control negotiations and treaties under the specter of a deployed BMD system."[9]

At a time when Russia was proposing a reduction in its nuclear strategic offensive arms, the United States was willing to embark on a highly speculative project that would at first glance be directed toward "rogue States," but which would also be able to neutralize hostile Russian warheads. Such a preponderance of American power would produce international fears and would be the source of worldwide instability.

4. NATIONAL MISSILE DEFENSE

With the closing down of the cold war and the break up of the Soviet Union national security policies have been reexamined. For example, the role of NATO is being reexamined, and new members are joining. A more important consideration is whether world conditions justify a trend away from offensive weapons and toward defensive weapons, such as the NMD system. This would involve, from a strategic point of view, a shield against foreign attacks, if, in fact, an effective shield is within the creative capability of science and technology and within the financial capacity of a State.

This would involve, from a legal point of view, the validity of such devices under the 1972 ABM treaty. From the perspective of world order and stability an effective NMD in the hands of the United States could be considered threatening to States which have since the end of World War II focused on bilateral arms reduction and the concept of "mutually assured destruction."

In July, 2000, the Department of Defense reported that such a NMD policy would best serve the security interests of the United States. In August, Secretary of Defense William Cohen recommended to President Clinton that limited steps, including the awarding of contracts, should be taken. This would allow for the construction of anti-ballistic missile sites in Alaska and an upgrading of radar and early warning systems.

Although a new NMD policy had not been adopted, there had been a number of studies conducted at the Defense Department. In assessing the issue, Mr. G.T. Allison, a former Department of Defense official, has raised the following questions: "Why the Urgency," "How Much Will NMD Cost," "Is There More to Come," "What Are the Key Arguments of the Advocates," "What Are the Key Opponent Arguments," "What is Gov. George W. Bush's Position on Missile Defense," "What is Vice President Al Gore's Position on Missile Defense," "Is the Technology in Fact Ready," "In the Hierarchy of Threats to American National Security, Where Do Long-Range Missiles from North Korea, Iran, or Iraq Rank," "What Will Be the Net Effect of NMD on U.S. Security?"[10] In the latter's view embarking on a NMD policy would contribute "nothing but trouble."

The response to the first question was based on CIA information. In its view North Korea was a present threat because of missiles capable of delivering chemical and biological agents to the United States, with the expectation that within the next 15 years it could effectively target the U.S. with nuclear weapons. Initial costs would be $60 billion. A second phase would entail an additional 100 launchers.

As to the key arguments of the proponents, Mr. Allison, relying on CIA estimates, noted that North Korea, Iran, Iraq, and others were trying to develop long-rang missiles, and that within 15 years ICBM threats might originate in Russia, China, and North Korea, probably from Iran, and possibly from Iraq. Further it was claimed, as has subsequently proven to be the case, that the ABM treaty "is a cold war relic: allowing Russia or any other State to veto actions necessary to protect American security is unacceptable."[11] It was concluded that support for terrorism exists in the countries mentioned above, except China and Russia. The Bush administration has seized on this fact in order to obtain support for its NMD policy.

The opponents, on the other hand, have urged that these threats are not so grave or so large as others faced by the United States. Further, they stress that "the current ballistic missile-defense does not work . . . [and] tests have so far failed and simple counter-measures such as decoys can render a system ineffective."[12]

Tests conducted up to the end of December, 2002, were far from conclusive, and it was highly speculative if the tested defense equipment could become more reliable. According to an editorial "A national missile defense system would be enormously expensive, and there are no indications it's feasible. The ABM Treaty shouldn't be junked for a 'maybe' defense."[13]

Mr. Allison cited as a third argument of the opponents of NMD the view that deployment would be opposed by Russia and China and could ignite an arms race with them.[14] A recent report indicates that China is engaged in nuclear modernization. It has a stockpile of about 400 nuclear warheads.[15]

In the quoted article Mr. Allison asked whether the NMD technology was in fact ready. He offered no immediate assurance that the NMD would be ready at any future date, while acknowledging that from the technological point of view it was very ambitious, but that over time there could be a feasible system that "has some degree of effectiveness."[16] On this last position there have been many expressions of view, which, on the whole raise substantial doubts concerning NMD reliability. Opponents have called attention to failures of launched missiles to hit the target, pointing to the difficulty of a bullet hitting another bullet, and the problems of determining which oncoming objects carry destructive devices and which are decoys. As a result it has been termed a high-risk project with editorial calls for an indefinite delay because of the unproven technical feasibility of a "dubious" project.[17]

However, in 2002 a successful strike was reported by an exoatmospheric kill vehicle. That device has been described as the most sophisticated weapon ever developed. Moreover, it was the third consecutive time that a hit had occurred. In order to be successful the NMD must "hit the warhead at its so-called sweet spot—measured in centimeters—where the nuclear munition is housed to prevent an errant nuclear explosion."[18] The program manager for the project described the event as "like hitting a golf ball across the country, from Los Angeles to New York, and getting a hole in one even though the pin is moving and there are a whole bunch of others that look just like it."[19]

President Clinton decided to take no final action on the NMD proposal. In accepting this approach Governor Bush indicated such a decision was appropriate. At the same time he indicated as president he would work for building effective missile defenses at the earliest possible date. Candidate Bush also called for American withdrawal from the 1972 ABM agreement unilaterally if Russia failed to agree to changes. Such changes, according to Mr. Bush would allow the United States to field a defense system that would "protect all 50 states—and our friends and allies and deployed forces overseas—from missile attacks by rogue nations, or accidental launches."[20]

By September of 2001 Congressional Democrats under the leadership of Senator Joseph R. Biden, Jr. of Delaware, began to attack the NMD project charging that it was a waste of governmental resources and would substantially increase world instability. Included in their concerns was the increasing display by Republicans of unilateralism in foreign policy matters. Senator Biden restated the often heard argument that the United States is more imperiled by destructive devices delivered in ships, aircraft, or personal backpacks. The Senator expressed his concern that the proposed Bush policy would oblige China to embark on a missile defense program.[21]

Earlier in 2001 Secretary of Defense Rumsfeld told America's European allies that the United States would press ahead with the NMD policy. Since they had already indicated disagreement with that approach they expressed the view that the American policy was destabilizing and if implemented would constitute a violation of the 1972 ABM treaty. Henry Kissinger told them that the ABM pact was outdated.[22]

In a subsequent review of the Bush administration's view toward the use of nuclear weapons, Senator Biden referred to a classified Pentagon document known as the "Nuclear Posture Review," which canvassed U.S. intentions on the use of nuclear weapons. Senator Biden reemphasized the real objective of the U.S. in the nuclear field, namely, to deter states from starting a nuclear war. He noted: "Nuclear weapons are weapons of retaliation of last resort. They are not handy military tools, and we must not allow ourselves to think of them in that way."[23]

Returning to the Allison question and answer report, the author addressed Vice President Gore's position on missile defense. He held that a global Star Wars system would not work. In his view the ABM treaty should be renegotiated so that an affected State would be allowed to engage in a "responsible and practical defense against a nuclear attack from a rogue state."[24]

The manner of delivering hostile long-range missiles from North Korea, Iran, or Iraq, was examined. Based on a CIA assessment it would be via "a non-missile delivery means [rather] than by missiles."[25]

The final question inquired into the net effect of NMD on U.S. security. Russia's response during the Clinton administration was to consider the abrogation of all of its arms control treaties. When the Bush administration began to promulgate the same approach for the 1972 ABM Treaty, Russia had to reconsider a policy of abrogation.

With a limited defense budget Russia was in no position to start on a NMD system of its own. Other Russian options would include a more efficient management of its existing resources. It was also thought that Russia would be unlikely to reduce weapons or its "bloated stockpiles of bomb materials."[26]

As for China, if it were to enhance its missile program, this could trigger further nuclear activity in India and Pakistan. In summing up his position Mr. Allison stated: "In the absence of a U.S.-Russia agreement, NMD deployment is likely to do more to undermine our security than to improve it. Having examined the issue, I believe that national missile defense is a secondary item on the larger defense agenda."[27]

From the foregoing it is evident that there are many considerations affecting many countries regarding the utility of a NMD system. The differences of opinion are manifest. Affecting the entire debate, and much to the consternation of America's allies, as well as potential adversaries, has been the clearly established willingness of the United States to embark on unilateral policies as the occasion might seem to require.

Unfortunately, the gravity of any situation depends on the availability of facts, which sometimes are closely held, and on the motivations of an adversary, which sometimes are somewhat cloaked, or not readily perceivable. The situation of the two Koreas, but especially North Korea, is a case in point. It has been listed by the United States as a country engaged in terrorist activities. News accounts regularly depict violations in North Korea of basic Human Rights, as enjoyed in democratic societies.

To carry the situation of North Korea a step further, the United States in recent years has depicted North Korea as constructing nuclear weapons and launching capabilities. During the Clinton administration the United States was endeavoring to curb the North Korean ballistic missile program. There are some who believe that the Bush administration has not put heavy pressure on the North Koreans to abstain from such programs, and, that the United States thereafter has cited North Korean action as grounds for building its NMD system. Following this line of argument, the United States would have two grounds for unilateral decision making: terrorism and nuclear danger. On October 16, 2002 the United States revealed that North Korea was engaged in an advanced nuclear weapons program with the probability that it had produced several nuclear weapons. This activity of several years constituted a violation of the 1994 commitment to halt all pursuits of nuclear weapons.

In 2003 the United States was forced to address North Korea's nuclear capabilities and the means to reduce potential threats. Affecting the American concern was the February notice by North Korea that it was considering the termination of the 1953 armistice with South Korea. At the same time North Korea restarted a nuclear reactor at Yongbyon which had been deactivated in 1994 as a result of an agreement to receive economic and energy assistance. The restarting of the plant along with the revelation of the intent to build four new reactors produced speculation that there was a plan to reprocess plutonium for nuclear bombs. In March North Korea also tested a short-range cruise missile. Although it traveled only about 66 miles the launch was considered to be a part of the running standoff with the United States.

The measures were designed to obtain bilateral negotiations with the United States regarding its continuing support for South Korea. However, in April representatives of the United States, North Korea, and China met in Beijing to consider Pyongyang's nuclear ambitions. Although the details of this meeting were not revealed it has been assumed that North Korea may have offered to suspend its nuclear program if the United States were to promise not to attack it. To further North Korea's sense of security it has been suggested that the United States could provide technical assistance and funding to North Korea to dismantle its weapon capabilities. This could be coupled with guidance in the development of energy and the fostering of trade relations. This would depend on North Korea's cooperation and proof of compliance, since in the past North Korea has not revealed its nuclear activities.

However, this approach was negated early in May when North Korea nullified its 1992 agreement with South Korea to keep the Korean Peninsula free of nuclear weapons. The United States has endeavored to address the situation from a regional perspective with four participants, namely the two Koreas, China, and Japan. In June it was reported that North Korea had suggested "bilateral contacts" in the context of the presence of the other countries. Through such multilateral efforts, including the prospect for economic assistance to North Korea, there is a possibility that it can be diverted from its present policy of nuclear brinksmanship.

The United States has solicited the advice of its allies on how to proceed. Several responses have been forthcoming. First, diplomatic negotiations might lead to reconsideration by North Korea of its initiative. Second, there could be a concession to nuclearization followed by an effort at nuclear containment. But, since North Korea is deemed capable of transferring nuclear materials to terrorists this option could be dangerous. Third, following the example of Israel in the Middle East there could be a bombing of the nuclear weapons plants and storage sites. This would cause contamination in those areas and could harden the resolve of North Korea to attack South Korea. Secretary of Defense Rumsfeld has stated that the United States has the capability of carrying on two wars at the same time. At the end of December 2002 Secretary of State Powell stated "Military action is always an option, but it is not an option that is in the forefront of thinking right now, because it doesn't seem necessary or appropriate. . . . There are no forces being put on alert on either side."[28] Clarification would require a higher degree of openness, including a treaty-based right for the United States, or its designee, to conduct unannounced inspections of nuclear facilities in North Korea.[29] The January 2003 decision of North Korea to cancel the 1968 Nonproliferation of Nuclear Weapons Treaty caused a dramatic escalation of American concerns. Following U.S. diplomatic efforts at the end of 2003 the posture of North Korea had become somewhat more conciliatory.

5. NEGOTIATING A NEW U.S.-RUSSIAN DISARMAMENT TREATY

The 1972 ABM treaty prohibited the deployment of a NMD system. It was designed to prevent the use of nuclear weapons following the assumption that a first user would also perish from a nuclear exchange. Mutual deterrence was seen as the salvation of the times.[30]

With the adoption on May 20, 1999 of the National Missile Act President Clinton candidly stated that the policy contained in the statute would require an amendment of the ABM Treaty. During campaign 2000 candidate George W. Bush expressed concerns over Russia's role in the spreading of weapons of mass destruction. He received advice from Dr. Condoleezza Rice, who was to become the new head of the National Security Council. She wrote:

> American security is threatened less by Russia's strength than by its weakness and incoherence. . . . Washington must begin a comprehensive discussion with Moscow on the changing nuclear threat. . . . The Russian deterrent is more than adequate against the U.S nuclear arsenal, and vice versa. But that fact need no longer be enshrined in a treaty that is almost 30 years old and a relic of a profoundly adversarial relationship between the United States and the Soviet Union. The Anti-Ballistic Missile Treaty was intended to prevent the development of national missile defenses in the Cold War security environment. Today, the principal concerns are nuclear threats from the Iraqs and North Koreas of the world and the possibility of unauthorized releases as nuclear weapons spread.[31]

Following his election President Bush expressed increasingly negative views of the ABM Treaty, despite the fact that through its assurances of restraint it had contributed to a steadying of the relationship between the United States and Russia. The increasingly unilateral approach by the United States on the status of nuclear arms caused major concerns in April-May 2000, during the Review Conference of the Parties to the Treaty on the 1968 Non-Proliferation of Nuclear Weapons. This led "nuclear weapons (NWS) and non-nuclear weapons States (NNWS) [to] oppose the United States' plan to amend the ABM Treaty both during the conference and throughout the entire year at every available convenience."[32] Such views were grounded in the fact that super-power parity had allowed for cold-war problems, but had avoided the outbreak of armed conflict between the two adversaries since the end of World War II.

Beginning with their meeting in June, 2001, Presidents Bush and Putin and their high foreign policy and defense advisors, entered into negotiations which led to the abrogation of the 1972 agreement and to the signing on May 24, 2002 of a treaty reducing and limiting strategic nuclear warheads. During this period both leaders engaged in personal diplomacy. In order to obtain the new agreement President Bush had to persuade President Putin that the ABM Treaty was outdated.

The first step occurred on November 3, 2001 when the Russian Defense Minister, Sergei B. Ivanov, stated that he agreed "partially" with the American contention.[33] He added, however, that it would be a mistake to scrap the agreement entirely and that before any modification might occur there would have to be something in its place. In August of 2001 the U.S. Department of State had denied that the United States had given Russia an ultimatum respecting its withdrawal from the agreement.[34] At that time and in the weeks that followed the United States continued to stress the dangers presented by "rogue States."

Two important meetings occurred between the leaders of the two countries prior to the summit meeting in Washington on November 13–15, 2001. Despite President Bush's position that both countries would benefit from a sharp reduction in the numbers of nuclear warheads from, in the case of the United States of about 7,013, and for Russia 5,858, at the end of September, 2001, the Department of Defense was not able to arrive at a preferred number.[35] Since this would have to be determined by knowing what Russia had in mind, Secretary of Defense Rumsfeld went to Russia for consultations with Russian defense officials while Secretary Powell met in Washington with Foreign Minister Igor S. Ivanov. In determining what reductions could be achieved, which at the same time would establish the numbers still on hand, it would be possible to determine the magnitude of the NMD system.

These negotiations were followed by a meeting between the two presidents in Shanghai on October 21, 2001. President Bush continued to express the fear that terrorists might be able to employ intercontinental missiles against the United States. President Putin considered this quite unlikely. Nonetheless, President Bush reported that the 1972 ABM Treaty, to the extent it prevented the United States from defending its citizens "is outdated, and . . . dangerous."[36]

The national security advisor, Dr. Rice, confirmed the American plan to withdraw from the agreement, adding: "We are not going to permit a program of testing and development to be constrained by a treaty that we think is outmoded. We think the important thing here is to move forward with some urgency to really begin to explore and to have a robust testing and evaluation program."[37] She added that the U.S. had not mentioned a "deadline" for its withdrawal from the agreement. Although no agreement was reached on the proposed termination of the treaty the two officials referred to a growth of good will and trust.

At their meeting in Washington on November 11–13, 2001, the agenda of the two presidents covered the 1972 ABM agreement, the prospects for cuts in nuclear arsenals, closer economic ties, efforts to combat terrorism, and NATO prospects. Commentators at that time referred to the "style" of the meeting, namely, the cooperative postures of the two leaders, as well as to the substantive issues. Mr. Bush indicated that their respective ties were strong enough to "endure this difference of opinion" on national missile defense and the future status of the 1972 treaty.[38] In a conciliatory mood President Putin stated that he understood the American concern regarding terroristic activity and that the problem was in figuring out the "ways and means" for "reaching the same objectives."[39]

At the close of the conference the two presidents made a joint statement in which they referred to a new relationship between the countries. Emphasis was placed on their commitments to the values of "democracy, the free market, and the rule of law."[40] Of first importance was their commitment to meet threats taking the form of terrorism, proliferation of weapons of mass destruction, militant nationalism, ethnic and religious intolerance, and regional instability. They pledged to create a "new strategic framework" designed to "ensure the mutual security of the United States and Russia, and the world community."[41]

These wide ranging promises were supplemented by those addressed to their beliefs that the "current levels of our nuclear forces do not reflect the strategic realities of today."[42] Therefore they confirmed their respective commitments to "implement substantial reductions in strategic offensive weapons. On strategic defenses and the ABM Treaty, we have agreed, in light of the changing global security environment, to continue consultations within the broad framework of the new strategic relationship."[43] They referred to mutual interests in the area of non-proliferation, and to the safeguarding of nuclear materials, including preventing illicit nuclear trafficking.

The joint statement was followed by separate statements by the two leaders. President Bush announced his intention to cut the U.S. strategic stockpile of nuclear warheads by roughly two-thirds within the next ten years. This action, to be taken unilaterally, would produce an arsenal of between 2,000 and 1,700 warheads. This figure is smaller than the number agreed to in 1993 under the START II treaty. That agreement called for each State to effect a reduction of between 3,500 and 3,000 by 2010. Since the number available to the United States under the Bush declaration and those which would be available under the START II limitation are not very far apart, it is believed that the strategic balance between the two countries would not be changed.[44]

President Putin in a separate declaration indicated that Russia would reduce its number of warheads by about two-thirds, with 5,858 warheads being used to calculate the result. President Bush added that: "President Putin and I have also agreed that my decision to withdraw from the treaty will not, in any way, undermine our new relationship or Russian security."[45] The above figures, assuming the ongoing availability of reserve weapons, would allow for the operation of the deterrence theory.

The immediate response of President Putin and high Russian officials was to describe the American action as "a mistake." The Russian Minister of Defense, Sergei B. Ivanov, commented that the decision would not unbalance the relations between the two States. He added that the unilateral action of the United States could serve to raise questions about the durability of other important international agreements that had been entered into in good faith. He noted that such agreements are conditioned on a spirit of international trust and cooperation.

Critics of unilateral declarations point out that the same process would be used to increase a nation's stockpile. Thus, they favor formal international agreements, including provisions for transparency and other suitable safeguards.

In a follow-up to the Russian observations the White House Press Secretary called attention to reduction of strategic nuclear weapons to the lowest level for the two countries in decades. Further, it was stated that the United States would work with Russia to formalize this arrangement, on offensive forces, including appropriate verification and transparency measures.

A. NATO and the 2001 Decision on National Missile Defense

The United States and Russia were aware that the members of NATO, and other major States, had a very substantial interest in the prospect for fewer strategic nuclear weapons. Thus, following reference to the commitment made on November 13, 2001 to implement substantial reductions of strategic offensive weapons, the two countries turned to the subject of NATO. Both wanted to "improve, strengthen, and enhance the relationship between NATO and Russia, with a view to developing new, effective mechanisms for consultation, cooperation, joint decisions, and coordinated/joint action."[46]

Although President Bush did not provide specifics of his plans for the relationships between the two entities, some experts have interpreted the statement "as a sign of momentum for an increased Russian role in NATO."[47] This outlook finds support in the view that the two entities are becoming increasingly allied because of their concerns for terrorism and regional instability. Russia has also objected to the possible future role of the Baltic States in NATO.[48] One prospect for Russia might be to obtain the same status in NATO that is exercised by France. France, unlike the other members, does not participate in alliance military activities.

B. Responses to the Decision to Withdraw from the 1972 ABM Treaty

Since the withdrawal constituted a disavowal of the mutually assured destruction doctrine, and since that doctrine had been supported by many leaders in many countries for a long time, much disapproval was immediately voiced. Portrayals of intended and unintended consequences were put forward. As noted, the U.S. action could be used as a reason or justification by other countries to opt out of prohibitory or regulatory treaties. The response of a Chinese arms control analyst was that the United States "doesn't want to be hemmed in by nuclear control regimes."[49]

The United States was aware that China was concerned that American missile defense plans might pose a threat to Chinese security. In 2001 Dr. Rice stated that the United States would tell the Chinese that "the missile shield is not aimed at them and they shouldn't feel threatened by it."[50] She added that they would receive the same briefing given to everyone else and that China's views would be considered. Unfortunately, neither the United States nor China are parties to the 1996 Comprehensive Nuclear Test-Ban Treaty, although both countries as well as France, Russia, and the United Kingdom have engaged themselves to a voluntary moratorium on nuclear tests.

Concerns were also expressed that India and Pakistan would interpret the American action as an expression of indifference as to compliance by other States with their arms control and limitation agreements. Such a reading by India and Pakistan would result in a devastating destabilization in a part of the world already in a condition of continual crisis. For such States the firmer are the commitments and expectations of compliance by powerful countries, the greater will be the prospect for stability. In the early 1990s when France broke its self-imposed moratorium on testing nuclear weapons it became the target of world-wide criticism.

A different argument is based on the timing of the withdrawal from the 1972 agreement. It has been urged that "testing that is compliant with the treaty can continue for years."[51] Thus, it was concluded that December, 2001, was the wrong time to antagonize Russia and China since there was at that moment a need to obtain their fullest cooperation on a more important foreign policy objective, namely, cooperation on winning the war against terrorism.

At the partisan political level the timing was identified as a benefit to conservatives in Congress. In applauding the action Senator Jesse Helms of North Carolina stated: "As long as our nation is vulnerable to nuclear threats from the likes of Kim Jong Il, Saddam Hussein and the ayatollahs of Teheran, we also will be vulnerable to blackmail, intimidation, and other efforts to influence our foreign policy."[52]

This was countered by the chairman of the Senate Armed Services Committee, Carl Levin of Michigan. In his view the Bush decision was likely to lead to a cycle of development of costly offensive and defensive weapons, "and that kind of arms race would not make us more secure."

While it is true that efforts to achieve an effective NMD will be expensive, it should also be accepted that money spent for the education, training, and employment of a large reservoir of highly trained and skilled scientists and technologists serves the cause of national security. No State can be an effective world leader if it cannot demonstrate leadership in these areas.

However, the same reasoning can be applied to the U.S. outer space program.[53] So the question arises whether there is a need to support both programs in order to maintain a full reservoir of such specialists. In achieving a suitable balance it is necessary to take into account the existing need to rebuild the decaying infrastructure of the United States. Unfortunately the cost of fighting international terrorism, and effecting a regime change in Iraq will be long and expensive, especially if there are provisions for humanitarian assistance to populations that have been caught in these situations.

On a technical level it has also been argued that the Bush decision was not necessary in 2001. Thus, it has been stated in 2002 that none of the tests, which the Pentagon wished to make of a missile launch, so that it could determine the suitability of the NMD, were then prohibited.[54]

It was also indicated that while President Bush favored mobile ABM systems, laser weapons on 747 aircraft, interceptors on Aegis cruisers (a component of the Aegis radar system), and space-based laser battle stations, all of which would fall under the ban of the ABM treaty, that "it will be several years before their development gets to the stage where the AMB Treaty becomes a barrier."[55]

Among the debatable issues raised by the Bush action are: whether those countries, whose ill-will to the United States has been demonstrated, possess now or may possess within the predictable future the technical capacity to launch long range or short range nuclear missiles able to hit or to harm the United States? Whether such countries or terrorist groups have nuclear devices that could be exploded in the United States via other delivery systems, such as in vehicles, or pizza deliveries, or other uncomplicated means? Whether American fact-gathering, e.g., intelligence operations, will be able to provide meaningful advice within an effective time frame? Whether in these different scenarios the United States will over an extended period of time be willing to fund such defensive measures, and preemptive strike measures, while at the same time being able to maintain the social programs required to guarantee the basic well-being owed to its citizens?

Also, on a more mundane level, but nonetheless important, is the question of America's claim to be an honorable and law-abiding country. In Article XV of the 1972 ABM Treaty the United States agreed that the agreement was to "be of unlimited duration." However, this was subject to the further provision that "Each Party shall, in exercising its national sovereignty, have the right to withdraw from this Treaty if it decides that extraordinary events related to the subject matter of this Treaty have jeopardized its supreme interests."[56] This was followed by a standard provision requiring the "Party," to give six months notice prior to withdrawal to the other "Party." This notice must contain a "statement of the extraordinary events the notifying Party regards as having jeopardized its supreme interests."[57]

President Bush's formal remarks, made on December 13, 2001, were addressed in part to the terms of Article XV. He stated: "Today I have given formal notice to Russia, in accordance with the treaty, that the United States of America is withdrawing from this almost 30 year old treaty. I have concluded the ABM treaty hinders our government's ability to develop ways to protect our people from terrorists or rogue state missile attacks."[58] From the foregoing it is clear that President Bush held the view that his powers under the U.S. Constitution were sufficiently comprehensive for him to make the identified decision.

Nonetheless, the argument has been made that since the Constitution provides for the manner in which treaties are made that the same process must be followed in effecting a valid withdrawal from the agreement. This would mean that a unilateral decision could not be valid, since by its own terms it did not receive the advice and consent of the Senate required prior to a presidential ratification. The contention rests on the principle of separation of powers in which the Congress, the President, and the Supreme Court are engaged in the governance of the United States. The President does not have exclusive control over U.S. foreign policy in all of its ramifications. Yet it is possible that in the ABM Treaty, because of concerns about terrorism or missile attacks, a president could base his action on the totality of his constitutional authority. It comes down to the gravity and the immediacy of the danger, at least, as seen by a chief executive. That, it can be argued, is a factual matter—an area in which appellate courts traditionally seek to avoid having to make decisions.

Those who consider that President Bush exceeded his constitutional authority can refer to the 1979 case of *Goldwater v. Carter*.[59] In that case which ultimately reached the U.S. Supreme Court, Senator Goldwater and other senators endeavored to get a ruling that the president had exceeded his power in unilaterally terminating the mutual defense treaty between the United States and Taiwan. Joining Senator Goldwater were Senators Orrin Hatch of Utah, Jesse Helms of North Carolina, and Strom Thurmond of South Carolina.

In disposing of this litigation the Supreme Court relied on the doctrine of the non-justiciable "political question." Its application enables the Court, for prudential considerations, to determine that its wisest course of action is to avoid dealing with certain substantive issues that may have been raised. In effect the case is dismissed, with the victory going to the defendants. In the cited case six justices voted to dismiss the appeal without addressing the substantive issue of presidential power. When members of Congress challenged President Bush's termination of the 1972 ABM Treaty in a judicial proceeding the court held for the president.

Additionally, an authoritative treatise on the meaning to be accorded in American courts to claims founded in international law suggests quite persuasively that a Head of State, unless the treaty contains contrary provisions, can be expected to speak on behalf of his/her country regarding the status of international agreements.[60]

The Bush administration, having completed a successful negotiation with President Putin on the termination of the 1972 ABM Agreement, turned its attention to the reduction of nuclear warheads. Both countries were vastly over supplied. By 2001 a different combination of weapons would be of greater utility against the threat of terrorism and for States not conclusively proven to constitute nuclear threats.

In furtherance of international security the Bush administration has proposed a comprehensive strategy entitled "The New Strategic Framework." It entails "reducing offensive nuclear weapons, creating limited defensive systems that deter the threat of missile attacks, strengthening nonproliferation and counterproliferation measures, and cooperating with Russia to combat terrorism."[61]

By 2002 President Bush had announced unilateral plans to reduce the number of deployed nuclear warheads from about 7,000 to between 2,000 and 1,700 over 10 years. With more intensive negotiations with Russia in January, 2002, at which time Russian leaders, including the Russian parliament were condemning the U.S.'s ABM withdrawal, negotiations were going on relating to the reduction in weapons. Aside from establishing applicable figures, negotiations required a decision on the form the agreement should take. Russia favored a formal treaty, while the United States urged the exchange of mutual declarations. The U.S. position was influenced by a Pentagon concern over a need to have a larger number of weapons on hand in the future. The

U.S. indicated that Russia would be protected via dissemination of predictability and transparency documents.

Initial bargaining centered around the ease with which a commitment could be altered. Also involved was whether the final quota was to count those in storage and those destroyed, and, if the latter, the disposition of the valuable residual, nuclear material.

During the negotiations the chemical weapons components of the Russian defense arsenal came under review. Russia in 1997 had become a party to the International Chemical Weapons Convention. At that time the United States pledged $880 million to assist in the destruction of the Russian stockpile, which included difference kinds of gases. American payments were suspended in 2001 when concerns were raised as to the rapidity of such destructions. In February, 2002, the United States agreed to release up to $620 million to accelerate work in progress.

In early March, 2002, a Pentagon study was leaked. Entitled Nuclear Posture Review (NPR) it identified contingency plans for an expanded use of nuclear weapons. They would be employed against countries posing a threat to the United States by virtue of their nuclear, biological, or chemical weapons. Identified in the plan by name were Iran, Iraq, Libya, North Korea, and Syria. China was referred to in connection with a military confrontation over the status of Taiwan. Russia was listed as a possible target, but not in response to an initial Russian attack against the United States.[62]

In assessing the situation Secretary of State Powell observed that when States were engaged in developing weapons of mass destruction the United States was entitled to engage in prudent military planning. He stated: "Prudent planners have to give some consideration as to the range of options the president should have available to him to deal with these kind of threats."[63] He indicated that the NPR was not a plan for an imminent attack.

The NPR called for a new generation of small nuclear weapons having the capability of deep penetration including the destruction of underground bunkers. With the explosion taking place under these circumstances it has been argued that there would be little if any contaminating fall-out. Critics have asserted widely ranging outlooks. Some have seen the project as a dangerous change in policy. Other have identified it as an important advance toward ending nuclear dangers. Others have noted that it is an example of a policy of unilateralism. These observations did not impede U.S.-Russian negotiations placing limits on strategic nuclear warheads.

In the spring of 2002 the negotiators were showing progress on the form of the agreement and on means to identify compliance. They were assessing common concerns in the Israel and Palestinian tragedy, the status of military activity in Afghanistan, and the role of Russia in Iran and Iraq, which Russia considered to be political allies. Russia was being asked to slow down the transfer of nuclear technology to Iran. On its side the United States was aware that in 2001 President Putin had withdrawn remaining Russian troops from Vietnam and Cuba, without asking any concessions from the United States.

As the military and political ledger was being totaled both presidents had to weigh the concerns of their respective armed forces and diplomatic advisers. Although grumbling on the part of some continued down to May 24, 2002, on that date the two leaders signed in Moscow a treaty consisting of five articles. In doing so they endeavored to establish the conditions for strategic nuclear stability.

6. THE U.S.-RUSSIAN NUCLEAR WARHEADS REDUCTION AND LIMITATION TREATY, MAY 24, 2002

The essential terms of the agreement are:

Article I memorialized the statements made by President Bush on November 13, 2001 and those of President Putin on November 13, 2001 and on December 13, 2001 whereby each party to the agreement promised that it "shall reduce and limit strategic nuclear warheads," so that by December 31, 2012, "the aggregate number of such warheads does not exceed 1,700 to 2,200 for each party."

Pursuant to Article II: "The parties agree that the START treaty remains in force in accordance with its terms."

Article III dealt with the implementation of the agreement. The parties promised to hold meetings at least two times a year "of a Bilateral Implementation Commission."

Article IV dealt with the formalities of the agreement's coming into force, duration, and withdrawal. It was to be ratified "in accordance with the constitutional procedures of each party." It was to enter into force on the exchange of ratifications. It is to remain in force until December 31, 2012. By agreement of the parties they may extend it. Further, they provided that it could be superseded earlier by a subsequent agreement. Additionally, "each party, in exercising its national sovereignty, may withdraw from this treaty upon three months written notice to the other party."

The final Article stated that the agreement "shall be registered pursuant to Article 102 of the Charter of the United Nations." Two copies were signed. One was in English; the other in Russian. Both texts are equally authentic.

The treaty's provisions are to be carried out over a period of years and at the end of the term there will be a very substantial reduction in the number of strategic nuclear warheads. The accompanying chart identifies the inventory of nuclear warheads between 1951 and 2012.

NUCLEAR WARHEADS, U.S., USSR, RUSSIA
(All Figures Approximate)
U.S. Left Column
Russia Right Column

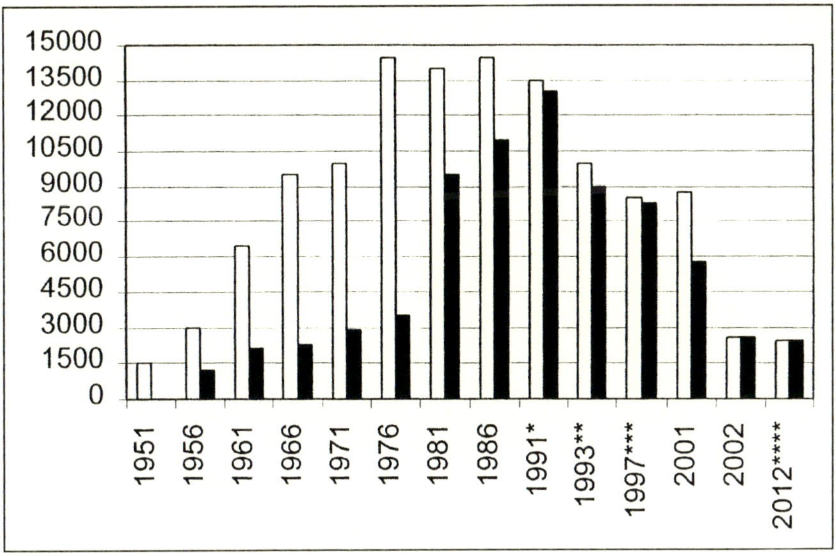

Chart 5.
***Under START I, Limit on warheads 6,000**
****Under START II, Limit on warheads 3,000–3,500**
*****Under START III, Limit on warheads 2,000–2,500 by end of 2007. Agreement not signed.**
******U.S.-Russian Nuclear Warhead Reduction and Limitation Treaty, May 24, 2002. Between 1,700 and 2,200 each party.**

Sources: Arms Control Association, the *Christian Science Monitor,* Carnegie Endowment for International Peace, Council for a Livable World Education Fund, Natural Resources Defense Council, U.S.-Russian Nuclear Warheads Reduction and Limitation Treaty, May 24, 2002.

The treaty is consistent with the American-Russian nonproliferation objectives of safe transportation of such warheads to places of dismantlement, meeting the need for increased security for storage of existing warheads, and for the employment of Russian scientists in the down-grading of all of their highly dangerous weapon programs, including chemical and biological.

The agreement did not invalidate the American plan for a NMD system. The purchase of nuclear fuel from Russia will reduce, over time, the hazards resulting from the domestic mining, manufacture, and use of nuclear materials for national power purposes, as well as all of the problems involved in the disposition of still active nuclear waste. Some of these actions will constitute a drain on the U.S. Treasury in order to aid in the costs incurred by Russia in its threat reduction plans. To the extent that the Russian economy can be improved, there is the expectation that the American subventions to Russia for different projects can accordingly be reduced.

The Cooperative Non-Proliferation and Threat Production Program, named after Senator Richard Lugar of Indiana and former Senator Sam Nunn of Georgia has cost the United States about $400 million a year, from its inception in 1991 to the present. The program has been referred to by a former Secretary of Defense, William Perry, as a "defense by other means."

In future U.S. funds will be needed to augment Russian costs for security at nuclear storage sites including those for spent reactor fuel. The latter can be exploited by weapons experts in order to fabricate "dirty bombs." At the time the treaty was signed it was estimated that "only about 40 percent of Russia's bomb-grade materials and less than a seventh of enriched uranium stocks have been secured."[64] A Russian source was quoted as saying the stocks of plutonium in storage will skyrocket in the next few years.

American funding of Russian security procedures may be money well spent, especially if it serves to deny nuclear materials to terrorists.[65] Further, polls indicate that President Putin's support for the treaty has not caught on among a large number of Russian citizens; anti-Americanism has strong roots.

President Putin has called for weapons cooperation with the United States, and with regard to nuclear weapons this has been referred to as an integrated approach. Yet, and this is despite denials from him, there is good reason to believe that Russia has been providing support to Iran as it seeks to upgrade its nuclear capabilities. Whether the integrated approach concept has equal application to chemical and biological weapons remains to be proven.

The existence of the new treaty highlights the need to address all security needs. The fact that progress has been made between the United States and Russia also highlights the need to consider in particular the relationship between these two States and China.

The need to establish an effective working relationship among like-minded countries in order to achieve gains has been demonstrated in many situations. In the Chapter on The Middle East it is pointed out that there are problems too large for any single State to resolve. It was mentioned that President Bush was seeking a forum consisting of European and Arab States to offer suggestions for the resolution of Middle-Eastern issues, and that the road map was the product of a Quartet.

With regard to nuclear weapons, and their presence in Iran, Iraq, and China, now that President Putin has agreed to a limited membership in NATO, perhaps that organization would find it attractive to engage them in the resolution of nuclear problems. NATO already is committed to fighting terrorism, engaging in peacekeeping operations, and curbing, in a more restrictive geographical area, the proliferation of weapons of mass destruction. The seriousness of the problem excludes an arbitrary decision in both of these regional situations.

With regard to the 2002 Treaty, one very important point has been left to the last. In this so-called "fast track" agreement there are no "way stations," that is, there is no scheduled requirement that any fixed number of warheads has to be destroyed at periodic intervals. For example, it does not provide that 25% of a State's quota must be destroyed by 2005, another percentage at a later date, and another percentage at still a subsequent date. The terms state that all reductions and limitations must have been completed on the last day on which the Treaty remains operative, i.e., December 31, 2012.

This suggests that although from a negotiating point of view the agreement was on a fast track that from the point of implementation it is on, or can be on, a very slow train. It need not arrive, absent any cargo, which has been destroyed along the way, until December 31, 2012. This being the case the views mentioned above may have some influence on establishing schedules for reductions and limitations.

7. THE NORTH KOREAN THREAT

In 2002 high officials in North Korea asserted it had a uranium nuclear and plutonium program. United Nations inspectors, prior to their forced departure, had viewed hundreds of spent plutonium fuel rods used in the processing of weapons-grade material. Remote sensing from outer space has identified manufacturing facilities and the presence of missiles needed to launch nuclear warheads.

The enmity held by Kim Jong Il toward the United States has been focused on its help for and presence in South Korea. The United States has enlisted the support of neighboring countries, particularly China, to obtain the dismantling of the North Korean nuclear program. In 2003 China began to host multilateral talks on the future of the Korean Peninsula. Their focus has been on the non-testing of such weapons. Such tests would have the effect of destabilizing the Asian continent, and would pose very great concerns throughout the world. Affecting the outcome will be the future relations between the United States and South Korea where recently there has been evidence of animosity toward the United States. Since the presence of a nuclear capacity is a threat to the peace and security of all nations the subject is ideally suited for consideration at the United Nations.

8. THE WORLD COURT'S ADVISORY OPINION ON THE LEGALITY OF THE THREAT OR USE OF NUCLEAR WEAPONS

This Chapter would be incomplete without reference to the World Court's Advisory Opinion on the Legality of the Threat or Use of Nuclear Weapons. The decision was rendered on July 8, 1996.[66]

The issue was referred to the Court by General Assembly Resolution 49/75 K adopted on December 15, 1994. The General Assembly asked for the Court's opinion on "Is the threat or use of nuclear weapons in any circumstance permitted under international law."[67]

Before examining this issue the Court asked States to file legal briefs and to make oral statements. Among those filing statements were Iran, North Korea, Russia, and the United States. Verbal statements were made by eleven States, including the United States and Russia. The United States was represented by lawyers from the Department of State and the Department of Defense.

Having satisfied itself that the Court possessed jurisdiction and that the question as framed asked a legal question, the tribunal, consisting of fourteen of its fifteen members, made several rulings. The judges were unanimous in the opinion that "There is in neither customary nor conventional international law any specific authorization of the threat or use of nuclear weapons."[68]

By a vote of eleven to three they held that "There is in neither customary nor conventional international law any comprehensive and universal prohibition of the threat or use of nuclear weapons as such."[69] The majority included the American, British, French, Japanese, and Russian judges.

The judges were unanimous in holding that "A threat or use of force by means of nuclear weapons that is contrary to Article 2, paragraph 4, of the United National Charter and that fails to meet all requirements of Article 51, is unlawful."[70]

They were also unanimous in holding that "A threat or use of nuclear weapons should also be compatible with the requirements of the international law applied in armed conflict, particularly those of the principles and rules of international humanitarian law, as well as with specific obligations and treaties and other undertakings which expressly deal with nuclear weapons."[71]

The Court was also asked to rule on whether a State had an obligation to pursue in good faith negotiations dealing with nuclear disarmament. Its holding was in the affirmative, and, in the Court's words: "There exists an obligation to pursue in good faith and bring to a conclusion negotiations leading to nuclear disarmament in all its aspects under strict and effective international control."[72]

On one issue the judges were not able to reach a unanimous decision. This involved the question of whether an exception to the basic rules relating to the threat or use of nuclear weapons could be made when a State's very survival was at stake. Under the rules of the Court, where there is an equal distribution of votes, the decision must conform to the conclusion supported by the President of the Court. His vote, in effect, is counted twice. Thus, by a vote of seven to seven, by the President's casting vote, the tribunal concluded that it followed that "the threat or use of nuclear weapons would generally be contrary to the rules of international law applicable in armed conflict, and in particular the principles and rules of humanitarian law. However, in view of the current state of international law, and of the elements of fact at its disposal, the Court cannot conclude definitively whether the threat or use of nuclear weapons would be lawful or unlawful in an extreme circumstance of self-defense, in which the very survival of a State would be at stake."[73]

The Court made very brief reference to a situation where a State may have unconditionally engaged not to resort to nuclear weapons. An inference may, perhaps be drawn, that such weapons are not permissible, even when the State's survivability is at stake.[74] It if were ever necessary to test such an interpretation, assuming that nuclear warfare had erupted, its time may well have passed.

9. CONCLUSION

In 1972, as at present, important countries possessed sufficient weapons of mass destruction—nuclear, biological, and chemical—to destroy easily all of Earth's inhabitants. The agreement between the United States and the Soviet Union in that year constituted a surrender by the parties of any meaningful right to defend themselves against the launch of a nuclear warhead by the other country. The massive oversupply of weapons and the resultant over-kill capability has continued down to the present. Now, such weapons and their components are multiply dangerous. If launched in anger there will be harm to the attacked. If retained there may be harm to the owner because of the deterioration of weapons, launching sites, and storage facilities. There is the additional danger that they may fall into the hands of irresponsible countries as well as the most recent scourge of humanity, the terrorist.

It would be futile to argue that times have not changed. Such a condition, provided for in the bilateral ABM Agreement, was invoked so that a new approach might be taken to continuing and basic problems of national security. This did not change the ongoing need for verification and transparency procedures. This is a matter of proof in which a high degree of cooperation is required, including some form of mutual inspection. With good relations existing between countries, such inspection, although sometimes with permission reluctantly granted, will provide assurance that the basic condition of security exists. The problem is very real because of the so-called rogue States. Even for the United States and Russia this verification requires further clarification.

President Bush was convinced that the ABM treaty stood in the way of a new defense strategy, namely, that of national missile defense. Since NMD was designed as a protection against the rogue States, they were expected to take notice of the termination of the ABM treaty. They were to construe this action as opening the door to a nuclear attack on any country which may consider the employment of nuclear warheads against the United States. The quotas retained are more than adequate as counsels of caution.

An even clearer warning to such States to restrain any aggressive planning, and such conduct, was the publicity given in March 2002 to the Pentagon's Nuclear Posture Review which identified by name States which are attempting to acquire nuclear warheads. The fact that specific States have been found to support terrorist activities has not helped their cases.

The debates leading to the May 24, 2002, Reduction and Limitation Agreement with Russia have served as a reminder that the entire world has an excessive supply of nuclear warheads, and that any reduction in volume and no matter how long it takes will increase world safety and stability. Both parties see the agreement as serving their respective self-interests. A strategic commitment was made.

In what has been referred to as the New Strategic Framework, there remains, additionally, a need for a political declaration. Under Secretary of State John R. Bolton in his May 6, 2002, statement on warheads observed: "We are also working to draft a political declaration on the New Strategic Framework that would cover the issues of strategic offensive and defensive systems, nonproliferation and counterproliferation."[75] When this is ready it may be hoped that it takes into account the relationships between the parties to the May 2002 treaty and such States as China, India, North Korea, and Pakistan. The value of international cooperation must be brought home to North Korea.

Heads of State must become aware of the World Court's 1996 Advisory Opinion.

Additionally there is a need for a new economic declaration between the United States and Russia identifying goals and means to achieve such goals in the economic arena. Such a declaration, at a minimum, will have to address the export by Russia to Iran of the science and technology related to the construction of facilities, both commercial and military, requiring nuclear fuel.

Many safety problems confront Russia, and to a certain degree, the United States, in the decommissioning of nuclear warheads. With this there is a new resource consisting of highly enriched uranium, for fuels for commercial use. The availability of this material for sale may affect the subsidization that the United States has accorded to Russia under the cooperative Threat Reduction Program. Favorable relations in the future between the United States and Russia will depend on a cooperative blending of their military, political, and economic interests. The fact that Russia has chronic and severe economic problems may condition the outcome. Future negotiations can accommodate competing interests when carried on in circumstances where mutual benefits will be realized.

DISCUSSION QUESTIONS

1. How do you assess the merits of the position taken by the United States regarding its withdrawal from the 1972 ABM Treaty?
2. What are the advantages and disadvantages of bilateral and multilateral agreements designed to achieve arms control and disarmament?
3. How long should the "defense by other means" policy between the United States and Russia be continued?
4. What needs to be done before the United States embarks on the policy of the NMD?
5. Do you feel safer today than five years ago from nuclear attacks initiated by countries now possessing nuclear warfare capabilities?

NOTES

1. The treaties referred to in this Chapter are printed in *International Legal Matters*, a publication of the American Society of International Law.

2. U.S. State Department and Time magazine. For a list of States possessing chemical and biological weapons, see Monterey Institute of International Studies. (www://cns.miis.edu/research/cbw/possess.html)

3. C.Q. Christol, "The Convention on the Prohibition of Military or Any Other Hostile Use of Environmental Modification Techniques," in N. JASENTULIANA, ed., MAINTAINING OUTER SPACE FOR PEACEFUL PURPOSES 189 (1984). D.L. Guruswamy and J.B. Armodt, "Nuclear Arms Control: The Environmental Dimensions," 10 *Colorado J. of Int'l Environmental L. and Policy*, No. 2, 267 (1999).

4. P.W. Mason, "Arms Control and Disarmament," 34 *The Int'l Law*, No. 2, 618 (Summer 2000).

5. *Id.*, at 619.

6. BMD stands for Ballistic Missile Defense.

7. J.H. Harrington, "Arms Control and Disarmament," 35 *The Int'l Law*, No. 2, 592 (Summer 2001).

8. *Supra*, note 4 at 612.

9. *Supra*, note 7 at 587.

10. G.T. Allison, "ABCs of ABM and Missile Defense," *The Christian Science Monitor*, 21, May 31, 2000. Mr. Allison was a former Assistant Secretary of Defense. J. Newhouse, "The Missile Defense Debate," 80 *Foreign Affairs*, No. 4, 97 (July–August 2001).

11. *Ibid.*

12. *Ibid.*

13. "Trading 'Good' for 'Iffy'," *Los Angeles Times*, B12, December 12, 2001. J. Schell, "The Folly of Arms Control," 79 *Foreign Affairs, No. 5,* 30, (September/October 2000). He builds his argument on the limitations of the relevant conventions or on their non-ratification.

14. B. Jasani, "U.S. National Missile Defense and International Security: Blessing or Blight?" 17 *Space Policy*, No. 4, 247 (November 2001).

15. B. Roberts, R.A. Manning, and R.N. Montaperto, "China, the Forgotten Nuclear Power." 79 *Foreign Affairs*, No. 4, 53 (July–August 200).

16. *Supra*, Note 10 at 21.

17. *Los Angeles Times*, B8, August 9, 2000.

18. *Los Angeles Times*, A12, March 26, 2002.

19. *Ibid.* The difficulty has been acknowledged by other defensive missile experts.

20. *Supra*, Note 10 at 21. Cited by Mr. Allison in his article.

21. *Los Angeles Times*, A10–11, September 10, 2001.

22. *Los Angeles Times*, A1, February 4, 2001.

23. *Los Angeles Times*, B15, May 16, 2002.

24. *Supra*, Note 10 at 21. The quoted words were those of Vice-President Gore.

25. *Ibid.* The quoted words were taken from CIA sources.

26. *Ibid.*

27. *Ibid.*

28. *Los Angeles Times*, A4, December 30, 2002.

29. The U.N. General Assembly's sixth committee, which is charged with the drafting of international agreements, is presently elaborating a Convention for the Suppression of Acts of Nuclear Terrorism.

30. C.Q. Christol, "The Role of Law in U.S.-Soviet Arms Control and Disarmament Relations," 21 *The Int'l Law*, No. 2, 519 (Summer1987).

31. C. Rice, "Promoting the National Interest," 79 *Foreign Affairs*, No. 1, 58–9 (January/February 2002).

32. *Supra*, note 7 at 581.

33. *Los Angeles Times*, A9, November 4, 2001.

34. *Los Angeles Times*, A3, August 23, 2001.

35. *Los Angeles Times*, A3, September 30, 2001.

36. *Los Angeles Times*, A6, October 22, 2001.

37. *Ibid.*

38. *The Christian Science Monitor*, 3, November 19, 2001.
39. *Ibid.*
40. White House, Office of the Press Secretary, *Press Release*, November 13, 2001.
41. *Ibid.*
42. *Ibid.*
43. *Ibid.*
44. *Los Angeles Times*, A20, November 12, 2001. White House, Office of Press Secretary, *President Discusses National Missile Defense*, 2, December 13, 2001.
45. *Ibid.*
46. *Supra*, Note 38 at 1.
47. *Ibid.*
48. *Ibid.*
49. *The Christian Science Monitor* 6, June 22, 2000.
50. *Los Angeles Times*, A3, September 2, 2001.
51. J. Peter Scoblic, "The Wrong Message, The Wrong Time," *Los Angeles Times*, B17, December 13, 2001.
52. Senator Jesse Helms, "Bush Was Right to Abandon Treaty," *Los Angeles Times*, B11, December 17, 2001.
53. M. Krepon, "Lost in Space," 80 *Foreign Affairs*, No. 3, 2 (May–June 2001).
54. Robert M. Bowman, "ABM Treaty Can it be Saved?" 19 *Space and Security News*, No. 1, 5 (February 2002). Reference was made to the findings of Lisbeth Gronlund of the Union of Concerned Scientists and John Rhinelander, Esq., who participated in the negotiations of SALT I and the ABM Treaty.
55. *Ibid.*
56. 23 U.S.T. 3435; TIAS 7503.
57. *Ibid.*
58. White House, Office of the Press Secretary, *Remarks by the President on National Missile Defense*, 1, December 13, 2001.
59. 444 U.S. 996, (1979).
60. The American Law Institute, *Restatement of the Law, The Foreign Relations Law of the United States*, Vol. 1, # 339, 226 (1987).
61. J.R. Bolton, "Beyond the Axis of Evil: Additional Threats from Weapons of Mass Destruction," *U.S. Department of State, Press Release*, 1, May 6, 2002.
62. R.S. McNamara and T. Graham, Jr., "A Pretty Poor Posture for a Superpower." *Los Angeles Times*, B13, March 13, 2002.
63. *Los Angeles Times*, A1, March 11, 2002.
64. *The Christian Science Monitor*, 13, May 23, 2002.
65. William J. Perry, "Preparing for the Next Attack," 80 *Foreign Affairs*, No. 6, 31 (November-December 2001). He refers to threats from individuals processing nuclear or biological weapons.
66. 35 *I.L.M., No.3,* 809 (July 1996). The case, as reported, runs to over 35 pages. The citations are a treasure-trove of resource materials for additional reading.
67. *Id.* at 815.
68. *Id.* at 831.

69. *Ibid*.
70. *Ibid*.
71. *Ibid*.
72. *Ibid*.
73. *Ibid*. The Russian judge voted with the prevailing judges; the American, French, and British judges were on the losing side. An analysis of the case appears in VED P. NANDA and DAVID KRIEGER, NUCLEAR WEAPONS AND THE WORLD COURT (1998).
74. *Supra* Note 61, at 1.
75. *Ibid.*

Chapter VIII

The Middle East Peace Process

1. INTRODUCTION

The vast problems of the Middle East for decades have challenged the world's leaders. The search for peace in the area requires agreement on the forum for negotiations and on the substantive issues to be resolved. The United States has consistently, but without success, endeavored to facilitate a peaceful, and hopefully, long-term resolution of the situation.

The issue is whether two peoples with different traditions, religions, and outlooks can live harmoniously in a small area possessing limited natural resources. What formula, illusive to the present, can be found to offer hope for the future? How can agreements dealing with future relations be respected and implemented? What role does the international community have? Where does American foreign policy fit into the larger picture? Answers to these questions will have to take into account the paramouncy of respect for the rights of others.

On May 14, 1948 Israel became an independent State. It became a member of the United Nations in 1949. Having watched Israel's progress to statehood, the United States under the presidency of Harry Truman accorded early recognition.[1] Statehood had long been the goal of Jews who had been in search of a national homeland.

The area now constituting Israel had been a part of the Ottoman Empire, and following World War I was administered by England as a part of the Palestine Mandate. Seeking relief from governing in the area England turned to the United Nations.[2] In 1947 the General Assembly adopted a resolution calling for the partition of areas inhabited by Palestinians and Jews, including a division of the city of Jerusalem between Israel and the Palestinians. The partition plan was not implemented.

Upon the formation of the new State it was attacked in 1948 by Arab States, who were defeated. The constant turmoil that followed the formation of Israel has continued to the present. At some periods it has lessened and hopes for reconciliation have been enhanced, only to be followed by attacks in which both Israel and the Palestinian Authority (PA) and its predecessor, the Palestine Liberation Organization, have been charged with terrorism and violations of basic human rights.[3]

New levels of violence in 2002 and 2003 have marked the uneasy relations between militant Jews and Palestinians. Questions abound as to the role played by officials of Israel and the PA in ordering, encouraging, and tolerating indiscriminate killings. Religious sanctuaries and their occupants have been attacked. Tanks and heavy artillery were used to destroy the Palestinian government compound in Ramallah. Jewish settlers have taken property owned by Palestinian citizens and have erected and occupied new settlements. Members of the Arab zealot Fatah group, and others encouraged by them, have become human torpedos. Human Rights Watch has estimated that between January and November 2002 suicide bombers have killed 250 civilians and injured 2,000 others. The totals are larger when account is taken of the role of the military forces of Israel. Unfortunately the heavy casualties have not improved the chances for peace so fervently wished by the ordinary people of both faiths.

The on-going tensions in the area have been of vast concern to neighboring Arab countries, to the United States, to other entities having special interests in the area, and to the members of the United Nations.

The Bush administration in reviewing its general approach to foreign policy has employed the term "integration" as a guiding consideration. Dividing policy issues into themes, the integrative approach requires that all of the themes by addressed simultaneously.[4]

This approach to be effective would have to rely on the common outlooks of the peoples and the governments in the region. In this connection it has been noted that following the 1991 Madrid Middle East Peace Conference "The essential bargain between Arabs and Israelis—that a fair settlement of their conflict could be achieved, but only through negotiations and not violence or intimidation, and that both sides had a mutual interest in confronting militancy—has broken down."[5]

These outlooks are consistent with President Bush's remarks of June 24, 2002. His search was for a Palestinian leader in whom he could have confidence. Yasser Arafat, considered as having significant political responsibility for Israeli deaths, was no longer regarded as that person. Thus, President Bush stated that "Peace requires a new and different Palestinian leadership, so that a Palestinian State can be born."[6] He also observed that Palestinians should not "live in squalor and occupation . . . [and that my] vision is two States, living side by side in peace and security."[7]

He favored a gradual process with the new State's sovereignty to be provisional until resolved as a part of a final settlement. The United States, he said, would be able to provide economic, humanitarian and security assistance. These were contingent on an end to Yasser Arafat's policy of terrorism.

Also affecting the American position is the relative instability of the government of Israel burdened by buffetings from extreme right-wing and left-wing politicians. Tactics as well as grand strategies are to be considered. It has been suggested that piecemeal solutions are more practical than more ambitions plans for the area. Also of substantial concern are the open allegations that Israel has violated provisions of the 1949 Geneva Conventions dealing with the rights of civilian persons in the time of armed conflict.

As the United States addresses the problems of the region, it is aware that foreign policy is an element of domestic policies. Such influences frequently call for public accommodations.

The United States has had a major role in seeking to ameliorate and improve the conditions of the people living in the areas controlled by Israel and by the Palestinians.[8] In monetary terms the U.S. has provided Israel annually for many years approximately three billion dollars. In May 2002 the House Appropriations Committee proposed an additional two hundred million dollars to be used in combating international terrorism. In April 2003, an additional one billion was appropriated for Israel. In 2002 the United States gave the Palestinians approximately $130 million of which $30 million was an increase for special relief purposes. The House in May 2002 decided to increase this sum to $50 million.

2. PARTICIPANTS IN MIDDLE EAST PEACE PROCESS

Concern for a peaceful resolution of the controversy in the Middle East has been expressed by international intergovernmental organizations, by States, and by ad hoc groups composed of both States and international organizations. While their principal focus has been on areas of foreign policy, with the attendant diplomatic activity, attention has also been given to principles of international law which have application in the area.

Both the General Assembly and the Security Council of the United Nations have attempted to achieve the political and economic stabilization of the area. The numerous resolutions adopted by these bodies identify policies and legal conditions applicable to Middle Eastern States and to the PA. The U.N. has created peacekeeping forces designed, for example, to protect refugees and displaced persons in Lebanon. The U.N. has been engaged in coordinating national efforts.

The League of Arab States has conducted conferences in order to formulate a consistent policy with regard to the disputes between Israel and the PA. These policies have been made known to Heads of State so that such persons may be aware of the Arab point of view. The European Union has become involved.

The United States has organized conferences designed to achieve greater stability in the area. The first, and perhaps the most successful resulted in the 1978 Camp David Accord, establishing a peaceful relationship between Israel and Egypt. Other conferences meeting upon the initiative of the United States were held in Oslo in 1993 and 1995, and at the Wye Plantation on the Wye River in the United States in 1998. In 2000 negotiations were resumed with meetings in Madrid, Sharm el-Sheikh, and Camp David. These were followed by meetings in Taba, Egypt, in January of 2001 and in Sharm el-Sheikh and Aqaba in 2003.

The United States was instrumental in the appointment of a committee headed by former U.S. Senator George J. Mitchell which presented its findings in a report in May, 2001. Additionally, President Bush appointed the Director of the CIA, George J. Tenet, to prepare a study on Middle-Eastern conditions, which has been useful in carrying on negotiations in 2002.

By 2002 it was evident that the Bush Administration would continue the policy of past governments and would defend the statehood of Israel. In a meeting with Prime Minister Ariel Sharon of Israel in early May 2002, President Bush made it clear the he would continue to work for the creation of the independent State of Palestine.

Although these general policies are known and accepted, there is still a need for the United States to determine how it will address the two foreign leaders. With respect to all important details the United States must fix its negotiating position. This involves the extent that the United States can be directory or mandatory, that is, should the United States put to one side the normal expectations of delicacy? By December 2003 in the United States there were many indications that the United States should take a more assertive stand.

Involved is the need to obtain concessions from both sides. This will require suitable proof that mutual accommodations will serve all interests. This may oblige the United States to make certain long-term commitments to each entity. Needless to say, in the United States there will be a vast difference in outlooks, with some of higher intensity than others.

A major issue to be resolved is the boundary between the two States, if Palestine becomes a State. Also to be resolved is the status of Jerusalem. On such matters, because they involve international peace and security, the

United Nations, and, in particular its dominant members expect to be consulted. Up to now there have been many summits and valleys. The challenge is to find an open and level road to benefit the people who are entitled to a safer way of life.

3. EVENTS AFFECTING THE SEARCH FOR ACCOMMODATION

During the first eight years of Israel's existence its main adversary was Egypt. Border skirmishes erupted into a major armed conflict in 1956, with Israel, France, and the United Kingdom attacking Egypt. Following negotiations with the U.N. the three countries withdrew their troops later in the year. On June 5, 1967 Israel and Egypt were at war again. In the "six-day" war Israel prevailed and occupied the Gaza Strip territories claimed by Egypt, the Golan Heights claimed by Syria, and the West Bank of the Jordan River claimed by Jordan.

An interesting, and quite complex, problem arose out of the manner in which military action was carried out in this war. In particular there was a question whether Israel, as a party to the 1949 Geneva Conventions, and particularly Article 2 of the Fourth Convention dealing with the protection of civilian persons in time of war, had respected the Convention. The government of Israel contended that it had no legal duty toward the civilians in the area of armed conflict, but that it had voluntarily accorded to them their lawful rights.[9]

Israel also took much of the Sinai Peninsula, as well as Old Jerusalem. This led to an effort on the part of the U.N. Security Council, acting under its Chapter VII authority to deal with threats to international peace and security, to prevent a dangerous acerbation of the situation.

On November 22, 1967, the Council unanimously adopted Resolution 242. The Resolution, with its legal ramifications, set the tone for the involvement of the U.N. in the matter down to the present. The Resolution emphasized, with regard to Israel and its adversaries, that the acquisition of territory by war was inadmissible, that the parties were committed pursuant to Article 2 of the Charter to refrain in their international relations from the threat or use of force, and that there was a need to work for a just and lasting peace in which every State in the area could live in security.

The Security Council decreed that, in order to establish a just and a lasting peace in the area, two principles must be observed:

"Withdrawal of Israeli armed forces from territories of recent conflict; Termination of all claims or states of belligerency and respect for and acknowledgement of the sovereignty, territorial integrity and political independence of every state in the area and their right to live in peace within secure and recognized boundaries free from threats or acts of force." The Resolution also referred to the "freedom of navigation in the area, to a just settlement of the refugee problem, and for guaranteeing the territorial inviolability and political independence of every state in the area, through measures including the establishment of demilitarized zones. . . ."[10]

With the outbreak in 1973 of the Yom Kippur war for control of the Golan Heights, the Security Council voiced its dissatisfaction over the failure of Israel and the Palestinians to give serious attention to the establishment of a just and durable peace in the Middle East. On October 22, 1973 it adopted unanimously Resolution 338. It called upon "all parties to the present fighting to cease all firing and terminate all military activity immediately". Further, it called upon the parties concerned to start immediately after the cease-fire "the implementation of Security Council resolution 242 in all of its parts."[11]

4. EARLY AMERICAN PEACEMAKING EFFORTS, CAMP DAVID, 1978

Brokered by President Jimmy Carter, the Camp David Accord produced the basis for relatively peaceful relations between Israel and Egypt from that date to the present. These two States were able to agree on many of the divisive issues which today are obstacles to peace between Israel and the PA. The success of the Accord can be attributed to the willingness of the parties to compromise on exceedingly small details.[12]

5. THE SECURITY COUNCIL

Charged by the Charter with the maintenance of international peace and security the Security Council has a clear duty to employ its powers in order to find a resolution to Middle Eastern problems. An examination of the terms of its Resolutions from 1976 down to the present indicates that it has approached its duty on the premise that the Arab-Israeli dispute can be resolved through political processes. Its most assertive measures have been to demand that Israel terminate its attacks on foreign countries, such as Lebanon, and the establishment of a Disengagement Observer Force containing up to 10,000 troops.

For example, Security Council Resolution 425 of March 19, 1978 demanded that Israel respect the territorial integrity of Lebanon and to withdraw "forthwith" its armed forces from the country. The United States supported the resolution. Czechoslovakia and the USSR abstained.

The Security Council addressed the Arab-Israeli conflict in 1980 with the adoption of Resolution 476 on June 30, Resolution 478 on August 20, and Resolution 672 on October 12. As violence increased in the area the Security Council responded by the adoption of additional resolutions. In 1982 the Security Council expressed its grave concern over the deterioration of the situation in Lebanon. It instructed the Secretary-General to induce the two countries to conform to their 1949 armistice agreements. The U.S. voted for the Resolution. Poland and the Soviet Union abstained. However, when the issue was raised as to the participation of the PLO in the debate, without a vote, the United States cast a dissenting vote.

6. RESUMED EFFORTS, 1988, ISRAEL AND THE PALESTINIAN AUTHORITY

During the administration of George H.W. Bush, a plan was devised to secure the implementation of Security Council Resolutions 242 and 338. In March 1988 a special group consisting of the five permanent members of the Security Council and all of the parties to the Arab-Israeli conflict were to meet.

A unique plan to allow for Palestinian representation was devised. Palestinians acceptable to Israel and approved by the PLO were to join the delegation of Jordan. This was intended to facilitate bilateral negotiations between Israel and Jordan, Israel and Lebanon, and Israel and Syria. The focus was to be on finding means for a limited Palestinian autonomy on the West Bank and in Gaza. The participants were not able to devise procedures to move ahead on Resolutions 242 and 338.

On October 12, 1990, the Security Council called to the attention of the warring entities the terms of Resolutions 242 and 338 as the bases for a just and lasting solution of the Arab-Israeli conflict. Numerous resolutions were also adopted calling for the recognition of the sovereignty of Lebanon and dealing with the presence of U.N. peacekeeping forces in the area.

A. Special Meetings

Madrid, 1991

In October 1991 President Bush convened the Madrid Middle East Peace Conference to consider the implementation of Security Council Resolutions 242 and 338. For the first time in history direct peace negotiations took place between Israel and all of its Arab neighbors. There was great hope that long-standing disputes would be resolved. Although the participants were unable to obtain compliance with the two Security Council resolutions the conference did have an impact on politics in Israel. In June 1992 voters provided Prime Minister Yitzhak Rabin with directions to pursue peaceful options.

Oslo, 1993, 1995

This was followed by two sessions in Oslo. The first, in September, 1993, produced an Israeli-Palestinian Declaration of Principles. Based on the theme of "land for peace," it provided for self-government arrangements for the West Bank, Jerusalem, and the Gaza Strip. Israel agreed to withdraw from 13% of the disputed territories. The Declaration also formalized the Palestine Authority. Plans were laid for eventual civilian elections to a Palestinian Legislative Council. Future statehood for Palestine was acknowledged, and promises were made to bring violence and terrorism under control.

The second meeting occurred in September of 1995. The conferees reached agreement on an "Interim Accord," which provided for Palestinian self-rule. It was signed by Prime Minister Yitzhak Rabin for Israel and by Yasser Arafat for the PA. It was a complex and detailed document running to over 400 pages.

The Accord was based on the 1991 discussions in Madrid. The Accord called for the Israeli withdrawal from additional areas, including Hebron. A timetable was fixed for elections to the Palestinian Council and the powers to be exercised by that nascent body. Plans were made for a follow-up meeting, which was prevented by unrest in the area. The Israeli military occupation continued.

3. Wye River, 1998, Washington Accords

The second Oslo meeting was followed by a session in the United States which produced the Wye River Memorandum of October 23, 1998. Entitled "Steps to Facilitate Implementation of the Interim Agreement on the West Bank and Gaza Strip of September 28, 1995" it was designed to allow the Palestinians to have more self-rule. It also called for the parties to carry out reciprocal responsibilities relating to redeployment and security.[13]

At this meeting President Clinton referred to some of his contributions to the improvement of Arab-Israeli relations. These included efforts to improve regional long-term economic growth and the negotiation of an agreement between Israel, Lebanon, and Syria designed to prevent terrorist attacks on Israel from Lebanon. He considered his remaining challenges to include brokering peace talks between Israel and Syria, further normalization of relations between Israel and all of the Arab States, including the termination of boycotts against Israel by Arab States, and the provision of additional aid to the Palestinian Authority.

On October 23, 1998 the Washington accord was signed by Prime Minister Netanyahu and Chairman Arafat in the presence of King Hussein of Jordan and President Clinton. It was the product of the Wye River negotiations, which had taken place during the preceding 10 days.

Commentators have emphasized that the Accord was the product of much courage on the part of the leaders of the three Middle Eastern States. In the view of President Clinton the agreement was good for Israel because of the creation of a comprehensive plan against terrorism, provisions for a support infrastructure, and strengthening of security measures. These included prevention of incitements by the PA against Israel and for the elimination of those articles of the Palestinian Charter calling for the destruction of Israel.

President Clinton found the Accord to be in the best political and economic interests of the Palestinian people. Through the transfer of 14.2% of jointly controlled territory to Palestinian control the PA achieved more political authority in about 40% of the West Bank. The agreement called for the phased release of 750 Palestinian prisoners. The economic future of the Palestinians was brightened with a new airport, an industrial zone, the promise of a seaport, and safe passage between Gaza and the West Bank.

As a part of the transaction President Clinton agreed to address members of the Palestinian Council upon their reaffirming Chairman Arafat's commitments and support for the peace process. He also indicated that, with the support of Congress, funds would be paid to Israel to meet the security costs of redeployment and to the Palestinian Authority to meet the economic costs of development.[14]

The Security Council continued its very high interest in the Middle East and Israeli questions at this time.

For example Resolutions 1223, 1243, 1254, and 1276 dealing with U.N. Observer Forces in Lebanon were adopted in 1999. In 2000 Resolutions 1288, 1300, and 1322 were adopted dealing with the continuation of U.N. Observer forces in Lebanon.

B. Continuing Efforts of the Clinton Administration, 2000

The high expectations generated at Wye River and confirmed by the October, 1998, Washington Accord, were dashed by ongoing violence in the Middle East. This led the United States to resume its diplomatic efforts. Meetings at Camp David were scheduled in July, 2000.

Israel was represented by Ehud Barak, who became Prime Minister in July 1999. The PA was represented by Yasser Arafat. The parties agreed to consider the relevance of Security Council Resolutions 242 and 338.

Prior to the meeting the Clinton administration had prepared a comprehensive peace plan and had obtained Mr. Barak's permission to present it to Mr. Arafat. Among its provisions were a demilitarized Palestinian State consisting of 92% (various figures have been identified) of the West Bank and 100% of the Gaza Strip, subject to adjustments for pre-1956 Israeli territory, dismantlement of most of the Israeli settlements, resettlement for Arabs living in the 8% of the West Bank to be given to Israel, establishment of the Palestine capital in East Jerusalem with Arab neighborhoods in the city to become a part of Palestine's sovereign territory or to have Palestinian "functional authority," Palestine to have sovereignty in one-half of the Old City of Jerusalem, Palestine to exercise custodianship over the Temple Mount, which is known to Muslims as an Haram or Al Sharif, Arab refugees were to be accorded a right to return to the prospective Palestinian State, but not Israel, and a large internationally sponsored rehabilitation program for refugees.

Since the proposal was an extensive one and a breakthrough from previous hardened positions Presidential Clinton expected that it would be subject negotiations. However, President Arafat rejected it immediately. There have been wide speculations for this approach. The most evident one is that Mr. Arafat was counting on demographic considerations, with the expectations that the Arab populations would continue to expand at a rapid rate. One immediate result was the resumption of infada activities in October 2000.

The two entities made grave charges. The government of Israel stated that in killing Arabs it was enforcing a policy of "counterterrorism," and was engaged in "armed force short of war" in order to prevent its own destruction. The Palestinians claimed that their responses were based on Israel's "assassination policy."

The matters soon took an even more ugly turn with the visit of Israel's head of the Likud party, and later Prime Minister, Ariel Sharon, to the Temple Mount in Jerusalem on September 28, 2000. The Temple Mount is one of the holiest areas for three faiths inhabiting Jerusalem. Because of the risks involved he was accompanied by Israeli security forces. When Arabs protested, the Israeli response resulted in many deaths.

General Sharon's action occurred on the day that Israeli and Palestinian officials were meeting in New York for the purpose of finalizing an agreement intended to reactivate the Middle East peace process. Earlier in September during the annual meeting of the U.N. General Assembly President Clinton had asked Chairman Arafat and Prime Minister Barak to defer reaching a political decision relating to Jerusalem and Temple Mount until it was evident that such a decision would receive peaceful approval. With the premediated act of General Sharon the entire peace process was reduced to chaos.

The United States wished to establish the facts of the confrontations. President Clinton in December 2000 invited representatives of the two entities to meet in Washington. This led to a more extended conference in the Egyptian resort of Taba at the end of January 2001. President Clinton had left office at that time and the Bush administration considered a bridging proposal involving concessions on the part of Prime Minister Barak. He was in the midst of a campaign against General Sharon, and did not have popular support nor that of the Knesset. Further, the Palestinian position had hardened since Camp David. With the landslide victory of Sharon in February 2001 the 1991 initiative of Oslo was halted.

C. The Mitchell Committee, 2000–2001

It was considered that all would benefit from a fact-finding committee. The committee consisted of former Senator George J. Mitchell, who became the chairperson, former Senator Warren Rudman, Suleman Demirel, former president of Turkey, Thorbjoern Jagland, foreign minister of Norway, and Javier Solama, the European Union high representative for foreign and security policy. In January 2001 the Bush administration gave it the green light to continue with its work.

The findings of the committee were made public on May 21, 2001. On that date the two Senators issued a joint statement in which they identified their key recommendations. These were: an immediate cease-fire; the total freezing of Jewish settlement construction; resumption of joint security cooperation; denunciation of "terrorism"; the requirement that Palestinian Authority persons should be prevented from firing on Israeli soldiers and civilians; the Israeli military establishment should be required to limit its use of lethal force; and, negotiations should be resorted to in order to resolve the underlying causes of conflict.[15]

The Report recommended that Israel and the PA recommit themselves to the spirit of Sharm el-Sheikh and that they implement the decisions made there in 1999 and 2000,[16] that they should engage in bold action, and that they should act promptly in light of the high level of hostility and mistrust. The principal message of the report, which involved six months of hard work, was that leaders on both sides agreed that

> "In virtually identical words, that life has become unbearable for their people. They said that violence has to end. But it has not ended. It has gotten worse. And it will keep on getting worse unless the government of Israel and

the Palestinian Authority take swift and decisive action to end the violence, rebuild confidence, and resume negotiations."[17]

It was evident to the committee, as it had been long evident to the inhabitants of the area, that a political decision was required. In such a decision, as was indicated, there would have to be a renewed spirit of compromise, reconciliation, and partnership. Only with this outlook would it be possible for negotiations to lead to a just resolution of the chaos that had been imposed upon their lives.

Secretary of State Powell announced immediately the support of the United States for the recommendations contained in the report. He reviewed the report's primary recommendations, and agreed that the two entities should reaffirm existing agreements and undertakings; that they should implement immediately and unconditionally commitments to cease hostilities and to resume security negotiations; that they must engage in confidence building measures through the avoidance of unilateral acts that would prejudice or prevent further negotiations or which would have a negative impact on the prospects for peace, and that in planning for the future they should be attentive to earlier calls for the cessation of hostilities.

The Secretary of State framed the U.S. policy in these words: "We believe that both sides should give every consideration, the most serious consideration, to the committee's recommendations and it is in that spirit that we endorse the report."[18] He added that American diplomats would assist in furthering the indicated goals.

Following his statement he was asked by a newspaper reporter if his expressions constituted a new and more active role on the part of the United States in trying to broker a lasting and just peace in the Middle East. The Secretary responded that the Bush administration had not approached the issues on a detached basis. He stated that the U.S. posture remained "in the same sequence" and it was "not putting forward peace plans today . . . [which dealt with] final status issues."[19]

D. The Tenet Plan, 2001

When the terms of the Mitchell Plan were not implemented because of the ongoing violence in the Middle East, President Bush instructed CIA Director George Tenet to draft a plan to advance the peacemaking process. Issued on June 13, 2001 it was titled "Israeli-Palestinian Ceasefire and Security Plan." The plan consisted of six courses of action to be pursued by a joint security committee. These actions were refinements of the security commitments set forth in the October 2000 Sharm el-Sheikh agreement and as embodied in the

Mitchell report on April, 2001. Resumption of negotiations were conditioned on their being a single week free of violence.

The leaders of the Government of Israel and the Palestinian Authority were not able to obtain a week in which there was no violence. In an effort to advance the plan the Israeli Prime Minister, Ariel Sharon, stated that he would be willing to forego the waiting period. However, by March 2002, Israeli armed forces had again invaded Palestinian areas. At this time PA leader Yasser Arafat's headquarters in Ramallah on the West Bank were under siege and remained so for over a month. Under such circumstances it became impossible to engage in meaningful security planning.[20]

The Security Council on March 12, 2002, taking into account the grave problems of the area, called upon the disputants to "cooperate in the implementation of the Tenet work plan and Mitchell report recommendations with the aim of resuming negotiations on a political settlement."[21]

E. The Zinni Negotiations, 2002

With the terms of the Mitchell report and the Tenet security work plan before him President Bush recognized the need to carry on negotiations to secure their implementation. He designated a retired General, Anthony Zinni, as Special Envoy to deal with the leaders of the Government of Israel and the Palestinian Authority. He met with them and their subordinates in March 2002. The United Nations Security Council on March 30, 2002, aware of the mission of General Zinni called upon the parties to the conflict to cooperate with him in the implementation of the Tenet security work plan. This was considered to be a first step toward the implementation of the recommendations of the Mitchell Committee. The members of the Security Council remained steadfast in their view that the problems of the Middle East could be resolved only through a negotiated political settlement.[22]

7. SECURITY COUNCIL RESOLUTIONS, 2000–2002

A series of resolutions dealing with special problems that have arisen during the Arab-Israeli conflict attest to the violations of international law. Thus, the Security Council on October 7, 2000, after referring to provocations occurring at Temple Mount on September 28, 2000, and resulting deaths, as well as deaths occurring in other areas throughout the territories occupied by Israel since 1967, called upon Israel to abide by its legal obligations and responsibilities in time of war. The Security Council condemned the excessive use of force against Palestinians as a violation of the

Fourth Geneva Convention relative to the Protection of Civilian Persons in Time of War of August 12, 1949.[23]

The Security Council repeated, as it had in so many prior Resolutions, the need for compliance with Resolution 242 of 1967 and 338 of 1973, and the obligation to resolve problems via an active negotiating process.

On March 30, 2002 the Security Council in Resolution 1402 took notice of the suicide bombings being carried out by Palestinians and the military attack on the headquarters of the President of the PA. On April 4, 2002 the Security Council in Resolution 1403 referred to the presence in Israel of foreign diplomats interested in a negotiated peace. These included the U.S. and representatives of both the Russian Federation,[24] and the European Union. The U.N. special coordinator joined the group.

8. NEW LEVELS OF DEATH AND DESTRUCTION, APRIL–JUNE 2002

Just at that time a round of extreme violence occurred at the Jenin refugee camp on the West Bank. Starting on April 3, 2002, and going on for several weeks, fire-fights and bombings occurred, with deaths and destruction of property.

On April 13 the Security Council adopted a resolution calling for an inquiry into the existing situation at Jenin. The United States voted in favor of the investigation. It did so following assurances from the Government of Israel that it would cooperate in the investigation. The Secretary-General appointed a 20 member fact-finding committee consisting of experts in the fields of human rights and refugee problems, including the head of the International Committee of the Red Cross. Only a few military experts were designated. When Israel learned of the composition of the Committee it revoked the permit for the inquiry. Israel also indicated if its attack on Jenin were to be investigated that the U.N. should investigate the support being received by Palestinian terrorists who were engaged in suicide bombings.

On April 30, 2002, after learning of the Israel decision, and knowing that a full inquiry would depend on the cooperation of Israeli authorities, the Secretary-General urged the Security Council to revoke its decision. At that time it was known that the first reported number of deaths had been exaggerated. By May 3, 2002 there was evidence that 54 refugees had been killed and that the death toll for Israel soldiers was 23.

An investigation would have disclosed under what circumstances the refugees lost their lives. Since such persons enjoy the status of protected persons under the 1949 Geneva Convention it would have been necessary to ascertain if war crimes had been committed.

The matter was then reviewed by the U.N. General Assembly. On May 8 it determined that the attack should be investigated. Some States, in voting for the inquiry, considered that the investigation might disclose facts justifying the Israeli attack, such as terroristic activities being staged from that area.[25]

Following the charge that Arafat had responsibility for the violence Israel placed his headquarters in Ramallah under heavy artillery fire. The attack was successful in destroying many of the headquarters buildings, including records and communication systems. Also, at the beginning of April Bethlehem's Church of the Nativity was entered by Palestinians seeking refuge. It came under siege while negotiations were instituted to determine the status of those who had claimed sanctuary. Releases occurred on May 9, 2002, with 13 captives being exiled.

On May 3, 2002 Israeli tanks entered Nablas and destroyed buildings and caused deaths and injuries.

These occurrences involving the devastating use of force by both sides have posed enormous concerns throughout the world. There is great sensitivity concerning attacking a church. The crisis became so acute that Prime Minister Ariel Sharon cancelled an appointment with President Bush prior to their meeting in Washington during the first week in May, 2002.

The enormity of this violence, with its loss of lives and large physical damage and destruction, resulted in a new position on the part of President Bush. According to the U.S. Ambassador to Israel, 1995–1997 and 2000–2001, Martin S. Indyk, in relying on the advice of Secretary of State Powell, the new position was "to move immediately to negotiations—a dramatic shift in the American position over the last 15 months."[26] Ambassador Indyk also took note of the fact that President Bush was the first Republican president "to have committed to establishing an independent Palestinian state."[27]

9. MAJOR MULTILATERAL EFFORTS TO BRING PEACE TO THE MIDDLE EAST

A. Council of Arab States, March 2002

As violence reached new heights in the Spring of 2002, and as the Security Council's efforts and those made by President Clinton and the Bush administration were proving to be wholly ineffective, despite their assertions to the contrary, the Council of Arab States made its policies known. In June, 1996, this body had declared in favor of a just and comprehensive peace in the Middle East. In March, 2002, the Council considered a proposal made by Crown Prince Abdullah bin Abdul Aziz, of the Kingdom of Saudi Arabia.

Its central theme was "land for peace." Thus, Israel was called upon to withdraw "from all the territories occupied since 1967, including the Syrian Golan Heights to the June 4, 1967 lines as well as the remaining occupied Lebanese territories in the south of Lebanon."[28] Further proposals included a solution of the Palestine refugee problem under the terms of General Assembly Resolution 194.[29]

The Saudi Arabian proposal also called for the establishment of a sovereign independent Palestinian state for the territory occupied since June 4, 1967 in the West Bank and Gaza Strip with East Jerusalem as its capital. A critical aspect was the rejection of "all forms of Palestinian patriation which conflict with the special circumstances of the Arab host countries." Following the meeting of these conditions there was to be the establishment of normal relations with Israel within the context of "this comprehensive peace."[30]

In order to promote these objectives it was agreed that the Secretary-General of the Arab League would arrange for contacts with the United States, the Russian Federation, Muslim States, and the European Union.

Prince Abdullah arranged to meet with President Bush on April 26, 2002 to provide him with an official briefing on proposal of the Arab League. Following his meeting with the Crown Prince the President told the press that the United States had a "unique relationship with Israel," which is "one thing the world can count on. It's part of our foreign policy—the Saudis understand that."[31] At the same time President Bush repeated a demand that he had made to the Government of Israel, namely that it should withdraw its armed forces from those areas of Palestinian territory in the West Bank that had been recently occupied.

One aspect of the meeting between the President and the Crown Prince, was the submission of a position paper identifying the Saudi position on eight subjects. They are: the withdrawal of Israel from occupied territory; an end to the Ramallah siege; the creation of a multinational peacekeeping force; the reconstruction of Palestinian areas recently damaged; a renunciation of violence; renewal of efforts to bring both sides into longer-range political talks; an end to Israeli settlement activity in the occupied territory; and a renewed emphasis on the implementation of the Security Council Resolution 242 of 1947.

B. The Bush Proposal, May 2002

On May 2, 2002 a new approach was announced by President Bush to bring peace and security to the area. It was based on the view that a few very powerful countries, through a blending of their outlooks, could produce results which had proven beyond the reach of the United States and the best efforts of the Security Council, which had quite clearly identified the areas of disagreement and distrust.

The proposed new conference would be given the mission of dealing with security and economic issues, with the objective of obtaining a final political settlement. The participants were to be the U.S. Secretary of State, U.N. Secretary-General, the Russian Foreign Minister Igor S. Ivabov, the Spanish Foreign Minister, Josep Pique, and the European Union's foreign policy chief, Javier Solana.[32] In approaching these issues, and in working with Jewish and Arab leaders, the consortium would identify critical areas and fix time-tables. In doing so it would be confronted by the policy announced by Israeli Prime Minister Ariel Sharon. He has "insisted that full security guarantees must precede any talk of a political settlement."[33] The magnitude of the difficulties facing the Prime Minister have been indicated by the adoption, which occurred over his objections, by his Likud party of a resolution stating "no Palestinian state will be established west of the Jordan River."[34]

In his "Rose Garden" speech of June 24, 2002 President Bush pointed to the need of the Mid-East leaders to address core issues, to resolve all claims, and to bring the conflict to an end. He stated: "This means that the Israeli occupation that began in 1967 will be ended through a settlement negotiated between the parties, based on UN Resolutions 242 and 338, with Israel withdrawal to secure and recognized boundaries."[35] He also pointed to the need to resolve questions concerning Jerusalem, refugees, and peace between Israel and Lebanon and between Israel and Syria.

The Bush administration during 2002–2003 frequently expressed its concern over the high level of violence in the area. Demands were made on President Yasser Arafat to contain suicide bombers engaged in terrorist activities. Prime Minister Ariel Sharon was also counseled to engage in restraint. The Bush administration expressed dissatisfaction with President Arafat's inability to restrain his supporters and indicated that it favored the appointment of a new prime minister. This resulted in the approval on April 29, 2003 by the Palestinian parliament of Mahmoud Abbas to that position. It occurred after weeks of wrangling between Arafat and Abbas over the composition of the new cabinet.

C. The Road Map, March 2003

On March 17, 2003 Secretary of State Powell announced that a new peace plan, referred to as a "road map." for the two entities would be released. It had been crafted by the United States, the United Nations, European Union, and Russia. Both Israel and the Palestinian Authority had been consulted prior to its finalization. Its major purpose was to create a Palestinian State by 2005.

The plan, referred to as "A Performance-Based Roadmap to a Permanent Two-State Solution to the Israel-Palestinian Conflict" was published on April 30, 2003.[36] Its scope and purpose are: "This settlement will resolve the Israel-Palestinian conflict, and end the occupation that began in 1967, based on the foundations of the Madrid Conference, the principle of land for peace, UNSCRs 242, 338, and 1397, agreements previously reached by the parties, and the initiative of Saudi Crown Prince Abdullah—endorsed by the Beirut Arab League Summit—calling for acceptance of Israel as a neighbor living in peace and security. This initiative is a vital element of international efforts to promote a comprehensive peace on all tracks, including the Syrian-Israeli and Lebanese-Israeli tracks."[37]

The five page plan was described as "a performance-based and goal-driven roadmap, with clear phases, timelines, target dates, and benchmarks aiming at progress through reciprocal steps by the two in the political, security, economic, humanitarian, and institution-building fields, under the auspices of the Quartet (the four proponents)." The roadmap called for the parties to perform their obligations in parallel, unless otherwise indicated.

The roadmap identified three recognized landmarks. The first beginning at once and lasting through May of 2003 provided for the "ending of terror and violence, normalizing Palestinian life, and building Palestinian institutions." Selected for special attention were security, Palestinian-institution building, humanitarian response, civil society, and settlements. The two parties were to conform to measures specified in the 2001 Tenet work plan and the Mitchell Committee Report of 2001. To the latter which called for the freezing by Israel of all settlement activity (including the natural growth of settlements) was added the requirement that there be a dismantling of the settlement outposts erected since March 2001.

The second dealt with transition within the June-December 2003 time frame. It was to begin following Palestinian elections and to end with the possible creation of "an independent Palestinian State with provisional borders and attributes of sovereignty. . . ." During this period emphasis was to be placed on security cooperation by the two entities, the continued normalization of Palestinian life and institutions, ratification of a democratic Palestinian constitution, the formal establishment of the office of prime minister of Palestine, and the consolidation of political reform. As a reward to Palestine for its favorable performance the Quartet were to promote international recognition of the State of Palestine including possible UN membership.

If both entities had demonstrated political and economic progress the Quartet was to convene an international conference, which was to occur in consultation with Israel and Palestine. The inclusivety of the agenda was reflected in the announced goal of a comprehensive Middle East peace, including Syria and

Lebanon, the restoration by Arab States of pre-intifada links to Israel, such as trade offices, and the revival of multilateral discussions on regional water sources, environment, economic development, refugees, and arms control.

The third landmark was a permanent status agreement and end of the Israeli-Palestinian Conflict during 2004–2005. Under the auspices of the Quartet a second international conference, in consultation with the parties, was to be convened early in 2004. Agreement was to be reached on a "final, permanent status resolution in 2005." The earlier "provisional borders" of the two entities were to be replaced by final and permanent "borders." The final comprehensive Middle East settlement would deal with Jerusalem, refugees, settlements, and relations with Syria and Lebanon.

The roadmap, in dealing with the ending of the occupation which began in 1967, specifically required "an agreed, just, fair, and realistic solution to the refugee issue, and a negotiated resolution on the status of Jerusalem that takes into account the political and religious concerns of both sides, and protects the religious interests of Jews, Christians and Muslims worldwide, and fulfills the vision of two States, Israel and sovereign, independent, democratic and viable Palestine, living side-by-side in peace and security." These goals were to be achieved ''as soon as possible."

This quite remarkable document is important on several accounts. It constituted firm proof of America's good intentions and efforts to bring peace, order, and the benefits of democracy to the warring entities. It was promulgated at a time when polls indicated that the Israeli public was increasingly attentive to the need for a peaceful resolution stemming from the violent deaths of their countrymen and Palestinians. In the 31 months prior to the new proposal 700 Israelis and more than 2000 Palestinians had been the victims of terrorism and governmental responses.

The new initiative was related to the military successes of the coalition States in the war against Iraq. That event had demonstrated a commitment to eliminate terrorists. The United States stressed that its troops would be withdrawn as soon as possible. At the same the United States announced the withdrawal from Saudi Arabia of military forces. These actions would deprive Osama bin Laden of some of his anti-social ammunition. American diplomats in Jordan, Lebanon, and Syria made the point that the United States was embarking on an even-handed approach without special benefits for Israel.

Timing of the initiative took into account that George W. Bush, Mahmoud Abbas, and Ariel Sharon would probably hold office for the next several years and could bring continuity to the negotiating process. All three had recognized the urgency of resolving the issues. All were in agreement that the status quo was not acceptable. All held the view that it would be impossible to achieve a comprehensive peace in the area under the existing circumstances.

In order to obtain success for the plan the Bush administration began a series of "confidence building" measures. They were designed to provide assurances to the immediately affected parties and also to neighboring States which would benefit from the restoration of peace and security. In May and June, 2003 President Bush and Secretary of State Powell traveled to Europe and to the Middle East to demonstrate, as had President Clinton, their personal involvement in the success of the plan.

Their commitment was rewarded when Prime Minister Sharon, after listening to Israeli politicians, who were divided on the issue, decided at the end of May following an affirmative vote of his cabinet to proceed with the plan. However, in the vote of 12-7 Sharon was obliged to accept a number of reservations. This was followed by a statement acknowledging the need to end the "occupation" of Palestinian areas, while at the same time calling for Prime Minister Abbas to prevent the terroristic activities of his followers.

The Bush administration has also seen the need to persuade Arab leaders to support the plan. To build their support he attended a meeting in Sharm El Sheik on June 3, 2003. At that time Arab Heads of State announced that they were taking steps to end the flow of financial support for the Palestinians through the Palestinian Authority thereby preventing Hamas, Islamic Jihad and other militant groups from engaging in terroristic activities.

In his address to the Arab leaders President Bush stated: "Tomorrow, I will go to Aqaba for a meeting with Prime Minister Sharon, Prime Minister Abbas, to discuss the responsibilities of the Israelis and the Palestinians. And if all sides fulfill their obligations, we can made steady progress on the road toward Palestinian Statehood, a secure Israel and a just and comprehensive peace." Each of the Middle East leaders promised to take steps to achieve the final goal. Prime Minister Sharon indicated Israel would dismantle some settlement outposts. Prime Minister Abbas pledged "full efforts" to end Palestinian violence. President Bush stated that implementing the road map was a "matter of the highest priority."

In relying on a principle invoked when confronted by major challenges the United States turned to multilateralism. The broad composition of the Quartet while giving considerable credence to its proposals indicated the United States could not shoulder all of the responsibilities and burdens required for success. What, for example, will be the role of the Quartet during Phase One if the government of Israel is not able to dismantle settlement outposts erected since March 2001 or freeze all settlement activity as delineated in the Mitchell Commission Report? Will the Quartet plan be able to withstand the analysis voiced by its early critics, for example, the charge that it is unfair in one or more of its provisions or assumptions?

While Israel and Palestine may both be generally committed to the peaceful resolution of their problems, one or the other, or both, may feel disadvantaged when the Quartet's general teams are converted into formal agreement composed of many details. At this point the members of the Quartet will have to respond.

In the United States the plan may become a part of domestic politics, with the input of private lobbies and congressional posturing already visible.

In the recent past the American people have been made increasingly aware of terrorism, violations of basic Human Rights, and the dangers posed by rogue States equipped with WMD. These events, when coupled with the huge economic costs associated with their control, may produce a greater interest in international affairs on the part of the voting public. This may have some impact on all American foreign policies and particularly those fixing the future of Israel and Palestine.

Within the U.S. government the Department of State will undoubtedly have the principal responsibility in working out the final details. The Department of Defense, however, has demonstrated a substantial interest in foreign policy issues. If the government is able to approach this function with the same tenacity exhibited by prior administrations it may be able to contribute to world order with the United States being a major beneficiary.

Factors, if maximized, leading to the success of this foreign policy, include building on the concept of land for peace. Prime Minister Sharon has given approval to the plan "in principle," and indicated in April and June of 2003 that there should be "concessions" respecting West Bank settlements. But, he also is building new "Berlin-like" walls. Recent polls in Israel reveal a strong and growing sentiment in favor of negotiated resolution of the enfeebling dispute. The inutility of armed force to resolve this conflict has provided a premise for action.

Prime Minister Abbas at the end of April told members of his government that "armed chaos" was not acceptable. He added that the "unauthorized possession of weapons" by Palestinians would not be tolerated. He states that terrorist attacks were poisoning the chances for a resolution of the standoff. He expressed the hope that the terms of the Quartet's plan would lead to serious negotiations.

Israel is in a more favorable position to negotiate following the downfall of Saddam Hussein and as a result of collective and separate pressures being addressed to Syria. Prime Minister Abbas had distanced himself from Saddam Hussein. This has been interpreted as a sign for Middle Eastern States to encourage the establishment of friendly relations between the Palestinian and Israeli governments.

The United States can expect that the reduction of terrorists in the Middle East will enhance its own security. The United States will have to demonstrate that its long and active support for Israel will not prevent it from providing the same kinds of support for the Palestinians. Arab States will take note and they may have a better understanding of U.S. foreign policy. This will be especially true if the final negotiations find mutual commitment to Oslo principles. So that none of the principal actors may feel slighted it will be necessary for the United States to maintain a strong and consistent pressure on the most directly affected States.

Russia's support will affect the outcome. It can actively seek support from U.N. members. Its involvement will allow Russia to address its own internal unrest and also to build the good relations with the United States that existed before Russia contested the timing and means to address Iraq in March 2003.

Factors which minimize the prospects for the performance-based road map are also identifiable. The possession and use of weapons in the Middle East has become a natural aspect of daily behavior. To restrict them only to security forces and to control their improper use will take time. In order to reduce concerns over personal insecurity it will be necessary to develop police professionalism and the reduction of street violence by partisans.

There was a legitimate fear during the tenure of Prime Minister Abbas that he might not be able to rein in terrorism which had become a way of life in the area. While he had denounced terrorism "by any party and by all its forms," it was not clear whether he would be undercut either actively or passively by Yasser Arafat, who had not relinquished fully the status he has occupied in the Palestinian Authority. Abbas was replaced in October 2003 by Ahmed Qurei, who, like his predecessor hoped to implement a more conciliatory relationship with Israel. He had indicated a willingness to resume peace talks if violence could be brought under control and there were a halt to the building of Jewish settlements in Palestine. He endeavored to persuade militant groups in Palestine to stop attacks on Israelis.

It is not clear that Ariel Sharon can muster enough support to meet the settlement conditions laid down for Phase I of the Plan. The people of Israel understand that the Palestinian population is growing more rapidly than theirs. There is concern that one day there may not be enough land to go around.

It will be a huge task to convert the Plan's principles into operative small print. Whether all of the affected parties have the staying power to see it through remains to be seen. Unfortunately, in a long contest, those promoting negative positions frequently are able to prevail.

Ever since the United States accorded recognition to the new State of Israel in 1948 it has been one of its chief supporters. The question never has been whether the United States should abandon Israel. That policy has endured to the present.

The formidable efforts identified in the foregoing were brought to a sudden halt on April 14, 2004. On that date, following a meeting between President Bush and Prime Minister Sharon, the former disclaimed the principal provisions of the road map for the Middle East. The existing position that all Jewish settlements in the Palestinian territories were an impediment to peace was abandoned. Accepting Sharon's proposed withdrawal of Israeli settlements from the Gaza strip and parts of the West Bank, the United States declared it would not object to the continued presence of a number of large Jewish settlements in the West Bank. President Bush also agreed with Sharon's declaration that Israel would reject the Palestinian demand for a "right to return" to occupied territories. The retention by Israel of West Bank settlements would bring to an end the historic efforts to achieve the condition of peace for land via negotiations.

In setting forth this vast modification of earlier American positions President Bush observed that it is "unrealistic to expect the outcome of final status negotiations will be a full and complete return to the armistice lines of 1949." He was influenced by the conclusion that Arafat was not inclined to bring terrorism under control and his inutility as a negotiator.

The dismay of the Palestinians was shared in many Arab countries which had considered the road map as the most viable process for success and that in time moderate Palestinians would prevail over the policies of Arafat. Also of concern to many was the manner in which the subject was approached. This unilateral American procedure replaced the multilateralism called for in relevant Security Council Resolutions, as well as the cooperative approaches leading to the promulgation of the road map. Observers have called attention to the suddenness, influenced by major concerns over wide-spread terroristic activities, with which a major U. S. foreign policy can be modified.

On May 2, 2004 Israel's Likud Party rejected the Sharon plan despite the public backing of President Bush. The vote repudiated the effort to make territorial concessions and abandon some Jewish settlements. The White House responded by stating that its view had not changed. Future consultations with Israel will occur. The UN Secretary-General invited the sponsors of the road map to meet. New initiatives will be required to revitalize disengagement plans.

The question remains whether effective international institutions will be willing to address proposals for an independent Palestinian State. It is fortunate that a consortium of States, including the United States, has accepted that responsibility. Their cooperative involvement will remain necessary particularly in light of the disposition attempted by the American President and the Israeli Prime Minister on April 14, 2004. In recent years it has been proved that NATO countries could contribute materially to the internal stability of the former Yugoslavia. Can the Quartet or others provide the same benefits for the Middle East? There is every reason for the United States to exercise leadership in this complex and sensitive situation. The joint statements of the two leaders on April 14, 2004 will not dispose of the matter.

10. POTENTIAL FOR CONSTITUTIONAL CONFLICT IN THE UNITED STATES

Almost immediately following the meeting between the President and the Crown Prince Abdullah in 2002 members of the Congress, who were becoming more alarmed over the upward spiraling of death and destruction in and around Jerusalem, began to draft resolutions so that their feelings might be known, both at home and abroad.

Following the adoption of numerous Congressional resolutions the University of Maryland's Program on International Policy Attitudes conducted a poll of 801 randomly selected Americans asking about the findings.[38] The Maryland poll takers compared their results with one taken by Fox News poll on April 16 and one taken by CBS News poll on May 13–14. The Maryland poll provided more options than those conducted by Fox and CBS.

Among the highlights were the views that, contrary to Prime Minister Sharon's beliefs, "only 17% of the survey's respondents said that Israel's struggle with the Palestinians was best understood as a Mideast version of the war on terrorism,"[39] and that the "vast majority thought the conflict was best described as a struggle between two national groups over the same piece of land."[40]

The majority of the respondents "blamed both sides equally for the failure to reach peace and expressed equal levels of frustration with each side. Of the remainder, less than one-third favorably viewed the Israelis; significantly fewer had a favorable view of the Palestinians."[41]

On this the authors commented: "Such even-handedness suggests a policy course quite different from one infused with the certain convictions of Congress."[42] With regard to the involvement of the United States in the area's problems, it was reported that two-thirds of the respondents did not wish the United States to take sides in the conflict, that the United States should put more "pressure on both sides to declare a cease fire and return to the negotiation table,"[43] that they favored President Bush's "renewed commitment to finding a peaceful solution in the Middle East,"[44] that "two-thirds approved the president's call for Israel to withdraw its military forces from Palestinian cities,"[45] that seventy-five percent "supported Secretary of State Colin Powell's recent meeting with Arafat, and a similar number backed Bush's endorsement of a Palestinian state."[46] The authors concluded that the respondents had a "more nuanced . . ., more complex and less partisan . . ." viewpoint than that held in Congress.[47] Further on the basis of outlooks disclosed in the survey it was suggested that the White House was in a position to exploit new opportunities in dealing with Middle Eastern problems. Among these could be the formalization of a plan by the United States to convene a new conference for the late summer or early fall of 2002.

The Constitution, Article II dealing with executive powers, assigns to the President the first authority to formulate and to administer U.S. foreign policy, subject to the right of the Senate to approve or disapprove of the formal international agreements submitted to it for advice and consent. The President also appoints ambassadors and other high foreign policy officials. Their appointments are subject to legislative approval, but serious opposition to such appointments rarely occurs. Together they constitute the basis for presidential action in this area. His war powers add a further dimension.

The two houses of the Congress play a substantial role in the implementation of U.S. foreign policy. Much of foreign policy involves the selection of beneficiaries for very substantial foreign aid, and since the appropriation authority is vested ultimately in the Congress (the President proposes and the Congress disposes), Congressmen have opportunities to provide funds for their favorite causes. Addressing this issue Presidents, often sadly, have called attention to a de facto presence in the Congress of 535 would-be secretaries of state.

Congressmen, addressing the wishes of their constituents and agreeing that their wishes are meritorious, although undoubtedly taking into account certain political realities, have been quite generous in their foreign aid grants. To facilitate improved economic conditions there is also a United States-Israel joint economic development group composed of public and private sector participants. The domestic implications of international beneficence demonstrate the overlap between legislative and executive claims to authority.

11. CONCLUSION

In assessing U.S. foreign policy in relation to the ongoing and ever-increasing violence in the Middle East it may be helpful to examine two situations. The first is how the United States acting alone can help in establishing livable, and, hopefully, peaceful relationships. The second is to determine what international procedures, if and when employed, are most likely to facilitate a resolution of problems dating back to 1948 and before.

To be successful there is the need for a U.S. plan of action or a program. This would consist of an assessment of existing facts and concerns and an acceptance that common goals are realizable. It would consist of management procedures built on a valid framework for action. It would consist of effective supporting measures.

In considering who should be involved and the availability of procedures it would have to be assumed that the two warring entities would be responsive. Jewish and Arab leaders should take into account the monetary costs to the United States of providing support in the past at the $3–4 billion plus year rate to Israel and the $100 million plus year rate to the Palestinian Authority. These sums have been augmented annually in recent years. There is a possibility, perhaps remote, of a lesser future drain on the U.S. Treasury. This would require cooperation on an economic jump-start for the area.

More importantly, a stable and democratically oriented Middle East would contribute very substantially to the protection and preservation of basic Human Rights which have been so seriously eroded by terroristic activities conducted by Palestinian suicide bombers and the attacks mounted by the government of Israel, using aircraft, artillery, tanks, and small arms fire against the residents of Palestinian refugee camps and numerous Palestinian cities and towns.

In responding to such events the United States, in the process of establishing a foreign policy, must ask itself whether it can justify support for those entities which knowingly engage in conduct which produces an escalation in violence. Such violence should raise grave doubts as to the utility, morality, and legality of such supportive actions. America's attack on terrorism must be consistent if it is to be effective. America must also insist on compliance with the laws or customs of land warfare.

Perhaps the kindest characterization of U.S. foreign policy toward the Middle East since 1948 is that has been a policy of good intentions. Another appraisal is that the United States has guided violence to the point where an international solution could be acceptable. Despite the dramatic, innovative, and costly efforts on the part of the United States during these long years, it can only be concluded that up to the present the U.S. policy has been one of failure.

Perhaps it could not have been otherwise. The very rapidly expanding populations of the Jewish and Palestinians have imposed economic problems. The natural resources of the area are limited. On the other hand, the inhabitants often are highly talented and well qualified to engage in advanced scientific, technological, humanitarian, and business activities. The violence has discouraged tourism, one of Israel's major sources of foreign exchange. The religious, cultural, and economic differences and disparities have all conspired to deflate many traditional expectations.

Although the U.S. enjoys membership in the U.N. Security Council it has not over the years taken an effective multilateral operational approach to the problems of the Middle East. Only in recent years, and then only with respect to a foreign policy addressed to the danger of terrorism, has the U.S. paid much heed to the benefits of a global approach.

Except for the subject of terrorism, and CBN weapons and particularly during the present Bush administration, many European States have expressed concern over U.S. foreign policies, although recently the European Union has expressed an interest in trying to work with the Bush administration with regard to the Middle East. At the Moscow May 24, 2002, signing of the Nuclear Arms Treaty the United States and Russia declared they would cooperate in trying to bring an end to terrorism. Even so, influential students of foreign policy have chided the United States for not having formulated or actively supported an international framework for the Middle East. Implicit in these criticisms has been the view that only a global approach has any chance of success.

The global approach must employ the same criteria as those available to the United States. Further, it must identify "bottom line" national commitments. For the world at large this requires an extended assurance of economic help and military direction. For the two parties it would be mandatory that they absolutely refrain from all forms of violence toward each other. Following the achievement of consensus by the international organization, there will be the need to identify the effective supporting measures. In theory such measures can be implemented by the pertinent institution, or there may be an assignment of such functions to members or even to just one member.

When States seek to resolve disputes and take collective decisions in a political context, there is always the prospect that physical force may be required, and this means that States, as the only legitimate possessors of such means, must be turned to for implementation. Assuming the best scenario, States with suitable means may agree to provide the required sanctions, but, they may not see fit to do so.

In that event a single powerful State may be requested by the international institution to volunteer or to engage in sanctioning measures. But, this may not be entirely satisfactory to a rival State which may have special interests or involvements in the affected area.

Thus, at least three practical scenarios could exist. They would allow for different procedures. In the first the Security Council, following consensus, could assign the sanctioning authority to a State or States. In the second the State considering itself at risk or best qualified to stabilize the problems could act unilaterally.

In the third situation two or more outside, e.g., non-party States, could act either on behalf of the Security Council or could volunteer to act for the community at large.

In an ideal situation the collective judgments of the Security Council members, followed by an assignment of responsibility or responsibilities to a State or States would be preferred. As an alternative approach, where there is an evident need to resolve a problem, the presence of a strong national capability, independently promulgated, but wholly consistent with the collective judgment, might be the process to produce the required changes.

By way of contrast the multilateral approach stresses the collective judgments of the participants. It could allow for sanctioning actions to be delegated to one or more States. Even though the United States might consider that its independent judgment should preempt a collective decision with regard to the Middle East, the nature of that situation is so wide-ranging that one dominant State can not be expected to resolve the matter.

In the light of the failure of a U.S. foreign policy that materially serves the interests of the United States in the Middle East, it may be desirable for it to focus more on the multinational institutions capable of responding to the challenge than to try to continue its effort to be the dominant, although seemingly reluctant, actor in the situation. In weighing this prospect occupants of the White House will have to consider the responses likely to be generated in the Congress of the United States and by public opinion.

A meaningful foreign policy for the Middle East must be based on cooperation between the President and the Congress. Together they must determine the degree of U.S. involvement. In the event they make decisions, which are then implemented, and the decisions turn out to be counterproductive, adequate turnaround time must be allowed for readjustments. Despite the most recent U. S. intitiative the relationships between the parties in and concerned with the Middle East will continue to be in flux.

DISCUSSION QUESTIONS

1. American presidents from Jimmy Carter to George W. Bush have made peace in the Middle East a part of their political agendas. Compare the depth and timing of their commitments.
2. In comparison with other major States, such as China, Russia, Britain, France, and Germany, why shouldn't they, rather than the United States, seek to bring peace to the Middle East?
3. How does the United States involvement in the Middle East peace process fit in with the view that the United States prefers to approach foreign policy issues from a unilateral perspective?
4. What relevance do the laws or customs of war, particularly the Third Geneva Convention, have with regard to the use of force by the Israeli army in the West Bank?
5. What influence will the force used by the coalition States in Iraq have on Arab States as they assess the 2003 Roadmap for the Middle East?
6. In recent years the United States has threatened to cut off foreign aid and subsidies to countries which opposed its policies. Do you have an opin-

ion whether this kind of diplomacy is likely to be applied to either Israel or the Palestinian Authority?

7. If the essentials of the Roadmap are agreed to, who (countries or international organizations) should be authorized to secure the implementation of the agreement?
8. At what point, if at all, should the theme of "land for peace" be introduced into the Middle East peace negotiations?
9. What is the optimum way for the president and members of congress to adjust whatever differences they may have relating to bringing an equitable peace to the Middle East?
10. Make an appraisal of how future leaders of Israel and Palestine will be able to respond to the efforts of Sharon and Qurei.

NOTES

1. H.W. BRANDS, INTO THE LABYRINTH: THE UNITED STATES AND THE MIDDLE EAST, 1945–1953 (1993).

2. T. SEGEV, ONE PALESTINE, JEWS AND ARABS UNDER THE BRITISH MANDATE (2000).

3. Yasser Arafat was elected on October 12, 1993 by the Central Council of the Palestine Liberation Organization (PLO) to be president of the Palestinian National Authority (PNA). In a general election held on January 20, 1996, he was reelected. He is the chairman of executive committee of the PLO, and in 1968 founded the Fatah. On March 30, 1989 the Central Council of the PLO selected him to be president of the State of Palestine. The *de jure* status of such statehood is questionable, although such statehood on a *de facto* basis may exist. Palestine is not a member of the U.N. nor does it exchange diplomatic representatives with U.N. members. Mr. Arafat, as a result of his leadership roles in the PLO and in the PNA does speak authoritatively for the Palestine people. The extent of his power and influence can be measured by the means employed by Israel to force him to adopt policies more acceptable to Israel. An account of two Palestinian religious-based terrorist movements can be found in Y. ALEXANDER, PALESTINIAN RELIGIOUS TERRORISM: A PROFILE OF HAMAS AND ISLAMIC JIHAD (2002). B. WASSERSTEIN, ISRAELIS AND PALESTINIANS, WHY DO THEY FIGHT? CAN THEY STOP? (2003).

4. M. Grossman, "American Foreign Policy for the 21st Century," Speech, October 29, 2002. Mr. Grossman is Under Secretary for Political Affairs, U.S. Department of State. The theme areas are global war on terrorism, globalization, free markets, democracy, cultural and national identities, and American power. www.state.gov/p/14810.html. For an assessment of the operational aspects of the Bush foreign policy see C.L. Powell, "A Strategy of Partnerships," 83 *Foreign Affairs*, No. 1, 22 (January/February 2004).

5. W.J. Burns, "Rebuilding Hope: American Middle East Policy in the New Years Ahead," Speech, November 8, 2002. Mr. Burns is Assistant Secretary of State for the Bureau of Near Eastern Affairs, www.state.gov/p.nea/rls/rm/15087pf.html.

6. "President Bush Calls for New Palestinian Leadership," Speech, June 24, 2002. Yasser Arafat in May, 2002 had pledged that his security forces would be ordered to prevent all terroristic activity. At that time Mr. Bush referred to this as "an incredibly positive sign." *Los Angeles Times*, A9, May 9, 2002. This appraisal was revised as a result of large-scale violence in 2001 and 2002 carried out by Palestinians over whom Mr. Arafat may not be able to exercise control. K. Shikaki, "Palestinians Divided," 81 *Foreign Affairs*, No. 1, 89 (January–February 2002). Suicide bombings have been referred to by G. Luft in an article entitled "The Palestinian H-Bomb," 81 *Foreign Affairs*, No. 4, 2 (July-August 2002).

7. *Ibid.*

8. I.J. BICKERTON AND C.L. KLAUSNER, A CONCISE HISTORY OF THE ARAB-ISRAEL CONFLICT, 3rd Edition (1997).

9. G. VON GLAHN, LAW AMONG NATIONS, 6th Edition, 770–771 (1992).

10. For the American record of its diplomatic activities following the adoption of this Resolution reference may be made to 20 *Foreign Relations of the United States, 1964–1968* (2001). It covers the period of 1967–1968.

11. China did not participate in the voting. W.E. Griffith, "The Fourth Middle East War, The Energy Crisis," 17 *Orbis* 1161 (1974).

12. Http://usinfo.state.gov.regional/nea/summit/cdavid.htm, September 17, 1978; LINDA B. MILLER, JIMMY CARTER AND THE CAMP DAVID ACCORDS (1992).

13. The White House, Office of the Press Secretary, *The Wye River Memorandum*, http://www.state.gov; ROBERT O. FREEDMAN, ed., THE MIDDLE EAST AND THE PEACE PROCESS, THE IMPACT OF THE OSLO ACCORDS (1998).

14. The White House, Office of the Press Secretary, 9, October 23, 1998.

15. Http://www.cnn.com/2001/WORLD/meast/05/21/mitchel.rudman.statement/.

16. There were two meetings at Sharm el Sheik. The September 4, 1999 accord was entitled "Memorandum on Implementation of a Timeline of Outstanding Commitments of Agreements Signed and Resumption of Permanent Status Negotiations between Israel and the Palestinian Liberation Organization." The agreement referred to Palestine as an "entity," not a State, and dealt with such matters as borders, Jerusalem, water, settlements, refugees, and security. The second meeting in October 2000 followed the eruption of hostilities following the presence of General Sharon at Temple Mount on September 28, 2000. Its focus was on emergency measures to quiet the violence.

17. *Supra,* 15 at 3.

18. *Ibid.*

19. Department of State, *Press Release*, May 21, 2001.

20. http://www.mideastweb.org.Tenet.htm.

21. S/RES/1397, March 23, 2002.

22. Security Council Resolution 1402, March 30, 2002.

23. Security Council Resolution 1322, October, 2000.

24. The United States and Russia had agreed that they would benefit from a common position on the Middle East situation. In a joint statement by Secretary of State Powell and Russian Foreign Minister Ivanov they called on both sides to "take parallel and reciprocal steps to reduce the violence, calm the situation and create an environment in which both sides can find a way forward. The U.S. and Russia welcome the decision by the parties to resume security cooperation and urge them to seek ways to promote a political dialogue on a mutually acceptable basis." U.S. Department of State, *Press Release*, April 12, 2001. Both countries at that time urged the hostile parties to proceed by way of "direct negotiation," and added that they were ready to stand by to assist their efforts. *Ibid.*

25. On April 19, 2002, the Security Council in Resolution 1405 asked the parties to facilitate the work of the International Committee of the Red Cross and the U.N. Relief and Works Agency for Palestine Refugees in the Near East. It referred to the need to ensure the safety of civilians, and to respect the universally accepted norms of international humanitarian law.

26. Digest of Speech to Town Hall of Los Angeles on May 21, 2002. 65 *Town Hall*, No. 10, 40 (May 21, 2002).

27. *Ibid.*

28. http://www.mideastweb.org/SaudiPeace.htm.

29. For discussions on this subject see *Yearbook of the United Nations, 1946–47*, 277–294 (1947).

30. *Supra*, note 28.

31. *Los Angeles Times*, A10, April 27, 2002.

32. *Los Angeles Times*, A10, May 3, 2002.

33. *Ibid.*

34. *This Week*, 3, May 24, 2002.

35. *Supra*, note 6.

36. U.S. Department of State, Press Statement, www.state.gov/r/pa/prs/s/2003/20062pf.htm.

37. *Id.* at 1.

38. S. Kull and S. Telhami, "Public, Leaders a Poll Apart," *Los Angeles Times*, M2, May 26, 2002.

39. *Ibid.*

40. *Ibid.*

41.*Ibid.*

42.*Ibid.*

43.*Ibid.*

44.*Ibid.*

45.*Ibid.*

46.*Ibid.*

47.*Ibid.*

Chapter IX

The Iraq Crisis of 2002–2004: Legal and Political Issues

1. INTRODUCTION

The Iraq crisis produced three major legal and political issues. First the negotiations leading to and the meaning to be given to Security Council resolution 1441 of November 2002 created substantial discord. Second, a major challenge to the legality of the use of force by the coalition States erupted and the Charter's principle of collective security has been denigrated. Third, highly controversial views exist as to the role of Iraq's new leaders, the United States, and the United Nations in the building of a democratically oriented Iraq. Entailed were claims over managerial authority and huge rehabilitation and reconstruction costs.

When George W. Bush became President there was little evidence that he had cause to be dissatisfied with his father's decision not to bring down the regime of Saddam Hussein. Not until after 9/11/01 did he demonstrate pressing concerns over two situations that have produced major changes in American foreign policy. One is the worldwide war on terrorism. The second is the effort to rid Rogue States of the capacity to produce and use weapons of mass destruction (WMD), particularly chemical, biological, and nuclear (CBN) weapons.

Attention was drawn to Saddam Hussein because of his violations of over 10 Security Council resolutions dealing with Human Rights and armaments adopted between 1990 and 2002. Such resolutions also dealt with the repression of minorities in Iraq, the failure to return prisoners of war, attempted assassinations of the Emir of Kuwait and the President of the United States, the removal of weapons inspectors in 1998, and illicit trade in the oil-for-food program.

Concerns in the White House began to mount when Saddam Hussein adopted a plan of promising to implement UN resolutions but consistently failed to do so. He argued that the presence of inspectors violated national sovereignty. This was interpreted as an intentional plan of delay so as to allow for further weapons' development.

In his State of the Union address on January 29, 2002 President Bush labeled Iraq and North Korea as "an axis of evil." In his address at West Point on June 1, 2002, he called for a unilateral response to threatened dangers if the UN failed to act. When he spoke to the members of the General Assembly on September 12, 2002 he questioned the relevance of the UN if it could not deal effectively with Iraq's failure to comply with Security Council Resolutions.

Unlike the West Point address with its emphasis on unilateral action his remarks at the UN emphasized international cooperation. He referred to the need for early action. In his words: "We cannot stand by and do nothing while dangers gather."

He affirmed that the United States would join in a common approach. It was clear that if the world organization failed to respond to threats presented by Iraq, that the United States reserved the right to invoke a policy of unilateralism. Unfortunately, major countries failed to heed this warning.

On September 12, 2002, Secretary-General Kofi Annan addressed the General Assembly. There were striking differences between the approaches of the two leaders. The Secretary-General stated that he was a "multilateralist by precedent, by principle, by charter and by duty." He called for States to be committed to the world rule of law. In his words: "All States have a clear interest, as well as a clear responsibility, to uphold international law and maintain international order." He argued that multilateralism best serves the interests of all States, particularly regarding terrorism and compliance with arms control and disarmament requirements. In directing his remarks to Iraq his words were different, but the meaning of them was not far removed from the outlook of President Bush. The Secretary-General stated: "I urge Iraq to comply with its obligations for the sake of its own people and for the sake of world order. If Iraq's defiance continues, the Security Council must face its responsibilities."

On October 7, 2002, President Bush told an audience in Cincinnati that Iraq was a grave threat to the peace, and that the "danger grows worse with time." The United States relied on CIA and Department of Defense sources to identify the nature of Iraq's WMD arsenal. Subsequent events have disclosed that their advice was faulty or mistaken. Grave errors were made. However, top administration officials continued to defend until 2004 the view that the Hussein regime possessed the capability to produce weapons of mass destruction.

These concerns led to the adoption on October 10, 2002, of a Joint Congressional Resolution, H.J. Res. 114, entitled "Authorization for Use of Military Force Against Iraq." The President was authorized to use the Armed Forces "as he determines necessary and appropriate in order to (1) defend the national security of the U.S. against the continuing threat posed by Iraq; and (2) enforce all relevant UN Security Council resolutions regarding Iraq." Presidential action was conditioned on his notifying Congress that U.S. reliance on diplomacy or other peaceful activity was ineffective in reducing the Iraqi threat or would not be effective in securing the implementation of Security Council resolutions. Further, the President was expected to continue actions designed to eliminate terrorist organizations. The resolution acknowledged that the United States would have humanitarian responsibilities in Iraq following the use of force against Saddam Hussein.

Iraq's potential for producing great harm and its avowed animosity toward the United States have produced different policy recommendations. For example, Vice President Cheney in August of 2002 suggested early unilateral action citing the inutility of resuming the weapons' inspections and concerns over Security Council politics. Members of the Cabinet were supportive, but wished to explore diplomatic alternatives first.

Within the administration different reasons were put forward for action against Iraq including President Bush's call on July 8, 2002 for a regime change. Close advisors grounded their advice on Iraq's prospect for or possession of nuclear and other mass destruction weapons and means for their delivery, long-time violations of relevant Security Council resolutions, the sanctuary accorded to Al Qaeda terrorists, support for Hamas bombers, efforts to assassinate former President Bush, and the mistreatment of minorities in the country. Although the emphasis changed from time to time, the cumulative weight of these concerns suggested a proper response.

2. THE PROBLEM OF NO-FLY ZONES

At that time the American leadership was influenced by the Iraq response to the aerial reconnaissance being conducted in Iraqi air space. Following the close of hostilities in the Gulf War the Security Council on April 5, 1991 had adopted resolution 688[1]. It dealt with ending the repression of civilian populations and for access by international humanitarian organizations to all in need of assistance in Iraq. In order to protect Kurds living in the north and Shiite Muslems in the south the United States, the United Kingdom, and France established "no fly" zones.[2] Iraq aircraft were warned not to enter such zones. Aircraft of the three countries were fired upon by Iraqi surface to air missiles and antiaircraft artillery. The allied aircraft targeted ground-based air defense and communications facilities, and kept Iraqi aircraft on the ground. Iraq continued to fire on American and British aircraft until the coalition attack on March 19, 2003.

Generally speaking the presence of allied aircraft in Iraqi air space would constitute a violation of its territorial integrity. This has raised the question whether there were legal grounds for the allied aerial presence and activities.

Several arguments have been raised. Iraq has asserted its sovereignty and the provisions of Article 51 of the Charter as a prohibition against a foreign "armed attack." The allies countered that the mere presence of its aircraft did not constitute an "armed attack," while also claiming their responses have been within the legal bounds of proportionality. At the same time Iraq could raise the claim of proportionality by claiming that its response to the hostile presence of allied aircraft was limited, reasonable, and not excessive. The allies stated that their military presence in Iraqi air space dated from 1991, when the Security Council adopted Resolution 688, that the Council had been aware of overflights since 1991, and had taken no action requiring the termination of the surveillance and the resulting use of force.

In May, 1999, during the debate on Security Council Resolution 1241 dealing with the humanitarian crisis in Iraq objections were voiced relating to the overflights. Russia condemned "the illegal pretext of the no-fly zones" and aerial bombardments. China called for the halt of bombing missions in the zones. They noted that while Resolution 688 referred to Iraq's duty to end the repression of its civilian population and the duty to provide access by international humanitarian organizations, that there was no reference to the use of force against Iraq. The flights continued since the Council did not order their termination.

3. THE SECURITY COUNCIL RESOLUTION 1441; ANTECEDENTS AND CONSEQUENCE

On September 26, 2002, the United States and the United Kingdom tabled a draft resolution with the Security Council. With amendments it became Resolution 1441 on November 8, 2002. The U.S.-British draft was wide-ranging. It declared that Iraq was in "material breach" of all Security Council resolutions relating to Iraqi use of force since 1990 and demanded compliance, called for armed escorts for returning inspectors, for an account of the prisoners held by Iraq following the Gulf War, and for authorization to use "all necessary means" in the event Iraq failed to agree. The latter was intended, in diplomatic terminology, to mean an armed attack.

The proposal's blunt terms, occasioned in part by the demands of the "hard-liners" in the Bush cabinet, had several effects. It demonstrated that the president's speeches, going back to his State of the Union address on January 29, 2002, in which Iraq was listed as an "axis of evil" nation, and those of June 1 at West Point, of September 12 at the UN, and of October 7 at Cincinnati, had to be taken seriously. It caused serious discomfort in countries that had acceded to Iraq's extended non-compliance with Security Council resolutions. It produced an awareness that the United States was considering taking unilateral measures against Iraq. It allowed for a reevaluation of the central peacekeeping and security functions of the UN and its utility if members failed to take forceful sanctioning measures for fear of confrontation.

With the ice broken the United States, following consultations with the United Kingdom, submitted a formal draft resolution to the Security Council on October 23, 2002. It referred to all previous relevant Council resolutions and to Iraq's extensive obligations dating back to 1990. Attention was drawn particularly to eight resolutions, 660, 661, 678, 686, 687, 688, 986, and 1284. Resolution 678 of November 29, 1990 had authorized member States to "use all necessary means . . . [to uphold and implement earlier 1990 resolutions]" and "all subsequent resolutions," and to "restore international peace and security in the area." The continuing applicability of these terms to the power of the Security Council to respond to the threats presented by Iraq in 2003 was to become a central issue in interpreting resolution 1441 in the early spring of 2003.

The American-British draft also called particular attention to resolution 687 of April 3, 1991. It also referred to non-compliance with the duty to disclose "all aspects" of Iraq's programs to develop weapons of mass destruction and ballistic missiles with a range greater than 150 kilometers. It also referred to terrorism and non-cooperation with the UN Monitoring, Verification, and Inspection Commission (UNMOVIC) and the International Atomic Energy Agency (IAEA). Attention was drawn to Resolution 688 of April 5, 1991 dealing with violations of the Human Rights of civilian populations.

The proposed resolution noted the "material breach" by Iraq of numerous promises to allow for weapon's inspections, including private meeting with officials and other persons, and entry into physical facilities including "any sites and buildings, including immediate, unimpeded, unconditional and unrestricted access to Presidential Sites equal to that at other sites . . ."

The draft provided that the foregoing agencies "shall have the right to be provided by Iraq the names of all personnel associated with Iraq's chemical, biological, nuclear and ballistic missile programs and the associated research, development and production facilities." The agencies were to be granted the authority to destroy or render harmless all prohibited weapons and production facilities.

The draft resolution called for the Secretary-General to notify Iraq of its terms with a deadline of seven days to acknowledge its receipt. The proponents based this mandate on the Charter-based authority of Article 51 to "restore" international peace and security.

A critical provision of the draft appeared in paragraph 4. It recited that "false statements or omissions in the declarations submitted by Iraq pursuant to this resolution and failure by Iraq at any time to comply with, and cooperate fully in the implementation of, this resolution shall constitute a further material breach of Iraq's obligations."

The October 23, 2002 draft paragraph 11 called for a "report" from UNMOVIC and the IAEA of any "interference by Iraq with inspection activities, as well as any failure by Iraq to comply with its disarmament obligations, including obligations regarding inspections under this resolution." In draft paragraph 12 the Security Council was to convene "immediately upon receipt of a report in accordance with paragraph 11 above, in order to consider the situation and the need for full compliance with all of the relevant Security Council resolutions in order to restore international peace and security."

In the original U.S.-British draft paragraphs 11 and 12 were separate requirements, e.g., in paragraph 11 a report and in paragraph 12 a meeting to consider what to do in light of the report. Draft Paragraph 11 did not refer to the imposition of the sanctions. Draft Paragraph 12 made reference to the authority of the Security Council to "restore" international peace and security, thereby allowing for sanctions.

The negotiators were in agreement that Iraq's position was untenable, and that corrective measures were necessary. They had to decide what action, including military force, could be employed, if Iraq were to impede the work of the inspectors. The proposed resolution called for the use of force if Iraq interfered with weapons inspections or did not comply with its disarmament obligations.

In Resolution 1441, paragraph 11, followed the language of the American-British proposal. Paragraph 12, made explicit reference to paragraph 4 which imposed strict duties on Iraq to provide full and truthful information and to cooperate fully in the implementation of the resolution. Failure was to constitute "a further material breach of Iraq's obligations." The monitors were to report such lapses to the Council for assessment. "Restore" had been employed in the draft since it is found in Articles 39, 42, and 51 of the Charter. As finally adopted paragraph 12 required that Security Council "to convene immediately upon receipt of a report in accordance with paragraphs 4 or 11 above, in order to consider the situation and the need for full compliance with all of the relevant Council resolutions in order to secure international peace and security." This change did not relieve the Security Council from bearing its responsibilities in imposing sanctions on a State which was in "grave breach" of duties set forth in its own resolutions.

Resolution 1441 stated that Iraq had not provided an "accurate, full, final, and complete disclosure of all aspects of its programs to develop weapons of mass destruction and ballistic missiles." Failure also included nondisclosure of "their components and production facilities and locations." The resolution cited non-compliance with commitments on terrorism and the repression of Iraq's civilian population. Also listed was the failure to provide access by international humanitarian organization to all those in need of assistance in Iraq.

During the negotiation of Resolution 1441 the question arose whether it would serve automatically as the legal basis for sanctions against Iraq or whether the adopted resolution would require a new vote following the receipt of the reports of the inspectors. To make clear the need for a second vote France, Russia, and China on November 8, 2002 issued a statement indicating the exclusion of "any automacy in the use of force." They also expressed their satisfaction that this interpretation had been confirmed by declarations from the American and British representatives. They had pledged to resume discussion before engaging in the use of force. The three countries also recorded their understanding that the U.S. and the United Kingdom accepted that the "goal of the resolution is the full implementation of the existing security council resolutions on Iraq's weapons of mass destruction disarmament."

On November 8, 2002 resolution 1441 was adopted by a unanimous vote. It repeated the reference to "previous relevant" resolutions contained in the American-British draft. References to the possession by Iraq of WMD and the violation of Human Rights were critical in establishing the legitimacy of the war.

The unanimous vote in favor of Resolution 1441 was a victory for the peace-keeping procedures established in the Charter. It was a defeat for go-it-alone preferences. At the end the United States, vastly influenced by its Secretary of State's recourse to diplomatic negotiations, was able to energize efforts for corrective actions. However, if it had not been for the more militant early demands by the President, reinforced by the Vice President and the Secretary of Defense, the prospects for a valid compromise on the timing of sanctions, would not have occurred. The United States adopted a global approach with the goal being to destroy the power base of Saddam Hussein.

Attached to the Resolution was correspondence between Hans Blix, representing the UNMOVIC, and Mohamed El Baradei, head of the IAEA with General Amir H. Al-Saadi, advisor to the President of Iraq. It described the conditions under which inspections and verifications were to occur.

Syria had agreed to Resolution 1441 following assurance from the United States that there was no truth in Iraq's claim that the United States was engaged in an anti-Arab campaign. Secretary of State Powell promised Syria that the United States would participate in a Security Council meeting if the inspectors rendered an adverse report on Iraq.

However, during both the negotiations leading up to the adoption of Resolution 1441 and in subsequent statements made by the Secretary of State, the United States "made it absolutely clear that we did not believe that the resolution as finally passed would require a second resolution to allow for sanctions against Iraq."[3]

Following the adoption of 1441 the 19 members of NATO on November 21 pledged to take "effective action to assist and support the efforts of the United Nations" to ensure Iraqi compliance without conditions or limitations.[4] On November 22 President Bush and President Putin issued a statement calling on Iraq to "cooperate fully and unconditionally" with the Resolution.

UNMOVIC and the IAEA were instructed to return to Iraq with the consent of Iraq. Inspections began on November 24, 2002. In his report of February 14, 2003, Hans Blix, the Chief U.N. arms inspector reported that his team had not found a "smoking gun," that Iraq's response to the inquiry "requires more than the opening of doors," and added that "many prescribed weapons and items are not accounted for." Specially noted by Mr. Blix were "anthrax, the nerve agent VX and long range missiles."

Secretary of State Powell characterized the monitoring system as one where the inspectors should not be required to discover needles in hay stacks, but rather where Iraq was obliged to disclose the facts identified by the Security Council. Other international leaders concurred as to the burden of proof.

In his February 2003 report the head of the IAEA found that there was "no evidence of ongoing prohibited nuclear or nuclear-related activities in Iraq." His organization had conducted 177 inspections beginning on January 27, 2003, with Iraq providing "immediate access to all locations." However, the Blix team in addressing the capabilities of Iraq's missiles found that some had a range of more than 150 kilometers and were in violation of resolution 687.

Mr. Blix, anticipating that the reports would be seen as incomplete, addressed the question of how much more time was needed. He responded that it depended on the task to be addressed. He mentioned the elimination of weapons of mass destruction, disarmament, and the need for monitoring to insure that no new prescribed activities occurred. The resolution contemplated that more time for inspections might be required. However, paragraph 5 of Resolution 1441 fixed February 28, 2003 as the date for the monitors to "update" the Council.

In January 2003 the United States pointed to the failure of Iraq to disclose the nature and quantity of its military arsenal. Its increasingly public alarm frightened France, Germany, and Russia.

In order to forestall any action deemed by them to be precipitous on February 10, 2003, these countries issued a joint statement saying that the potential of 1441 "has not been fully exploited," while also noting that the past and ongoing inspections "have already produced results."

They wished to continue the inspections including a "substantial reinforcement of their human and technical capacities through all possible means and in liaison with the inspectors."

Ultimately the role of inspectors was to become crucial. Hastily gathered and positioned in unfamiliar surroundings they needed time to make objectively supportable and confirmable findings. It was understood that unless Iraq were willing to provide critical data the monitors would be obliged to search for an extended period of time. The United States and its allies considered the passage of time as dangerous since this would allow Iraq to improve its military position and the prospect of its threat to use WMD.

With the unanimous adoption of Resolution 1441, with its recitation of the relevant Iraq-oriented resolutions dating back to 1990, augmented by the new proposals and memoranda of February-March 2003, it had become evident that members would have to review the Council's voting procedures set forth in Article 27 of the Charter. Of vastly more importance was whether the Iraq situation, as interpreted by France, Germany, and Russia, was grave enough to challenge and destroy the UN's principle of collective security and the UN as an instrumentality charged with the maintenance of international peace and security.

President Bush and President Chirac appraised the facts differently with the former calling for a deadline and the latter demanding an extended fact-finding period. The latter urged that recourse to force, as a final alternative, be delayed. The vagueness of French proposals made it difficult for the coalition States and their supporters to know how to respond within the principles of the Charter when the charge of aggression was at issue.

In order to save the Charter and at the same time avoid the delaying tactic favored by Mr. Chirac, it was suggested that he articulate an acceptable standard of proof that would be applied to the findings of the inspectors. It would be one, which if met, that would justify the adoption and implementation of military measures designed to remedy an admittedly dangerous situation. To avoid the consequences of the often repeated statement by the United States that it was prepared to engage in preventive or anticipatory action it was necessary that the French standard of proof be announced immediately.

Refusal by France and its supporters to provide specific criteria would lead to the view that the underlying purpose of their position was to avoid the imposition of force on a guilty Iraq. It could also be justified on the moral ground that the use of force against a government would certainly imperil thousands of innocent civilians.

What at first seemed to be restricted to the issue of timing erupted into a challenge to the Charter's principle of collective security. Two fundamental issues were presented. The first was addressed to the scope of 1441, particularly the continuing applicability of the referenced resolutions. The second consisted of the often repeated statement of the United States that it had the legal right to engage in anticipatory or preemptive measures despite the understanding that resolution 1441 called for consideration of the reports of the monitors before there could be the use of force.

By February, 2003, it was becoming clear that Resolution 1441, which had been hailed as proof of the acceptance of collective security, and as practical means to reduce the Iraqi threat, was faltering. While there was little doubt that Iraq had misbehaved very badly and that there was not a substantial legal basis for challenging the legitimacy of relevant Security Council resolutions, yet American fears as to the presence in Iraq of WMD and the intent to make use of them had not been diminished.

Serious questions were raised by many as to the utility and the legality of the use of armed force against Iraq. There were grave doubts whether international peace and security would be served by the precipitous use of armed force while the monitors were still searching and whether the final decision on the use of force should be that of the UN or of countries that considered themselves to be threatened. The wisdom of 1441 was under siege. Doubt existed whether the monitors could provide persuasive reports by February 28.

To address this matter members of the Security Council began to consider additional resolutions. This brought into focus the prospect of vetoes or, alternatively, the failure of a proposal to receive the required number of votes.

Convinced that there was an urgent need to apply Resolution 1441 the United States, the United Kingdom and Spain on February 24, 2003 proposed an implementing resolution. It recited Iraq's non-compliance with all "previous relevant" council resolutions and the dangers to international peace and security presented by the proliferation of WMD in Iraq. It called for full compliance with the relevant resolutions and expressed a determination to "restore international peace and security in the area." The proposed resolution employed "restore" rather than "secure," which was used in 1441. The proposal concluded with the statement: "Describes that Iraq had failed to take the final opportunity afforded to it in resolution 1441 (2002)."

It did not use the terms armed force or war. However, in light of the use of "serious consequences" and "material breech" to describe Iraq's failure to comply with 1441, the prospect for the use of military force was evident. The proposal did not set a specific date, which remained open to negotiation. Nonetheless it was understood by all that "the clock was running."

On March 5, 2003 the foreign ministers of France, Germany, and Russia issued a statement in which they reviewed the application of Resolution 1441. They stated that their common objective was to achieve the full and effective disarmament of Iraq. They expressed the hope that by peaceful means there could be "a comprehensive settlement for the Middle East" through putting together a general framework for the area "based on stability and security, renunciation of force, arms control and trust-building measures."

In arriving at this position they called attention to the accomplishments of the inspectors, while at the same time calling for Iraq to cooperate more actively with the efforts to "fully disarm" that country. They also urged that the inspections be speeded up and rendered more effective. This was to be accomplished on a program by program basis by prioritizing remaining issues, and at each point the establishment of a "detailed timeliness." These considerations resulted in a declaration by the three countries asserting they "will not let a resolution pass that would authorize the use of force." They explicitly referred to their status as members of the Council and their readiness to assume all of their "responsibilities on this point."

This statement has been criticized for being overly general and vague as it addressed policy considerations. Why, it has been asked, did it not identify with specificity the proof of the presence of the WMD that the monitors would have to meet in order to satisfy them that such weapons were actually present? The monitors, with such guidance, would be able to make their reports, which might then be used in determining on military action against Iraq. The three countries identified the continuity of the Council's involvement when they referred to the goal of achieving the full and effective disarmament of Iraq in accordance with relevant Security Council resolutions. They concluded that priority means "would have to be achieved peacefully through the inspection regime," with the military option being "only a last resort." This outlook was based on the view the inspections had not provided sufficient evidence that Iraq was still in possession of WMD or intended to use them.

In support of this approach the three urged that the "unity of the Security Council must be preserved," and, at the same time the pressure on Iraq must be increased. The three countries proposed a more precise program of inspections, in accordance with resolution 1284, to which France had initially abstained. Reports were to be made to the Council at periodic intervals with one report to be submitted 120 days "after the adoption of the program of work according to resolution 1284."

On the whole no urgency was seen for the completion of the inspections. Thus, the memorandum proposed that "inspections should be given the necessary time and resources. However, they cannot continue indefinitely." The memorandum considered that the foregoing plus a "military build-up [would] provide a realistic means to reunite the Security Council and to exert maximum pressure on Iraq."

On March 7, 2003, considering the intransigence of Iraq and fearing the delays contained in the foregoing proposals, the U.S., the United Kingdom, and Spain restated their position. They fixed March 17, 2003 as the date for Iraq to meet the "final opportunity" afforded by Resolution 1441 to meets its obligations under existing resolutions.

However, Iraq was to be given time beyond the March 17 deadline if it were able to provide the Council with information allowing it to conclude that it had "demonstrated full, unconditional, immediate and active cooperation in accordance with its disarmament obligations under Resolution 1441 (2002) and previous relevant resolutions." The proposal of the coalition countries also required Iraq to yield possession to the UN inspectors of "all weapons, weapon delivery and support systems and structures, prohibited by Resolution 687 (1991) and all subsequent resolutions, and all information regarding prior destruction of such items. . . ." They suggested that a vote should take place during the week of March 9.

France, which had been uneasy about resolution 1441 from the outset, was the first to denounce the coalition proposal. President Chirac, encouraged by Germany and Russia stated that the deadline of March 17 was unrealistic. He considered the employment of armed force to be inopportune, and that the effectiveness of the Council required decisions by consensus. Commentators have also pointed to internal factors affecting the French response including the presence in France of a Muslim population consisting of about 20% of its residents, and important commercial interests in Iraq and other Middle Eastern and North African countries. Strong anti-war activities in France and throughout the world and concerns over the increasing hegemony of the US affected his thinking. He based his opposition on the need to subscribe to the principles of law and morality. He suggested the availability to France of the veto.

While calling for more time to complete the work of inspection, President Chirac also pointed to the need to continue cooperation against terrorists and the need to focus more intensively on relations with Pakistan, Iran, and North Korea.

The Russian Foreign Minister on March 10 also indicated his country would vote against the March 7 proposal of the U.S., U.K., and Spain. In doing so France and Russia failed to pursue the invitation contained in the "final opportunity" coalition proposal. If the coalition proposal were passed it would automatically allow for the use of armed force against Iraq unless a member of the Security Council offered a new resolution which was adopted before the March 17 deadline. It would have to provide according to the coalition that Iraq had "demonstrated full, unconditional, immediate and active cooperation in accordance with its disarmament obligations. . . ." If such a proposal were introduced by the European States, and if the United States and the United Kingdom considered that it was not factual, then they might either vote "no" or exercise their vetoes. If this were to occur they, and their allies, would be able to employ armed force, subject to the legal limitations dealt with below.

Russia's veto threat to the deadline resolution was based on the need to continue inspections, that military action on the part of the United States and its allies would result in a war against Iraq, and could trigger unpredictable consequences. The Russian officials also pointed to the hegemonic tendencies of the United States and that, while the positions of the three European countries might not modify the U .S. proposed action, that each would not have to experience the criticisms of the United States alone.

In an effort to refine the Security Council's central role on March 12, 2003 the United Kingdom put forward a six-point "benchmarks" program for Iraqi compliance. It was designed to obtain the support of undecided members of the Security Council.

The proposal called on President Hussein to make a TV statement that Iraq possessed a concealed arsenal and that he had made a "strategic decision" to surrender it to the UN. He was to notify Iraqis that failure to engage in the turnover would be a crime. He was also to ensure the adoption of comprehensive laws making the production of WMD a crime. Thirty key Iraqi scientists were to be allowed to go to Cyprus for interviews with UN inspectors. Biological and chemical weapons were to be delivered to inspectors or destroyed. The means used to manufacture such weapons were to be disclosed. A commitment to destroy banned missiles was to be made, and there was to be an accounting of drone aircraft. Failure by Iraq to comply with these measures would result in enforced disarmament. In order to allow for a consideration of the proposal the United States indicated a willingness to suspend the date for compliance from March 17 for as long as a week.

The French government on March 13, 2003 rejected the plan on the ground that if it were rejected by Iraq it would allow for "automatic recourse to war" without further action by the Security Council. The British viewed this as a failure on the part of France to avoid the prospect of the use of armed force.

By March 14, the United States believing that France, Germany, and Russia would oppose both the coalition proposal and the separate one of the United Kingdom, began to focus on acquiring the support of nine members of the Security Council so that the United Nations would continue to be engaged. President Bush embarked on a diplomatic effort to obtain support for a resolution, based on the reports of the inspectors, authorizing the Security Council's approval of the use of armed force. The United States again referred to Security Council Resolution 687 (1991) creating the cease fire in the Gulf War. As previously noted it required Iraq to destroy its biological and chemical weapons with failure being a "material breach" constituting legal grounds for the use of armed force.

Before embarking on a U.S. led military attack on Iraq on March 14 President Bush announced a further meeting with the United Kingdom and Spain to make a "last push" for peace. It had become evident to the three allies that the quest for nine members to support either Resolution 1441 or any other resolutions calling for an early deadline for Iraq's compliance had been unsuccessful. They then announced on March 17 they would no longer seek approval of their latest resolution.

In his briefing on March 17 the Secretary of State referred to the joint proposal of March 7. He stated that it was not a resolution "that we believe was necessary" to implement resolution 1441. Rather, he said, it was a "resolution" that would help some of our friends to show to their publics and to the world that we had taken one last step, we had made one last effort to see if Saddam Hussein would come into compliance."[5] The United States did not ask for a vote on the proposed resolution. It was allowed to die because of its built-in date of March 17 and because of resistance by members of the Security Council. The maneuvers of the outside three might have proposed a delay in the attack on Iraq forces. They were a challenge to the stature and influence of the United States.

At that time the United States also made a major statement on Israel and Palestine. It has been construed as an effort by the United States to keep the anti-Iraq coalition of Arab States from splintering and being helpful in the contest with Iraq. It was also announced that the U.S. would make public a plan for the creation of a Palestinian State by 2005 on land controlled by Israel in the West Bank and the Gaza Strip. This resulted from the announcement by President Arafat that a prime minister was being appointed and would be confirmed.

The inability of the United States to gather nine votes meant that diplomacy had failed. Perhaps this was preordained in the light of the national prejudices and diplomatic mistakes on the part of the permanent members of the Security Council. The United States previously had lost much political capital through its unilateral approach to many critical issues, excluding that of terrorism. It had transgressed against an outlook which many countries, especially France, were very sensitive about, namely, a unanimously interpreted Security Council Resolution 1441 in which Iraq would be given a "final opportunity" to meet U.S. disarmament demands going back to 1990 or to "face serious consequences."

As previously suggested, a rational approach to the use of Security Council authority is through the formulation of "benchmarks" by its members for countries chargeable with misconduct. Such lists have been suggested by the United Kingdom, Canada, and others. It would have been desirable to provide a reasonable opportunity to respond to consensus-based benchmarks, taking into account the most recent reports of the UN inspectors, and allowing for a reasonable time for a response before reaching "a final decision." The decision of the coalition States to go to war was made without specific authorization of the Security Council. It did not adopt a resolution implementing Resolution 1441 relying on reports from the appointed monitors. Nonetheless, it is important to understand the legal and political arguments addressed to it since they involve the ongoing peacekeeping responsibilities of the United Nations.

4. LEGALITY OF COALITION ACTION UNDER RESOLUTION 1441

Resolution 1441, with its reference to all relevant prior Security Council resolutions, was intended to provide the legal basis for the UN's employment of armed force against Iraq. When threats to veto subsequent implementing proposals were made the question arose as to the necessity of such resolutions. Coalition States decided that the Charter and resolution 1441 provided legal authority for them to employ armed force against Iraq. The extent of the legal authority created and conferred in resolution 1441 has produced a critical legal debate having vast policy ramifications. It has centered on the fact that the resolution did not expressly state that armed force could be applied to the transgressions of Iraq. The resolution used "serious consequences," "material breach," and "all necessary means." It restated and reconfirmed the action-based provisions of previously adopted Security Council resolutions.

There can be no doubt that the UN Charter constitutes the world's supreme law, subject to meanings to be accorded to it as a result of the conditions that have emerged during the more than half a century since it became operative.

One approach to the meaning of Article 51 is to read the term "armed attack" literally. Opposed is an interpretation holding that a State threatened with a WMD attack can act preemptively to protect itself.

Supporting the literal reading of Article 51 the Secretary-General on March 10, 2003, stated if the United States were to attack Iraq alone or without the approval of the Security Council that it would violate the Charter. This interpretation of the Charter has received the approval of many of the world's international lawyers, especially if their legal training were in countries following the civil law system. They point to the need for all States, weak and powerful, to be subject equally and evenly to the rule of law. They assert if one State consulting only its own interests engaged in the use of armed force this would destroy any prospect that the law may be applied fairly and beneficially for all.

In accepting that general proposition, the coalition States made an effort to except Iraq from that principle. They pointed to the international use of force in such situations as Kosovo when Russia was threatening to veto any military action, as well as the numerous situations were States acting under the aegis of humanitarian intervention have employed armed force.

In other instances neither States nor the UN acted to prevent genocidal massacres, as in Rwanda by the Hutus and the Tutsis. In such situations passive States have been faulted for their inaction.

In arriving at a judgment relating to the conduct of a particular State it is also necessary to examine its historical record. Has it achieved the reputation of an aggressor, or has it fostered humanitarian benefits and repatriated its troops when law and order has been restored? Also to be considered is the duration of a State's unlawful conduct, which in the case of Iraq can be traced back to 1990.

Taking the foregoing into account, and relying on the relevant Resolution, is has been asserted that the provisions of the Charter relating to the relations of States in the areas of international peace and security must be accorded a value-oriented interpretation rather than a strictly literal one. The proponents of this point of view start by accepting the applicability of the Charter. In their view Iraq had violated Security Council resolution 660 of August 2, 1990 which had determined that the invasion of Kuwait constituted a breach of international peace and security as identified in the Charter.

This and all of the other resolutions dealing with the action or inaction of Iraq are treated as a closely-knit fabric in which all of the resolutions are considered applicable. Supporting this approach is the fact that each resolution repeats and reaffirms the continuing applicability of earlier resolutions. Thus, 1441 referred to 10 previous relevant resolutions including 678 of November 29, 1990. The latter demanded that Iraq "comply fully with resolution 660 (1990) and all subsequent relevant resolutions and decides, while maintaining all its decisions, to allow Iraq one final opportunity, as a pause of good will . . ." to withdraw its forces from Kuwait. Resolution 678 authorized member states to "use all necessary means to uphold and implement resolution 660 (1990) and all subsequent relevant resolutions and to restore international peace and security in the area."

Resolution 1441 also made reference to Resolution 687 of April 3, 1991. It affirmed 13 prior resolutions and referred to the formal cease-fire between Iraq and Kuwait as set forth in Resolution 687. Resolution 687 also imposed on Iraq the duty to destroy, remove, or render harmless, under international supervision chemical and biological weapons and ballistic missiles with a range greater than 150 kilometres. It imposed the duty to eliminate all actions, methods, and practices of terrorism. It announced its continuing jurisdiction to take such steps as "may be required for the implementation of the present resolution and to secure peace and security in the region."

Resolution 1441 stated that Iraq "has been and remains in material breach of its obligations under relevant resolutions, including resolution 687 (1991), in particular, through Iraq's failure to cooperate with United Nations inspectors and the IAEA, and to complete the actions required under paragraphs 8 to 13 . . ." which refer to the disposition of the identified weapons.

The question has been raised whether the inability of the Security Council to respond to the reports of its weapons monitors as indicated in paragraph 12 of resolution 1441 would prevent the use of force by the coalition States against Iraq acting without specific Security Council authorization in order to implement the foregoing resolutions. A valid response depends on whether resolution 687 was legally applicable in 2003 and, if so, whether it could be invoked prior to the council's approval or disapproval of the reports to be presented by the monitors.

The status of Iraq's compliance on March 17, 2003 with resolution 1441 depended on whether on that date Iraq were still required to meet the terms of resolution 678, and the terms of resolution 687 as well as the terms of 1441 which referred to the failure of Iraq to comply with the disarmament provisions of that resolution. The extent of such compliance had been reported to the Security Council by its arms monitors in February, 2003.

On March 17, 2003 there was some doubt whether the monitors had discovered biological and chemical weapons. They had found weapons capable of firing nuclear weapons beyond the permitted range.

Legal opinions have identified the status of compliance by Iraq with the relevant resolutions. The Attorney General of the United Kingdom on March 17, 2003 issued an opinion, referring to the above resolutions. It was his conclusion that "it is plain that Iraq has failed so to comply and therefore Iraq was at the time of resolution 1441 and continues to be in material breach." He concluded that the authority to use force established in resolution 678 on November 29, 1990, which was never rescinded, was valid in March, 2003. On

March 20 Britain's representative to the Security Council submitted a letter to the same effect. On the same date the United States representative submitted a statement calling attention to the on-going validity of resolution 678. This was confirmed by Secretary of State Powell when he stated that Iraq's "flagrant violations of obligations that it had entered into over the past 12 years" justified the use of force. There was no reference in the British and American opinions to a regime change.

Secretary Powell in interviews conducted on March 24 and 25 stated that resolution 1441 "established more than adequate justification with its underlying resolutions, 678 and 687, to support what we are doing." He added that "We need no further legitimacy for what we are doing."

In his interview on NPR on March 25, Secretary Powell indicated there would be no need for a resolution adopted after a regime change had taken place to provide legitimacy for the original military action. He added that "as we move forward, clearly, coalition leaders will be in charge of Iraq initially." He also pointed out that any country which "wants to contribute in some way will be able to do so."

In urging support for this interpretation of resolution 1441 he stated that the action of the coalition States would serve the interests of all countries. He asked that this be considered when plans for the rebuilding of a defeated Iraq were being formulated. The timing and the extent of the contributions of non-coalition States will undoubtedly be the subject of critical negotiations in the post-war period.

Disagreement with the British and American interpretations has been vigorously asserted. It has been noted that while resolution 678 had authorized the use of force to remove Iraq from Kuwait and to restore international peace and security in the area the other 1990 resolutions did not explicitly authorize force to overthrow Saddam Hussein.[6] It has also been suggested that the American president in 1990 did not regard the existing resolutions as mandates to attack Baghdad.

Those taking issue with the coalition governmental positions have urged that the UN resolutions lack precision and that before force could be employed that there would have to be more detailed resolutions.

These objections have been rejected by lawyers who consider that resolution 678, which had demanded that Iraq comply fully with resolution 660, and which authorized the use of "all necessary means" to secure its implementation, was applicable in 2003 to deal with Iraq's behavior. Support is also found in resolution 687 which called for Iraq to rid itself of WMD. It was asserted that Iraq was in violation and that this allowed unilateral sanctions to be employed against the offender. Reference was made to President Clinton's ordering an air attack on Iraq in December 1998 when Iraq removed the UN arms inspectors. Reference was also made to post-Charter uses of armed force to protect community interests.

It is in situations such as these that extreme tensions exist between law and policy. Violations of law are expected to be punished. The question is "by whom?"

Nonetheless, it was urged that the efforts of the U.S., United Kingdom, and Spain to secure nine votes for their March 7 proposal was an acknowledgment that it was necessary to go beyond 1441 and all of the other existing resolutions, in order to provide legal authorization for the use of force. It was thought that nine supportive votes would signify a more authoritative position to overcome the negative positions. If it were not possible to obtain nine votes for the allied proposal it could be urged that the critical legal element of consent for the use of force was lacking.

Opposed to this approach was the argument of the U.S., the United Kingdom, and Spain that they were following standard U.N. procedures, and were giving diplomacy a final chance. This point of view was consistent with their belief that it was not necessary to obtain a new authorization for the use of force, since the pre-1441 resolutions were reaffirmed in resolution 1441. This position was a challenge to any permanent member wishing to secure the adoption of a new resolution repealing Resolution 1441. In the post-1441 negotiations neither the coalition countries or the outside three were able to marshal sufficient votes to repeal 1441 or to meet the criticisms of their adversaries. This standoff posed a grave test to the Charter's principle of collective security.

In March 2003 practical considerations affected the conduct of the members of the Security Council. The reports of its monitors were not complete with no certainty when new reports would be available, and, if available, if they would be accepted as conclusive by members of the Security Council. The coalition forces were in an attack mode, and weather conditions were likely to become more hazardous. The position of the United States was not consistent. It had promised that following reports from the monitors that a second vote in the Security Council would occur before an attack would occur. China, France, Germany, and Russia were aware when they voted for resolution 1441 that the United States had reserved the right to engage in unilateral action. It was no secret that the United States in addressing the feared threat posed by Iraq had announced support for the controversial concepts of anticipatory and preventive self-defense.

On March 17, 2003, President Bush having failed to persuade nine members of the Security Council of the gravity of Iraq's capacity for harm warned Saddam Hussein to abdicate within 48 hours or to face certain destruction. The president stressed that the risks of inaction were greater than the risks of war. He stated that free nations had a duty to their people to unite against the violent. America, and her allies, he said "accept that responsibility."

National appraisals of the gravity of the situation, and the corresponding national responses at a time when States were still very worried about the prospect of new terrorist attacks, revealed the need to reexamine the roots of world order. These concerns have produced a critically important inquiry into the substance and the implementation of international law and the role of the United Nations. It has required a reconsideration of what is meant by a "common interest," and made relevant the policy question: "Where are your friends when they are really needed?" An immediate response may suggest that the Iraq war will turn upside down the international institutions upon which the United States has relied since World War II. While that is possible, it is unlikely to be a complete scenario. Even in the Iraq incident following the threat of vetoes, the United States continued to regard the UN as the appropriate forum, as opposed to an earlier option to engage immediately in the unilateral exercise of armed force. The United States, until the very last doubt was removed, sought the moral approval of at least nine members of the Council.

At the same time world alliances were being reviewed. New roles may emerge for NATO and the European Union. Respected persons have called for U.N. reform.

On March 19, 2003 the United States and the allies targeted Baghdad with precise weaponry hoping to hit a target of opportunity, leading to an early capitulation by Iraq. As plans were made for winning the war accompanying plans had been made for winning the peace.

The United States at that time endeavored to portray its vision of a future Iraq. This was the focus of Secretary Powell's remarks at the time of the entry of American forces into Baghdad. Iraq would be "free of weapons of mass destruction; a nation that has a representative form of government that is living in peace with its neighbors, no longer abusing its own population, using the wealth of Iraq for the people of Iraq; [and] hasn't splintered into different parts." There were no warnings of the high costs to be entailed in achieving such results.

5. INTERNATIONAL LAW, THE UNITED NATIONS, AND IRAQ

The use of force brought with it many foreign policy and legal considerations. Had the United States and the allies violated the U.N. Charter? Would the combatants conform to the laws or customs of war? How would violations be dealt with? Would Iraq embark on a scorched earth campaign including intentional harms to the natural environment and the incineration of natural resources? Could there be a use of WMD? Would Iraq, or its cohorts unleash terrorists? How would the victorious forces deal with internal disorder? If Iraqi leaders were apprehended would they be charged with international crimes. If so, what court or courts would possess or be granted jurisdiction? What institutions and which nations will become actively involved in meeting the challenges of winning the peace? Would the United States work through the UN or NATO? Who will pay the costs for reconstruction? Whose firms will receive remunerative contracts? Would the United States go forward with the plan announced on February 26, 2003 to be more actively involved in bringing peace to Israel and Palestine?

The coalition's use of force in Iraq will require worldwide foreign policy appraisals. Of critical importance to the world community will be the survivability of the United Nations. With the appropriate political will of its members in areas less contentious than the maintenance of international security, can it play a useful role? This will involve building the fundamental foundations upon which peace can rest. These are social, economic, humanitarian, and political in their nature. Lessons learned from the rehabilitation of Europe after World War II and more recently in the Balkans will have to be applied in Iraq and other volatile areas in the Middle East. Tensions among the permanent members of the Security Council will have to be dissipated. Or, is power politics bound to prevail?

While the world responds to such enormous challenges, it must also form a clear perception of the United States. Others must make a major effort to see the United States as it is seen by itself. By leading in the peaceful rehabilitation of Iraq, in which it seeks no ill-designed preferences for itself, the United States can offer evidence of its democratic commitments. Those who have been fearful or distrustful of the United States must be careful observers. Substantial evidence of its commitment to freedom must be offered by the United States. One example might be an insistence by the United States that the new constitution for Iraq contain guarantees for a diverse and pluralistic media. Another would be the guarantee of free religious choices. America's unilateral propensities of the past must be replaced by a commitment to multilateralism. The remainder of the world must be perceptive in its judgments and act accordingly. Cooperation may take on a new meaning and there can be a positive reshaping of global order.

The United States in claiming that its use of force in Iraq served community interests through the elimination of a dangerous threat and also was supported by valid legal principles has been obliged to prove its case. This has not been easy since many believe that it is not the function of one country to use armed force to advance even the most worthy of community interests and that the terms of the UN Charter cannot be interpreted as the United States has insisted. At issue is the meaning to be given to the Charter's key provisions, particularly Articles 2 (3), 2 (4) 24 (1), 42 and 51, and whether these are the only valid legal principles applicable to the measures taken against Iraq.

Ever since the Charter was adopted in 1945 statesmen and scholars have debated whether a State, reasonably believing on the basis of objective facts that it was about to be the object of an "armed attack," had to actually be attacked before it could mount a rollback response. Prevention of such an attack, with its dramatic consequences, has been referred to as both anticipatory and preemptive self-defense. A very fine line exists between anticipation and realization. Support for the use of unilateral preventive force in such circumstances is based on the principles of territorial integrity and national sovereignty.

Critics of the United States position have stated categorically that if the United States and its allies were to engage in preventive or anticipatory action it would violate both customary international law and the Charter. Some urged that resolution 1441 was unlawful and should be referred to the World Court for an opinion. Undoubtedly policy makers were being influenced by, and their public statements contributed to, the massive worldwide demonstrations calling for restraint.

What at first seemed to be restricted to the receipt of factual reports from the UN and the IAEA inspectors and the timing of sanctions erupted into a challenge to the Charter's principle of collective security. Particularly circumspect was the often repeated statement by the United States that it reserved the right to engage in preemptive measures while also having announced that it supported a post-1441 Security Council resolution in which agreement was to be reached on the employment of armed force.

In making its case the United States has had to overcome a considerable amount of foreign and domestic cynicism on the part of those who perceive the United States as inclined to operate outside and above the law. They ask whether it is the function of the United Nations or the United States to determine who is violating international law and all of the pertinent Security Council resolutions.

International lawyers have pointed to the contradictions between the mandate of the Charter and the American response to Iraq's threatening behavior. They have asked: What has happened to international law and the Charter's precise terminology? The U.S. response has been to confirm generally the role of international law, even in the presence of grave situations, including the threat of the use of weapons of mass destruction and terrorism, but to urge the fundamental legal right of self-defense. While accepting the importance of collective security, it has been contended that in special circumstances unilateral forceful action is permissible.

The announced policy of the United States to embark on unilateral measures has produced major concerns that it has appointed itself to be the world's policeman, even an international "bully", with an undeterrable and misguided policy of unilateralism. The United States, according to such critics, is committed to a form of world order dominated exclusively by its own concerns and lacking in the sensitivity to the interests of other States which favor widespread international cooperation.

When confronted by a State thought to possess nuclear capabilities, questions have been raised whether international law and institutions can address this situation, and, if so, what law and what institutions. Fascinating and opposing legal and political responses have resulted. They extend all the way from the dogmatic legal proposition that the use of armed force by the United States against Iraq would be aggressive war and unlawful to the view that the UN Charter properly understood, while calling for collective security, contains necessary and limited exceptions.

Conclusions depend on the manner in which the Charter is understood. It can be read literally. Its terms are also subject to interpretation since it, like the U.S. Constitution, is a constitutive document.

The Charter, like the U.S. Constitution, consists of an evolving set of principles. The U.S. Supreme Court, through its interpretive process, has provided a gloss which has allowed for the acceptance of new approaches to meet the needs of changing times.

The Charter absent the structure for access to national court processes, also has taken new directions over time. The forces for such change have been the product of the incremental work of the institution, the impact of political forces manifested by its members, new legal perspectives, and the opinions of the International Court of Justice. No great constitutive documents, such as the Charter and the Constitution, are immune from the expectation of viability. To be meaningful they require visions of an orderly future and the enduring support of diplomacy. When these waver little remains except the application of force.

International lawyers are influenced by many considerations in construing international law. Among them are their interpretations of the 1969 Vienna Convention on the Law of Treaties, their backgrounds in different legal systems, such as the Common Law or the Civil Law systems, with the weighting of changing values, the extent to which they allow themselves to be guided by the national law of their respective countries, whether they are supportive of positivist or literal readings of the law as opposed to more value orientated approaches, their appraisals of the role of politics in the formation of substantive legal principles, philosophical outlooks, an awareness of social, economic, scientific, and technological trends, and a whole host of identifiable personality oriented considerations. With such factors at work it would not be surprising that formal international agreements, as well as the real but more abstract concepts contained in the general principles of international law, may receive different interpretations.

This is particularly true respecting the meaning of self-defense including anticipatory and preemptive self-defense. International law is applicable to all of the aspects of the Iraq situation even though there are assertions that it is illusory to accept the international dimensions of law, especially as it governs the right to embark on armed conflict and the conduct of hostilities.

6. AGGRESSION, COLLECTIVE SECURITY, SELF-DEFENSE, AND HUMANITARIAN INTERVENTION

Aggression by one State against another by violent means has been universally condemned. Defense against such conduct is considered to be an inherent right. The question arises whether a State which is obliged to keep the peace, including an aggressor, can take action to forestall the aggressor.

International lawyers have analyzed the legality of the use of force by the coalition States against Iraq from several perspectives. Each has a long history. All are designed to protect the basic rights of States. All command varying levels of approval depending on the extent to which international peace and security are considered to be in jeopardy. All assert that the rule of law has application to world order. Some lend themselves to a nation's unilateral determination that its vital interests are threatened. Others prefer a collective approach for their implementation. Their sources may be found in customary international law based on the practices of States and in the UN Charter.

International lawyers accord preference to collective decisions, since they avoid the vagaries of unilateral determinations. These may be suspect because of their probable reliance on self-interest only.

A. Legal Theories Justifying the Use of Force

Both the UN Charter and customary international law contemplate the use of force by the United Nations and by its members. For such force to be legal it must conform to existing norms.

The legality of the use of force against Iraq has been examined from the perspective of the Charter's collective security provisions, the right to engage in self-defense, the right to engage in anticipatory self-defense, the right to engage in preemptive self-defense, and from the doctrine of humanitarian intervention with its accompanying concepts of humanitarian interposition and responsibility.

1. Collective Security: The Charter, Articles 24 (1) and 42

Under Article 24 (1) the members of the UN have conferred on the Security Council "the primary responsibility for the maintenance of international peace and security." They have granted to it the right to act "on their behalf." Article 42 gives the Security Council when it is confronted by "a threat to" or a "breach of the peace" the power to take "such action" as is "necessary to maintain or restore international peace and security." This approach is founded in multilateralism and can be effectively used when the conduct of a State is so harmful to the well-being of all countries, such as an unquestioned act of aggression, that they almost automatically decide to come to the aid of the country under attack. When Iraq attacked Kuwait in 1990 the principle of collective security was applied. When the United States and the coalition States voiced their concern in 2003 respecting the post-1990 conduct of Iraq they invoked the help of The Security Council in order to obtain the benefits of collective security.

For collective security to function States must acknowledge that they have common interests and act accordingly. Failure by China, France, Germany, and Russia to understand this basic fact caused them to reject the principle of collective security. They forced the coalition States to rely on other principles, and ultimately to proceed without meeting all of the conditions contained in Resolution 1441.

If a State cannot count on the members of the Security Council when it is in extreme peril it has no choice but to engage in balance of power alliances or to go it alone.

2. Self-Defense: The Charter, Articles 2 (3), 2 (4), and 51

Articles 2 (3) and 2 (4) impose critical constraints on the conduct of members. They are obliged to settle international disputes by peaceful means and must refrain from the threat or use of force so that international peace, security, and justice are not endangered. Recognizing that States might engage in an "armed attack" against a member Article 51 reaffirmed existing international law enabling a State to engage in "individual or collective self-defense." Such military action was to occur pending the Security Council's taking "measures necessary to maintain international peace and security." The term "armed attack" was intended to limit the conditions in which unilateral measures might be taken so that such measures would not be treated as aggression. The term "armed attack" has raised vast problems as to its interpretation.

3. Anticipatory Self-Defense

Although "armed attack" has not been defined or described in a manner fixing the boundaries of its meaning, and hence a consistency regarding its application, it is the reference point for "anticipatory self-defense." This term has a long history and has served as the foundation for national defense policies even though it suffers from the uncertainties surrounding the meaning of "self-defense." This is augmented by varying views of what specific facts could justify the taking of "anticipatory" action. This doctrine is invoked by a State under a threat of attack.

The concept of anticipatory self-defense grew out of the events referred to as the *Caroline* case.[7] In 1837 the vessel was anchored near Niagara, N.Y. It was being used by the Canadians who were seeking to oust Great Britain from Canada. The British military forces entered the United States, attacked the insurgents, and sent the vessel adrift over the Falls. In the ensuing negotiations Secretary of State Daniel Webster supported the right of a foreign State to take anticipatory action. In his 1842 memorandum he stated that there must be a "necessity of self-defense, instant, overwhelming, leaving no choice of means and no moment for deliberation."[8] At the close of World War II the Nuremberg Tribunal affirmed the rule stating "It must be remembered that preventive action in foreign territory is justified only in case of 'an instant and overwhelming necessity of self-defense leaving no choice of means and no moment of deliberation.'" These words indicate that the threat must be imminent and impending. The question has been raised as to how long or how short the time frame of the threat must be prior to resort to preemptive actions. In 1837 military service, although a full-time profession allowed for a rather leisurely preparation for months although the British presence in the United States was a matter of days. It was an era of muzzle-loading rifles and short-range howitzers.

Contrasting with the time frame of 1837 is that available for decision-making and action today. Events and decision- making now take place in a "collapse of time" setting, meaning that there can be a very short span between the formation of an intent to act and the act itself. Within a shorter framework the margin for error has been reduced and levels of tolerance may be lower.

On October 7, 2002 President Bush stated: "Some ask how urgent this danger is to America and the world. The danger is already significant and it only grows worse with time. If we know Saddam Hussein has dangerous weapons today—and we do—does it make any sense for the world to wait to confront him as he grows even stronger and develops even more dangerous weapons?"[9] He also stated in his October speech that "approval of this resolution [1441] does not mean that military action is imminent or unavoidable."[10]

On the other hand, perhaps the urgency condition is not the presence of nuclear weaponry, but rather the presence of a sufficient intention on the part of a hostile regime to obtain and employ it. This was influenced by the persistent refusal of Iraq to comply with arms commitments and Security Council resolutions governing the possession of weapons dating back to 1990.

The factor of intent was referred to in a January 13, 2003 opinion of the State Department's Legal Adviser. It noted that because a country possesses "significant military power, or seeks to enhance the military power that it has, would not, in the absence of any evidence that it intends to use its power against others aggressively, justify a preemptive strike against it." He also stated that a State had the right to defend itself from catastrophic harm where, after the exhaustion of peaceful remedies "and after careful consideration of the remedies" there was "overwhelming evidence of an imminent threat." Reliance on the *Caroline* case is evident.

In trying to assess the status of such intent, ranging all the way from immediate to non-existent, other factors reflecting an unfriendly or hostile outlook, could be considered. For example, to what extent, if any, was Iraq harboring or supporting terrorists whose purpose is to cause harm to America? This also would have to be assessed in terms of the instancy or overwhelmingness of the potential or actual nature of the posited action.

It has been noted that "the move from reactive to anticipatory self-defense required replacing the objectively verifiable prerequisites of an 'armed attack' with the subjective 'threat' of such an attack . . ."[11] Since anticipatory self-defense was marked by its subjectivity its authority "remained cloudy and much of formal legal doctrine rejected its lawfulness."[12]

4. *Preemptive Self-Defense*

Preemptive like anticipatory self-defense deals with a response to a "beforehand" situation. It is used unilaterally. Preemptive self-defense, which has been referred to as the Bush Doctrine, like anticipatory self-defense, is premised on the expectation that imminent enemy action is forthcoming. In President Bush's words "If we wait for threats to fully materialize, we will have waited too long." He added that the United States could not accept the risk of inaction.

In September 2002 President Bush endeavored to clarify the U.S. position on this matter. He stated: "For centuries, international law recognized that nations need not suffer an attack before they can lawfully take action to defend themselves against forces that present an imminent danger of attack. Legal scholars and international jurists often conditioned the legitimacy of preemption on the existence of an imminent threat—most often visible mobilization of armies, navies, and air forces preparing to attack. We must adapt the concept of imminent threat to the capabilities and objectives of today's adversaries . . . [namely] rogue states and terrorists . . .

He added:

"The United States has long maintained the option of preemptive actions to counter a sufficient threat to our national security. The greater the threat, the greater is the risk of inaction—and the more compelling the case for taking anticipatory action to defend ourselves, even if the uncertainty remains as to the time and place of the enemy's attack. To forestall or prevent such hostile acts by our adversaries, the United States will, if necessary, act preemptively."[13]

This approach allows for a response earlier in point of time than anticipatory self-defense and with a lesser factual basis for action. It links the potential for doing harm with an intent to achieve harm even though that intent may not have been fully disclosed or implemented prior to the resort to preventive action. In military terminology it is a more "trigger-happy" response than that contemplated by anticipatory self-defense.

The fear of terrorists contributed to this newer and more extreme claim to engage in self-defense. In September, 2002, President Bush stated: "While the United States will constantly strive to enlist the support of the international community, we will not hesitate to act alone, if necessary, to exercise our right of self-defense by acting preemptively against such terrorists, to prevent them from doing harm against our people and our country. . . ." In the following months, since Iraq was perceived as possessing WMD, a violator of basic Human Rights, and as a haven for terrorists, the Bush doctrine was implemented. From its outset it had referred to the need to "convince" or "compel" sovereigns to "accept their sovereign responsibilities."

Applying the foregoing to the use of military force in 2003 against Iraq, as urged by the United States, depends on several considerations. If it were contended that the rule applied to the presence in Iraq of WMD, which may have been developed since 1998, it would appear that the urgency identified by the rule's language is not evident.

Reflective of policy appraisals it has been suggested that intent must be proven beforehand beyond any reasonable doubt rather than by a preponderance of the evidence since the lives of thousands of persons could be in jeopardy. Unless and until the higher proof were available it can be argued that preemptive action should not be employed.

Only weak and ambiguous evidence of the presence of biological and chemical weapons in Iraq had been revealed at the time of the attack. Nothing of any consequence was ever found, although on April 21, 2003 a *New York Times* article reported that an Iraq scientist had disclosed "precursors for a toxic agent" banned by chemical weapons treaties.

In each situation the instancy and overwhelming nature of harmful action must be viewed from the present status of weaponry. In 1837 the time frame of attacks was measured in weeks and days. Today weapons of mass destruction can be triggered in a matter of minutes. It should by evident that a country that has been selected as a target for an attack with such weapons is placed in vastly more serious jeopardy than when the weapons of choice were rifles and artillery. Neither the Charter nor international law require a State to have been struck by weapons of mass destruction before it resorts to its inherent right of self-defense.

Preemptive action is permissible when the continued existence of the State being targeted is objectively threatened. Such action enjoys greater moral support when it is employed by a collectivity of States. It can be a successful deterrent against aggressors. It can be claimed as a right by the lesser as well as the greater States. If such use of force by one or several States can be demonstrated to be in the best interests of the larger community it enjoys a higher moral and legal condition.

Interpretation of or as an exception to the language of Article 51 to claim acceptance must be found in customary international law founded in the practices of States. Customary law is handicapped by evidentiary considerations which do not apply to written instruments. When proven, it is as authoritative as treaty law. A large concern is that the claim of preemptive self-defense is unilateral, with all of the potential faults inherent in a decision by a single party in a threatening environment. Recourse to preemptive strikes is subject to the practical danger of inadequate information.

In assessing the role of self-defense it has been noted that "By their nature, all acts of self-defense are initiated unilaterally and evaluated for their lawfulness only after the fact. In all claims to self-defense, the international legal review of the action will be based on a prudential contextual assessment of factors such as the degree of the threat presented, the availability of a meaningful organized international response, the urgency of unilateral action to prevent or deflect the attack, and the proportionality of the means chosen to the necessity presented by the threat. Thus, on a case-by-case basis, the legal danger of an abuse of preemptive self-defense is no greater than for anticipatory self-defense, which also does not required an 'armed attack' to justify it."[14] Under such circumstances, when a regime change is an announced objective and when a determination has to be made regarding the acceptance and incorporation into international law of the Bush doctrine, critical criteria must be weighed. To be acceptable it must "serve the common interests of the aggregate of actors."[15] Thus, the proper goal allows or justifies the use of the doctrine. This has been summed in the observation that "regime change may be internationally lawful when it is the contextually appropriate *instrument* of an intrinsically lawful action."[16]

5. Humanitarian Intervention and the Just War Theory

Humanitarian intervention has a long history traceable to the just war views of St. Augustine of Hippo in the 4th century. He had urged that the forces of "Good" could be employed to modify the conduct of those engaged in "Bad" or immoral conduct. Its controversial and complex prescriptions are mirrored in the concepts of anticipatory and preemptive self-defense. The *Caroline* case with its focus on the safeguarding of the territorial integrity and political sovereignty of a State is basic to such an approach.

States invariably make the claim that their collective use of armed force is taken in the interest of justice and that the UN Charter provides the necessary processes to assist in resolving the problem. However, when an acceptable outcome is not realized a State may turn to a unilateral response couched in terms of anticipatory or preemptive self-defense.

Humanitarian intervention, which also allows for the unilateral and limited exercise of armed force, was employed in the 19th century when countries engaged in large scale persecutions of religious minorities. It also was used by States whose nationals while living in a foreign country were deprived of basic Human Rights. With the ascendancy in recent years in the importance of protecting Human Rights, there has been an expanded use of humanitarian intervention. This exercise of extraterritorial jurisdiction has been justified on moral grounds even though an aspect of national interest also may have induced the protecting State to take action.[17]

Humanitarian intervention can be compared with anticipatory self-defense. Both are geared to respond quickly with force to unacceptable violations of Human Rights. Both rely on customary international law for their support, unless a specific treaty exists. Such intervention is subject to the same evidentiary problems as anticipatory self-defense.

Since its use disregards the territorial integrity and sovereignty of the affected State an active intervention must be justified by the need to protect individuals and to serve the common interests of the world community.[18] Its use must not be the product of a national bias. A failure to take collective action has also been subject to serious criticism, for example when genocide and ethnic cleansing are occurring.

Like the other principles and doctrines that have emerged relating to the maintenance of international order and justice, humanitarian intervention requires the use of armed force. In doing so the intervener is expected to establish and maintain order and justice.

The principle of humanitarian intervention may serve to blunt the charges that the use of armed force by the coalition of willing States against Iraq violated the literal language of the Charter and that it violated the authority of resolution 1441, and its incorporated resolutions.

The principles contained in the Charter, on their face, are the most restrictive of the use of armed force; those set forth in anticipatory and preemptive self-defense and humanitarian intervention establish a lower threshold for the use of armed force. The manner in which armed force is used and the causes which are being served must advance the well-being of nations and peoples.

Critics fear that humanitarian intervention will be used as an excuse for placing unlawful restrictions on a State's sovereignty and territorial integrity. The term "humanitarian interposition" has been introduced to require the use of force to be confined strictly to basic humanitarian needs; political and economic maneuvers are to be avoided. In recent years it has been used effectively to protect Human Rights in numerous developing areas of the world.

Such efforts have been carried out by States and by regional international organizations such as NATO in Kosovo. When authorized and engaged in by the United Nations it is referred to as "peace keeping".

Opposition to humanitarian intervention comes from those scholars who have called for a literal interpretation of Article 2 (3), 2 (4) and 51 of the Charter. Opposing this reasoning are the terms of Article 2 (7) of the Charter which deprive States from making a valid claim that Human Rights are subject to the exclusive domestic jurisdiction of the State of residence.

The increasing respect given to humanitarian intervention has also contributed to a diminution of the ancient vestiges of sovereign immunity. In recent times there has been a shift in terminology with emphasis being placed on a State's right or responsibility to engage in humanitarian "protection" rather than on humanitarian "intervention."[19]

The literalists, intent in finding international law in treaties, have noticed the absence of treaties assuring the right of humanitarian intervention. With their emphasis on the need for such agreements they are reluctant to accept that practice or customary international law may have reached the point where an embryonic *opinio juris* is emerging or has emerged which is able to sustain humanitarian intervention. They also point to few international court decisions giving limited support to humanitarian intervention.

The opponents of the literalists are not silenced by these outlooks. On their part they point to a fundamental principle of international law that what the law does not prohibit is permitted. They contend that since the Charter and other sources of international law have approved of the use of force in peace, and in particular since there has been no prohibition against humanitarian intervention, that the doctrine supports the use of force against governments that have thwarted for many years the basic rights of citizens and residents, especially minorities. Prevention of genocide has resulted.

Although humanitarian intervention has not been put forward in order to eliminate existing regimes, the charges made in 2002 against Saddam Hussein entailed the practice of genocide against minority populations in Iraq. Humanitarian intervention requires the pre-emptive use of force. An alternative to such action is prosecution in a suitable, preferably permanent, international criminal tribunal.

This was the situation in November 2002, when the Security Council initially decided to deal with the past transgressions of Saddam Hussein and to obtain a more secure world order.

The relevance of the legal principles analyzed in this Chapter, must, of course, depend on the facts. Was Iraq in possession, as continually stated by President Bush, Vice-President Cheney, Secretary Rumsfeld, Secretary of State Powell, and by the United States representatives at the United Nations, of WMD and did it have both the intent and capability to make imminent use of them? Very substantial doubts on these matters had been raised by inspectors authorized by the United Nations and by the IAEA prior to the coalition attack.

In the following months American inspection teams, unhindered by a defeated Iraq, engaged in detailed and extensive searches and came up wanting. At the end of January, 2004, David Kay, the head of the U. S. Iraq Survey Group, reported that Iraq had no significant WMD nor any programs to develop them in the months prior to the invasion. At the same time Hans Blix, the head of the UN inspection team prior to the attack, restated his earlier conclusions, namely, Iraq's dangerous capabilities had, under UN pressure following the 1991 Persian Gulf War, been eliminated. He observed that his team had looked at the situation "with a critical mind."

Absent such weapons the prospective threat of harm resulting from the impossible imminency of their use vanished. In early February, 2004, Mr. George J. Tenet, CIA Director, stated to the public that the agency had never advised President Bush that Iraq posed an "imminent threat" to the United States. He acknowledged that the government may have "overestimated" Iraq's nuclear weapons program and that the CIA "did not know" if biological weapons were being produced before the war. It was also admitted that undue reliance had been given to "unreliable" Iraqi defectors who had asserted that Iraq had a germ-weapons laboratory. Mr. Tenet stated that the CIA had provided "an objective assessment" of a brutal dictator who only "had the intent and capability" to produce biological and chemical weapons. In defending the findings of the agency he noted that intelligence obtained in the United Kingdom and other friendly countries were supportive of the American conclusions,

Prior to the Tenet statement congressional leaders in both houses had initiated hearings to determine why the intelligence "estimates" were incorrect. President Bush then established a fact-finding commission to investigate prewar misadventures and to advise on procedures suited to the acquisition of trustworthy data. Prime Minister Blair embarked on the same course of action.

The evidence presented by the inspectors demonstrated that Iraq did not have WMD stockpiles. They acknowledged that "intent and purpose," while subjective, did not equate with capability for use, since the absence of weapons would prevent possible or prospective uses.

Because of the difficulty presented in the acquisition of intelligence information the gatherers often assert that they are making "estimates" rather than "guarantees." While this is understandable such estimates should not be allowed to become the basis for concluding that the posture of a potential enemy is factually "imminent and impending." To counsel an armed attack on the basis of the facts gathered respecting Iraq can best be described as surmise. For this reason the waging of war against Iraq cannot be supported by the theories of anticipatory or preventive self-defense.

In February, 2004, Secretary Powell in commenting on his 2003 statement to the Security Council that Iraq was a "grave and growing danger" stated that this represented "the best judgment we could make at that time on Saddam Hussein's capabilities." He defended his 2003 position as having been based on "solid intelligence."

The devastating effect of inadequate intelligence has challenged the credibility of America's decisions in the areas of military and foreign policy. On February 8 President Bush admitted that the intelligence was flawed but that the United States had done the right thing when confronted by a gathering threat in Iraq. He placed emphasis on the context of the situation and stressed the war on terrorism and the irrationality of Hussein. In retrospect Secretary Powell has observed that the nonexistence of a stockpile of banned weapons has changed "the political calculus." Secretary-General Annan in commenting on America's flawed basis for the war stated that it had produced "damage that will probably take some time to heal."

Absent proof of WMD heavier reliance will be placed on the theories of humanitarian intervention or engagement in a just war. In appraising this position it should be recalled that the United States, as it has ascended in its hegemonic role in recent years, has with some frequency sent its troops into foreign lands. The concept of humanitarian intervention in its most benign condition has been used to protect the safety of Americans when a foreign government is unable to do so. A not unmeaningful gloss in the form of implementing foreign democratic processes often has been added.

Quite often an American presence encourages the intervened-in country to favor policies supportive of U. S. interests. A recent study covering the period between 1954 (Guatemala) and 1993 (Somalia) has disclosed that an American military presence has not strengthened democratic principles and procedures. The announced goal of a high level of democracy in Iraq, although certainly fundamental, and based on a highly commendable instinct, may not fare much better.

Approaching the Iraq war from a foreign policy point of view it has been urged that America's instincts were basically sound and that regime change, encompassing bringing Saddam Hussein before an appropriate criminal tribunal, plus the elimination of a source of international terrorism, made this use of force legitimate and lawful, the terms of the U. N. Charter notwithstanding. Or, it may be argued that this use of force was justified for practical reasons. This, of course, is a policy and not a legal contention.

From a foreign policy perspective the improvements which hopefully may occur will have to be measured against costs in America lives, material expenditures, status at the United Nations, and influence in foreign capitals. For the moment a multinational approach has been invoked to deal with the high levels of unrest in Iraq and the transition to a responsible government. The American appeal has been addressed to friendly countries acting alone, and also to the United Nations, and through it to all member countries.

6. Implementing the Peace

American forces were hailed as liberators when they entered Baghdad in the second week of April 2003. With surprising ease coalition troops destroyed the will of the government of Saddam Hussein to resist. Implementing the peace will be a major foreign policy issue for the United States for many years. It will involve the birthing of a new and responsible democratically oriented government, coping with the interests and concerns of those claiming the right in Iraq to become the new leaders of the country, organizing vast economic and humanitarian support, understanding and dealing with the outlooks and needs of all of the neighboring States, and addressing and ameliorating the claims of significant involvement by members of the United Nations, notably the permanent members of the Security Council.

Particularly in immediate need of resolution are the lifting of sanctions imposed by the Security Council, the opening of investment opportunities for all competitors, and the continuation of weapons' searches by the UN and the IAEA monitors.

Success in these areas will facilitate the effective delivery of humanitarian relief and the elimination of social unrest including the conditions productive of terrorism. Following a return to stability it will be possible to go forward with an interim administration led by the United States in consultation with its allies and with Iraqi leaders, followed by an Iraqi intermin authority, and thereafter a representative government.

The coalition countries, known as the Coalition Provisional Authority, will undoubtedly be credited for their willingness to assume enormous risks at great costs if they bring a measure of democracy and well-being to Iraq, while at the same time demonstrating a sufficiently multilateral approach to satisfy the critics. In not a few countries there may be, at least initially, strident condemnation when their advice is not taken and their participation in the economic and physical repair of Iraq is not so substantial as they might have wished. Paradoxically, the vast military strength of the United States may pose problems.

The coalition countries in viewing the prospective roles of the side-line countries will be challenged by the probable formation of regional alliances. It will be determined if the United Nations will remain as important to world order as it was when Resolution 1441 was adopted. It will as Secretary Powell stated on April 9, 2003, have a "vital" role to play through endorsing the authority of the coalition States in the governance of Iraq particularly as they arrange for the sale of oil supplies and engage in humanitarian activities. To this he added: The suggestion . . . that now the coalition has done all of this and liberated Iraq, thank you very much, step aside and the Security Council is now going to become responsible for everything, is incorrect."[20] For the transition from conflict to reconstruction he indicated that an early UN resolution "would be to give an endorsement of some kind [to] an interim authority representing the Iraqi people."[21]

Because many States possess concern over the ascendancy of the power of the coalition States in Iraq and in bordering States, they will test the extent of the "vital" role of the UN in the area. It will have to be determined how primary or central that role will be.

At the beginning it can be expected that the coalition States will exercise the principal or central authority based on their physical presence and the need for law and order including the provision of basic services. Before hostilities were over U.S. military civil affairs teams and the U.S. Office for Reconstruction and Humanitarian Assistance were seeking responsible Iraqis with whom they could cooperate in restoring a presence sufficient to prevent looting and to provide an infrastructure for the operation of public utilities and for the provision of hospitals, public transportation, food distribution systems, and access to religious structures.

The United States Office of Reconstruction and Humanitarian Assistance is to be directly engaged in effecting a transition from military occupation into the first stages of the new Iraqi Governing Council. Composing this body would be anti-Hussein elements, returning exiles, cooperative academics, former military personnel, and experienced business leaders. A delicate balancing of religious preferences will be critical to success. Among the first responsibilities of this nascent body will be to reopen the schools and hospitals, and to find and train competent judges, and to secure the administration of justice. Of even more importance will be the drafting and acceptance of a democratically oriented Constitution.

More immediately, depending on how rapidly it will be possible for the people of Iraq to assume the responsibility for their own governance, there may be a trend away from accepting the coalition forces as liberators and to treat them as occupiers. In that event the *jus in bellum* aspect of the laws of war will have to be obeyed, and in particular the rules relating to the treatment of prisoners of war and to a belligerent occupation contained in the Fourth Geneva Civilian Convention of 1949. Protected persons pursuant to Article 27 are to be treated humanely at all times. Respect is to be accorded to their persons, honor, family rights, religious convictions and practices, and their manners and customs. Particularly to be avoided are adverse distinctions founded on race, religion, or political opinion.

With Iraq's history of extensive violations of Human Rights and riven by religious and tribal disputes the need for the implementation of the Geneva Civilian Convention will be particularly acute. The treaty applies following armed conflict with both the United States, Iraq, and the United Kingdom being parties.

Military investigators will search for evidence of the war crimes committed by and unlawful weapons held by Saddam Hussein and his governmental subordinates. This could lead to judicial prosecutions. At the end of September 2003 the Iraqi Governing Council, an interim body appointed by U.S. authorities, explored the possibility of the prosecution of General Ali Hassan Majid, a Hussein subordinate, who allegedly used chemical weapons against Iraqi Kurds.

The capture of Saddam Hussein on December 13, 2003 raised the issue of his prosecution. The question became: which court and under what circumstances? He was a prisoner of war. He was in the hands of the Coalition Provisional Authority which had fixed July 1, 2004 as the date when full sovereignty would be transferred from the Iraq Governing Council to the State of Iraq.

American jurisprudence calls for an early and speedy trial in which all of the elements of a fair trial are present. Recent international prosecutions have set the same standard.

International lawyers began to explore past practices in order to ascertain the court which could provide the best operational capabilities to deal with the prosecution of a former Head of State. The number of interested parties is legion since underlying the prosecution of this defendant is the whole cause of world order. The legitimacy of the tribunal must be established. Without meeting this condition the entire proceeding would be written off at best as a lost opportunity and at worst as a monumental farce.

The Department of State in its Future of Iraq project formed a Transitional Justice Working Group which drafted the "Statute of the Iraqi Special Tribunal for Crimes Against Humanity." It was issued by the Iraq Governing Council on December 10, 2003. It went into force on that date. It calls for the prosecution of violations of international law, namely, genocide, crimes against humanity, and war crimes. Provision is also made for violations of Iraq law. The domestic crimes include manipulation of the judiciary, the wastage and squandering of natural assets and public funds, and engaging in policies likely to lead to wars with Arab States.

Domestic Iraq law will govern penalties. This allows for the imposition of the death sentence.

Judges are to be "persons" having the very highest qualifications. The judges for trials and appeals and also for separate investigations do not have to be Iraqi nationals. Both courts are to have the assistance of non-Iraqi nationals who will act in advisory capacities or as observers. In each case such non-nationals must have "acted in either a judicial or prosecutorial capacity in his or her respective country, or . . . shall have experience in international war crimes trials or tribunals."

Article 20 of the Statute deals with the procedural and substantive rights of an accused. Of first importance is the entitlement to the presumption of innocence prior to finding of guilt. Among the guarantees, which follow those available in American criminal courts, is the right to an early and public hearing following the identification of the cause and content of the charges being levied.

Procedural rules designed to advance the prospects of a fair trial are to be drafted by the President of the Tribunal and are to be adopted by a majority of the permanent judges of the Tribunal.

The choice of the foregoing Tribunal, with its mixed Iraqi and foreign composition, but with its emphasis on independence from excessive foreign control, meets several important criteria. In the first place it emphasizes an early return on July 1, 2004, of Iraq's control over its national government. Due respect is to be accorded to its national sovereignty. This choice accepts the view that a responsible government is entitled to make use of its domestic institutions before an international tribunal is empowered to prosecute citizens who held positions of authority in the offending State. Iraq would be responsible for funding the court.

Of major importance in selecting the model best suited to Iraq is the issue of the death penalty. Since this penalty is opposed by a vast majority of members of the United Nations, and since this penalty was rejected by the Security Council in creating the ICTFY and the International Criminal Court for Rwanda, it is unlikely that this penalty would be approved for a trial of Saddam Hussein and his subordinates. A failure to allow for the death penalty would also create a public issue in the United States which could lead to policy repercussions. However, the United States, when it participated in the formation of the Nuremberg Tribunal for the prosecution of Nazi war criminals, supported the death penalty.

Other models that could be pursued for Iraq are the Security Council-established tribunals mentioned above, or a mixed international/national court of the kind set up for the prosecution of similar crimes in Sierra Leone. In that situation a treaty between the United Nations and Sierra Leone provided that a majority of its judges and its Chief Prosecutor were to be appointed by the Secretary-General. Among these alternatives it has been suggested that "the national model with international support is the most viable one."[22]

The permanent International Criminal Court has also been considered as a suitable venue. Practical reasons have been advanced against a prosecution in this tribunal. Its jurisdiction is limited to crimes committed after July 1, 2002. The Baath Party came into existence on July 17, 1968, with Saddam Hussein becoming president in 1979, with Hussein's misdeeds occurring before July 1, 2002. Before the ICC could exercise jurisdiction the matter would have to be referred to it by Iraq or by the Security Council, and neither of these seems so inclined. Further, America's disavowal of the tribunal, particularly following its war with Iraq, has made this choice "inconceivable."[23]

While many non-Iraqi's have voiced support for either an *ad hoc* tribunal, including the hybrid tribunal in Sierra Leone, as well as others now operation in Kosovov and East Timor, none can assess the death penalty. It has been stated that "Neither the United Nations nor most of the United States' European allies would participate in a court that could impose capital punishment."[24]

Under these circumstances it is likely that the major Iraqi defendants will be tried in a domestic court. The proposed court will have to issue detailed procedural rules and create an environment as solemn as the charges that will be made. The tribunal will have to exploit the learning and the skills which have evolved through the experience of the tribunals mentioned above.

It has also been noted that Hussein as a prisoner of war could be transferred to the United States for trial in a Federal District Court on the same charges listed above. Further, there might be a trial in the U.S. military commission situated in Iraq. At the same time the United States "cannot lawfully turn him over to an entity that would foreseeably violate his rights to due process under Geneva [Conventions] and human rights law."[25]

The United States has shown no disposition to remove Hussein to the United States for prosecution. If he were to be turned over to Iraqi authorities America's recent emphasis on building democracies in totalitarian States would be put to a test. As a condition for the turn over it would have to insist that the domestic court apply and respect the procedural and evidentiary principles employed in either international criminal tribunals or in American criminal courts. The terms of the December 10, 2003 Statute offer the hope that this can be brought about.

It is evident that tyrants, and Hussein is not alone in this category, are willing to risk prosecution for violations of Human Rights. New black letter legal summaries must be introduced periodically into their operational procedures. The extended interests of mankind will be served only if Hussein, after a fair trial, goes into history as this century's example of the expectations so solemnly pronounced at Nuremberg.

The cost of the Iraq war is to be measured in human and economic terms. For the United States and its allies the number of fatalities before the door to door fighting for control of Baghdad and other metropolitan cities in April 2003 was about 200. By October it was over 300 with more than 1,100 wounded. All coalition prisoners of war had been accounted for.

At the beginning of the year the administration asked for $379.9 billion for military needs. In October Congress and the President agreed to a defense budget for 2004 of $368 billion. In April Congress had approved a $79 billion defense expenditure. Of this about $62.4 billion would pay for costs through September 2003. An early estimate of ultimate costs was $120 billion running through the next decade.[26]

Included in the April legislation was $1 billion for Turkey, $1 billion for Israel, $1.1 billion for Jordan, and $2.5 billion for reconstruction in Iraq. Additional sizable sums were appropriated to American firms which had experienced losses produced by the hostilities.[27] By comparison the national budget for 2004 will be about $202 trillion.

With the realization in mid-2003 that militant groups in Iraq were offering determined resistance to peacemaking operations by the Coalition Provisional Authority, attention was drawn to the financial costs of a Pax Americana. Such costs can have a critical impact on the overall economy.

In September the administration asked Congress for an additional $87.8 billion for ongoing operations in Iraq and Pakistan. This package included military and rebuilding and reconstruction activities. Of this $67.5 billion was earmarked to complete the military task with $20.3 billion for rebuilding and reconstruction of Iraq. The latter would modernize municipal services including water and electrical systems, police, fire fighting, streets, schools, and hospitals.

The wisdom of U.S. foreign expenditures of this magnitude has also prompted an assessment of the September proposal to make a loan to Turkey of $8.5 billion, repayable at the end of ten years, to help restore its uncertain economy. It suffered during the preliminary stages of the military operations in Iraq.

In July the United States expressed the intent to provide the government of Afghanistan with a grant of $300 million, which was increased to $1.2 billion in September. In 2002 it had received $1 billion. In 2003 it would be more than $2 billion.

To alleviate such national burdens President Bush told the General Assembly in 2003 that a unified effort was required for the revival of Iraq. This followed an earlier American presentation to the Security Council seeking additional peacekeeping forces for Iraq and for monetary contributions. This presented the members of the Security Council with an opportunity to raise the issue of the return to Iraq of all of its sovereign powers and the extent to which the United States and the coalition forces should continue to exercise a dominant position in Iraq. They have been reluctant precipitously to forego this position as a result of the presence of their troops and their monumental allocation of their economic resources.

Speculating on governmental expenditures, especially when large-scale military operations are being conducted, is a very risky undertaking. It is clear, however, that a national debt, already of very substantial proportions, will increase.

In August 2003, the Congressional Budget Office estimated a deficit of $480 billion for that year. For 2004 it was estimated at $500 billion and rising to $5 trillion at the end of the next decade.

In assessing Iraq's economic condition account must be taken of Iraq's private and public debt. Russia and France hold claims for about $8 billion and Germany an additional $4.3 billion. Other countries have even larger claims, including $171 billion in unpaid claims to Kuwait going back to 1991.

While the sale of Iraq's oil will be the principal source for rebuilding the country there will first have to be a large modernization project to make the industry competitive. Many skills and commensurate costs will be required to use Iraqi oil for rebuilding and for honoring existing debts. While some creditors might be willing to scale down their claims this involves world politics, since many debtor countries, especially in Africa, might make claims for similar relief. Iraq with a frugal budget and relieved from military costs and the construction of ornate palaces will have to find capable leaders whose democratic instincts will produce a governable entity. Many countries will identify their preferences, including the powers to be exercised by the new government.

Since the United States and members of the coalition were the greatest beneficiaries of the regime change they will be asked to bear the essential burdens of rehabilitation. But, since all of the members of the United Nations will benefit from a higher measure of stability in the region they must also share in the burdens. Arranging for such an outcome during the period in which the United States and its allies intend to exercise central responsibility constitutes and will continue to be a major challenge to world order.

While other countries may wish to make contributions for humanitarian relief, and even though numerous private groups have identified particular beneficiaries, it is very unlikely that the Coalition Provisional Authority will allow such initiatives to deny to it the central management for at least the near future of affairs in Iraq. It is to be expected that private firms will be awarded short term contracts to restore much of the country's infrastructure. Long-term development projects can be assigned to the specialized agencies of the United Nations.

Over time with the growth of confidence in the successes of the local institutions the foreign management would be replaced by Iraqi authorities. The last areas of government to be returned to full Iraqi authority would be national defense and intelligence gathering. In April, 2003, President Bush and Prime Minister Blair assured the world that their countries would leave Iraq when a peaceful and representative government was functioning.

At the same time that the United States was enacting legislation enabling it initially to carry on a dominant role in Iraq the leaders of Russia, Germany, and France met to assess their objectives. They favored a leading role for the United Nations. President Putin called for early action "in accordance with the U.N. Charter." Chancellor Schroeder advocated following the path "as set down by international law" lest the rebuilding of Iraq "look like a colonial situation." President Chirac stated that only the UN had the "legitimacy" to restore the political, economic, and social systems of Iraq.

At that time the contest between how to rebuild Iraq, and by whom, was enlivened by a proposal of the U.S. Deputy Defense Secretary Paul D. Wolfowitz who suggested that loans emanating in the three countries for the extravagances of Saddam Hussein could be forgiven thereby relieving the new government of such burdens.

Destroying the final phase of the regime of Saddam Hussein took only a matter of weeks. Following the removal of very stubborn pockets of resistance rebuilding a peaceful Iraq will take years. The longer this takes the greater will be the need for the full-fledged cooperation of all States, especially including those in the region. This automatically will result in an increasing supervisory role by the members of the UN. Its Office for the Coordination of Humanitarian Affairs will have to be consulted. Much will depend on America's character. How many soldiers can be killed and how many dollars are there available to complete a well-intentioned policy?

The United States in reassessing the legality and relevance of its role in the Iraq crisis cannot escape weighing the future utility of the United Nations. This will depend on the UN's continuing role in maintaining the principle of collective security particularly in light of the positions taken by France, Germany, and Russia on Security Council Resolution 1441. The United States can ask: Considering the misdeeds of Saddam Hussein why did these members combine against the coalition States with their commitment to democracy rather than unite against him?

In examining the Security Council with its delegated responsibility of enforcing international peace and security it is necessary to recall that it is composed of selected sovereign States each with its perceptions of self-interest and world order. They, like the United States, must weigh the advantages and disadvantages of unilateral or multilateral policies.

Nonetheless, the Security Council constitutes the collective source of authority required to meet at least the minimum expectations of an organized society for international peace and security. In their search for safety in times of stress the members of the United Nations must turn to the principles of the Charter. The wisest approach for the United States to this end is to contribute effectively to multilateral policies.

Through a multilateral approach States are able to rely on common allegiances which are the product of common concerns, which have been arrived at following the acceptance of similar values, and which do not depend entirely on the power status of the several participants. Such alliances and predispositions will emphasize the importance of resolving basic security problems through the United Nations reliance on democratic values. Human Rights, and the rule of law will contribute to success.

Whether the UN can recapture its role as the principal guarantor of collective security remains to be seen.[28] Hard lessons will have to be learned again. Saddam Hussein found that he could not thwart forever action designed to protect against his transgressions. France, Germany, and Russia learned that their substantial efforts to prevent the implementation of resolution 1441 by the United Nations were useless and created substantial ill will. As a sign of the times it has been suggested facetiously that a White House response might be to punish France, ignore Germany, and forgive Russia.

Yet, political leaders come and go, and the memory of ill-fated decision diminishes over time. The three outsiders and the members of the coalition will have to respond to their common interests. International goals and benefits are best served by multilateral policies. Equal responsibilities and opportunities will again prevail. By accepting the mutuality of their interests they can again enhance the principles contained in the UN Charter including the role of international law. And, on a lesser scale but of substantial importance, the concerns of the coalition States respecting terrorism and the development of WMD may give pause to the leaders in Iran, Israel, North Korea, Palestine, and Syria.

DISCUSSION QUESTIONS

1. If a dictatorial State, where it is believed that WMD are being manufactured, refuses to provide assurance that this is not the case, how can the "outside world" determine what the facts are?
2. How can one measure the reliability of the "facts" obtained from such sources?
3. What are your views concerning the impact of the development and fairly widespread distribution of WMD on the provisions of the UN Charter that have identified in this Chapter?
4. On the basis of the negotiation leading to the approval of Security Council Resolution 1441 is it fair to conclude that the United States is engaged in "bullying tactics" at the United Nations?
5. Some States have formed the opinion that the United States is lacking in sensitivity during multipartite diplomatic negotiations. In what situations may they feel justified in this view?
6. Is there any room in the UN Charter's Chapter VII provisions for the lawfulness of "humanitarian intervention," "humanitarian interposition," or "humanitarian responsibility"?
7. Did Resolution 1441 allow for the use of armed force against Iraq?
8. Can the UN Charter be interpreted as providing a legal basis for the doctrine of anticipatory or preemptive self-defense?
9. Did the difference between the coalition countries and their opponents regarding the use of force against Iraq immediably invalidate the principle of collective security?
10. What and by whom must be done to turn Iraq into a democratically oriented country?

NOTES

1. Two days earlier the Security Council had adopted Resolution 687 which imposed heavy obligations on Iraq. A cease-fire between the parties was to occur when all of Iraq's obligations had been met.

2. France later ended its participation.

3. Secretary of State Powell, "Briefing on Situation with Iraq," U.S. Department of State, 2, March 17, 2003. On March 3 Secretary Powell had stated that "The United Nations is damaged when there are members who do not want to stand up to the requirements of . . . resolution [1441] and take the action that was clearly intended in the absence of Iraq's compliance."

4. Prague Summit Declaration, NATO Press Release, November 21, 2002. Article 25 of the Charter requires all members of the UN to comply with Security Council resolutions.

5. *Supra*, note 3 at 1.

6. While analyzing the legality of the action of the coalition States critics have had to assess the meaning of the resolutions of the Security Council. In deviating from the terms of all of the resolutions some have attempted to demonstrate that their provisions did not sustain the use of force. See Mary Ellen O' Connell, "Addendum to Armed Force in Iraq: Issues of Legality," www.Insights@asil.org, April 2003.

7. J.B. MOORE, 2 DIGEST OF INTERNATIONAL LAW 409, 412 (1906); R.Y. Jennings, The Caroline and McLeod Cases," 32 *AJIL*, No. 2, 82 (1938).

8. *Ibid.*

9. *Los Angeles Times*, A9, October 8, 2002.

10. *Ibid.*

11. W. Michael Reisman, "Assessing Claims to Revise the Laws of War," 97 *AJIL*, No. 1 84, (2003). For a wide-ranging discussion of the legal and political aspects of the U.S. military involvement in Iraq see "Future Implications of the Iraq Conflict" with contributions of 10 American lawyers. 97 *AJIL*, No. 3, 553 (2003).Four additional articles addressing the same subject appear in 97 *AJIL*, No. 4, 803 (2003).

12. *Ibid.*

13. *The National Security Strategy of the United States of America*, 15 (2002), In December 2002 a poll revealed that two-thirds of Americans believed that President Bush had failed to a make a factual case to support preemptive action. *Los Angeles Times* A1, December 17, 2002. Despite the use by the United States and other countries of preemptive measures in the past it has been suggested that the Bush Doctrine is a radical foreign policy initiative and reflects a heightened bellicosity. As noted earlier a function of international law is to keep policies within identifiable bounds.

14. W.M. Reisman, *Supra*, Note 11 at 88.

15. *Id.*, at 89.

16. *Ibid.*

17. J.L. HOLZGREFE AND R.O. KEOHANE, eds., HUMANITARIAN INTERVENTION (2003), N.J. WHEELER, SAVING STRANGERS, HUMANITARIAN INTERVENTION IN SOCIETY (2001).

18. *The Responsibility to Protect*, Report of the International Commission on Intervention and State Sovereignty (December 2001). M. FINNEMORE, THE PURPOSE OF INTERVENTION (2003).

19. G. Evans and M. Sahnoun, "The Responsibility to Protect," 81 *Foreign Affairs*, No. 6, p. 99, (2002), M. Locke and J. Landier, "Criteria for Military Intervention in

Internal Wars: The Debate," FfP Reports (no date), P.S. TEMES, THE JUST WAR (2003), N.C. Crawford, "Just War Theory and the U.S. Counterterror War," 1 *Perspectives on Politics*, No. 1, p. 5 (March 2003).

20. *Los Angeles Times*, A12, April 10, 2003.

21. *Ibid.*

22. M. Cherif Bassiouni, Chicago Tribune, December 21, 2003. He is the president of the International Human Rights Law Institute at DePaul University.

23. D.F. Orenlicher, "Venues for Prosecution Saddam Hussein: The Legal Framework," insights@asil.org, December 2003.

24. *Id.* at 2.

25. J. Paust, "Saddam's Fate and Due Process Requirements," jpaust@central.UH .edu, December 16, 2003.

26. W.D. Nordhaus, "Iraq: The Economic Consequences of War," *The New York Review of Books*, p. 6, December 5, 2002.

27. *Los Angeles Times*, A29, April 13, 2003.

28. M.J. Glennon, "Why the Security Council Failed," 82 *Foreign Affairs*, No. 3, 16 (May/June 2003).

Chapter X

Conclusion

To write about international law and U.S. foreign policy is a substantial challenge; to practice them is an even greater responsibility. For the international lawyer the hazard is an inculcated commitment to the rule of law in world affairs. This includes the employment of accepted and orderly procedures for the establishment and implementation of world and national policies and laws. For political figures the risk is the disavowal of their policies.

For Heads of State, and especially for their advisors on diplomatic and security measures, the hazards are occasioned by transient opportunities to act unwisely, that is, without a reliable appraisal of all available facts and a suitable weighing of the consequences of their conduct.

Such challenges have been intensified in recent years with the progressive development of globalization. Yet States seeking to maximize their wants, interests, needs and values still can choose between multilaterally or unilaterally based policies. In adopting one of such approaches lawyers, diplomats, and political leaders must appraise the world forces within which they operate. For the lawyer much influence is accorded to science and technology as they have universalized the world's economy, and have led to a long-awaited recognition of universal Human Rights, including the expansion of international tribunals having dispute-resolving capabilities. For the diplomat there is a need to be tuned to perceived interests of States and the moods of their leaders.

For the political leaders a proper balancing of national security against individual rights and liberties remains a responsibility of the first order of importance. Currently the issue of worldwide terrorism, which is a most formidable problem, has produced, by necessity, a multilateral approach. But, in other areas, unilateral preferences have prevailed. This is based on the assumption that a State's sovereignty-based needs are so predominant that it cannot collaborate advantageously with others. Unilateralism may also be the product of hardened national practices with historic justifications.

In an era of unrivaled violence, especially in the former Yugoslavia, Rwanda, Iraq, the Middle East, and even in the United States, principles of law and considerations of policy should be aligned so as to protect civilized values. At the world level the choice for States is between cooperation, an inactive holding pattern, and noncooperation. The first is represented by multilateral support for globalization. The last is reflected in unilateralism with its rejection of multilateralism. The second allows for delaying a choice. Support for all have different levels of intensity.

The priorities assigned by the United States in recent years to the policies favored by it are quite evident. The United States has very actively solicited international support for its war on terrorism, including the invasion of Afghanistan. It has been heavily preoccupied with a regime change in Iraq, where it has worked hard to obtain the support of the U.N. Security Council and the members of the United Nations. At the bilateral level it has been able to join with Russia for a reduction over time of nuclear war heads and launching equipment. On the other hand, the United States has vigorously rejected the most recent international effort to establish an international criminal court, to outlaw anti-personnel land mines, and to improve the human environment. Much American political capital has been expended by its insistence on negativism in these areas.

In examining the on-going problems of Israel and the Palestinians the United States had for a long time adopted something akin to a holding pattern. During the early years of the Bush administration, the issues were studied with great care. Calls for changes were made. An American plan was said to exist. In fact extremely large financial subventions were made to both of the warring parties. But there was an absence of the urgency displayed by the United States in fighting terrorism or resisting Iraq's perceived challenge to world security. The mix of Islamic extremism and Israeli violence has changed that policy. A structure of limited multilateralism has been installed.

The issue of the nuclear capabilities of North Korea, long dormant, requires attention. The choice between multilateralism and unilateralism will have to be made. The United States will have to persuade the rest of the world on how to address this situation.

For there to be a measure of peace in the world, the world rule of law must be accepted, and this requires respect for and compliance with the rule of law. There is always the danger that States will be tempted to violate such law. Violations on occasion may benefit the lawbreaker, but they invite others to set aside the law for transient purposes.

The expression "rogue State" carries with it the opprobrium of law breaking. Thus, American policies must be fashioned in such a way to stay within legal boundaries. One of the gravest policy issues confronting current policy makers is to keep their activities within existing legal boundaries, while remaining aware of the living qualities of law.

In the Chapter dealing with Iraq attention was given to several interpretations of the expression "armed attack." The question was raised whether a State bound by the Charter could engage in anticipatory or preemptive "self-defense." In light of the kinds of weapons that are now in many national arsenals it has become increasingly plausible for the potentially harmed State to engage in lawful preemptive "self defense." This conclusion is highly controversial, but, in light of existing circumstances, it is supported both by the practical consideration of prudence and also by the right of a sovereign State to maintain its territorial integrity. How is a State to know if it is targeted for an imminent attack? And, how "imminent" is "imminent"?

It is also necessary for the United States to uphold its traditional Constitutional guarantees while coping with the world's new-found dangers. Prosecutions for well-defined crimes must proceed in a normal way in civilian courts. These courts in all but the most exceptional circumstances should be able to deal with unlawful combatants and military detainees. Numerous cases where contending aspects of a fair trial and the need to protect intelligence sources have been wending their ways slowly from trial courts to the United States Supreme Court. Oral arguments before the latter took place in April, 2004, and decisions are expected in June.

The contest between an outward looking (global) and an inward looking (unilateral) approach toward world relations is not a new invention. Much of the attention of students of law and diplomatic policy is given to trying to understand how, on the basis of choices, the best interests of nations and peoples can be served.[1]

In examining the relationship between international law and U.S. foreign policy during the Clinton and Bush administrations, with respect to globalism and unilateralism, there has emerged a feeling that President Clinton was inept and missed many favorable opportunities, and that President Bush, aside from his need for very broadly-based help on terrorism, and for bringing the Iraq war to closure, has been purposely opposed to a multilateral approach. Bush's negativism has placed him in the position that he must react to existing forces, being denied recourse to multilateralism, which would allow for a more creative outlook. By electing to reject the opportunities flowing from a policy of multilateralism, at least initially, the United States no longer is able to participate effectively in major and significant diplomatic conferences. This has prevented the United States from putting forward creative proposals that might serve common interests. The United States is not engaged in the "fine tuning" of the ICC. On the other hand, the United States treasures its membership in the Security Council and looks to it as efforts are made to bring Iraq back from the misadventure of Saddam Hussein.

The Bush approach, with its highly specific focus on violent threats to America, has resulted in a lesser commitment to the construction of a world community in which America's traditional values would be more in evidence. With a highly specific focus on terrorism and the recent dialogue with Russia on ballistic missiles, limitation of nuclear warheads, and the construction of NMD system, the Bush administration has given less attention to the plight of the developing nations, particularly in the area of climate change. While generally accepting the adverse impact of greenhouse gases, the Bush administration has scornfully depicted the Kyoto protocol as "fatally flawed." In saying so his administration has been more attentive to the position of America's major industrial leaders, including many in the automobile industry, who suggest that pollution is a necessary ingredient of large scale employment opportunities and a vibrant economy.

Unilateralism has allowed for a freer disposition of U.S. dollars in order to buy different kinds of benefits for America. Russia, for example, has received billions of dollars in order to take care that its nuclear warheads are destroyed or suitably safeguarded. The two warring entities in the Middle East have for many years received an accumulated total of billions of dollars from the American Treasury, with Israel receiving the preponderant share.

The financial costs of funding the U.S. anti-terrorist program, both at home and abroad, has become a new drain on America's economic resources. Since the war on terrorism has been described as a long-term project, it is uncertain what the future holds in this respect. However, there can be no doubt that, even though there cannot be an absolute protection against terroristic activities, the result will be a large need for a very costly vigilance. The Bush administration has insisted on an unproved NMD system, with its unrivaled cost.

The case for nation-building will have to be taken into account. Funds will have to become available to prevent areas of former hostilities from reverting to the chaotic conditions of the past. Particular candidates will be Afghanistan, Pakistan as a reward for providing military bases in the war against terrorism, Iraq, the former Yugoslavia as it proceeds to rebuild, and the expected Palestine State if and when it is allowed to become a responsible legal entity in the Middle East. Having forced a regime change in Iraq the United States must accept the on-going duty of restoring normalcy for the people of that country. Pragmatic interests will be served. It also should be considered to be a matter of conscience.

It should be evident that the United States, although perceived by some as seeking hegemony and wishing to become the world's new "policeman," cannot and should not be asked to perform that function. This means that in the matters identified above there will have to be a multilateral approach.

From the foregoing it is evident that at the present time the United States, within the context of globalism and unilateralism, is applying different approaches to several rather specific foreign policy issues. This should not be allowed to detract from the larger question: What is the purpose of foreign policy? The answer is not hard to find. It should advance the interests of the American people. The trouble is that there are so many interests. This means that at different times and places the purposes may be somewhat different, although there should be some constants.

Thus, while foreign policy may address itself to the issue of national security a State's foreign policy has the purpose of protecting the citizens or residents of a given country. By the same token the economic foreign policy of a State addresses itself to the needs of its inhabitants.

A foreign policy dealing with systems of justice must focus on the rights and duties of residents when appearing in its courts of law. The very expression "Human Rights" deals with the status of inhabitants and is now a fundamental element in the workings of foreign policy. A foreign policy addressed to climate change and the human environment deals with the lifestyles and enjoyment of the amenities of life of human beings.

A purpose of foreign policy is to liberate the minds of people. This is effected through the importation and exportation of ideas, from international educational opportunities, and from international travel. In order to advance such purposes as these a State formulates and implements its foreign policy. And since such purposes are common to almost all countries, their respective foreign policies indicate great similarities. The beneficial exploitation of common interests and the vast freedoms flowing from communication call for globalism. They do not achieve their maximum potential under policies of unilateralism.

It is better to have a singular wide-ranging habit than a series of narrow provincial ones. States taking a narrow and restricted view have the burden of proof to demonstrate that there is good cause for restricting the rights and duties of the persons they serve. Many doubt that such a burden of proof can be met—the mutuality of interests in the modern world is simply too great.

The timing of foreign policy decisions must be taken into account. Since people do not like to be surprised the September 2001 terrorist attack on the United States galvanized them into action. At the governmental level the executive department issued decrees and orders, with a principal one addressing the judicial approach to those prosecutions favored by the administration. At the congressional level over 200 bills were considered and passed into law. A reorganization of federal institutions involved in security matters was adopted. With Congressional approval a new Department of Homeland Security, with cabinet status, was created. Its function is to monitor and enforce security-based laws and to streamline communications. Greater attention will be given to the presence of illegal aliens.

This Department has the power to impose restrictions on the behavior of residents. The extent of such powers, and the manner of their enforcement, is subject to constitutional limitations. The concern is that the traditional rights of residents may, in some manner, be unduly restricted. In a word, terrorism, or the threat of terrorism, should not produce limitations on judicial standards acceptable in the past, and in no event violate the U.S. constitution.

Public opinion has a larger role to play in the critical area of U.S. foreign policy. It must be formulated, measured, and applied by America's political, diplomatic, and legal leaders. There must be a high degree of mutual respect between such persons as they apply their respective talents to the resolution of disputes. This results from the fact that although issues frequently arise in a political context they are resolved in a legal framework. This is particularly true in important matters where decisions are memorialized in formal international treaties.

In the United States foreign policy proposals must conform both to American constitutional law and to international law. They make it clear that claims invoking national sovereignty, which do not have a foundation in U.S. constitutional law and in the existing principles, standards, and rules of international law, have no merit.

It was with this in mind that in Chapter II it was stated that foreign policy could be likened to a machine, where if the machine is to be effective, it must come equipped with a regulator. The purpose of the regulator is to prevent the machine from embarking on conduct that is beyond the capacity of the machine, so that, if tested, the regulator would prevent the destruction of the machine.

Law, as the regulator, would serve to protect against unlawful policies. International law would lose its authority if it were to be seen as the handmaiden of the foreign policies of nations. In defining the lawful reach of a State's foreign policy, international law would be performing its function, i.e., identifying the rights and duties of States and of their peoples.

International law, like law in general, is subject to growth and to change. It can be creative and innovative. It can examine foreign policy proposals from such a perspective. In addressing the application of law to both foreign and domestic issues, Chief Justice Earl Warren once stated: "It is our great mission both at home and abroad to keep the terms law and justice synonymous."[2]

It is evident that the legal analysis of the foreign policy problems of the United States, that have been identified, has been based on the view that if human beings are to enjoy the advantages and opportunities open to them in today's world, and that if the legitimate goals of States are to be realized, it is necessary to approach foreign policy issues and problems from a multilateral perspective. Unilateralism, with its narrow and self-centered outlook, will produce failed policies and uneconomic friction and turmoil. Policy makers must have the capacity to think globally. Humans will benefit accordingly.

The world's leaders in addressing the mix of foreign policy and international law need look no further for guidance than to the recent words of U.N. Secretary General Kofi Annan. In responding to the award to him of the 2001 Nobel Peace Prize he stated, "When States undermine the rule of law and violate the rights of individual citizens, they become a menace not only to their own people, but to their neighbors, and indeed the world."[3]

DISCUSSION QUESTIONS

1. In the realm of international affairs who are the true "realists," the lawyers or the politicians?
2. Are the terms "multilateral" or "global" as opposed to "unilateral" helpful in identifying the goals and means to achieve such goals in the relations of nations?
3. What benefits and detriments result from adopting the term "rogue States" in describing political adversaries?
4. Financial resources available to governments to carry out programs and policies are limited. What, if any, concerns do you have as to the costs of the policies identified in this book?
5. Students of U.S. foreign policies are concerned over the present "image problem" of the United States. Assuming that their concerns are justified, what can be done to improve the situation? What role would you play?

NOTES

1. Recent books address the subject. I.H. DAALDER AND JAMES M. LINDSAY, AMERICA UNBOUND: THE BUSH REVOLUTION IN FOREIGN POLICY (2003); D. M. MALONE AND YUEN FOONG KHONG, eds., UNILATERALISM

AND U. S. FOREIGN POLICY (2003); C. PRESTOWITZ, AMERICAN UNILATERALISM AND THE FAILURE OF GOOD INTENTIONS (2003); J. MEARSHEIMER, THE TRAGEDY OF GREAT POWER POLITICS (2001) AND J.S. NYE, JR., THE PARADOX OF AMERICAN POWER: THE WORLD'S ONLY SUPERPOWER CAN'T GO IT ALONE (2002). Interesting articles include A. Chua, "Globalization and Ethnic Hatred," 83 *Phi Kappa Phi Forum*, No. 4, 13 (Fall 2003); R. Kagan, "America's Crisis of Legitimacy," 83 *Foreign Affairs*, No. 2, 65 (March–April 2004); D. K. Simes, "America's Imperial Dilemma," 82 *Foreign Affairs, No. 6,* 91 (November–December 2003); J. Rubenfeld, "The Two World Orders," *The Wilson Quarterly*, No. 4, 22 (Autumn 2003).

2. E. Warren, "Convocation Address," *University of Illinois L. Forum*, 278 (1956).
3. *The Los Angeles Times*, A15, December 11, 2001.

Addendum: The Private Citizen and the Formulation of Public Policy

The citizen's first step is to become informed. Set aside a brief period every day for reading one or two newspapers and listening to national and international news broadcasts. If you have a deeper interest in the subject consider subscribing to *Foreign Affairs*, published by the Council on Foreign Relations, 58 East 68th Street, New York, NY 10021, www.foreignaffairs.org.

For students enrolled in undergraduate and graduate courses in international law ask the American Society of International Law about discounted memberships in that organization. Included are a subscription to the *American Journal of International Law* and the *Newsletter*. 2223 Massachusetts Avenue, NW, Washington, DC 20008-2864, www.asil.org.

The American Society of International Law publishes *International Legal Materials*. It provides detailed coverage of official documents of international organizations including Resolutions, Treaties, Court Decisions, Reports of International Organizations, U.S. court cases, and the statutes or treaties to which the U.S. is a party.

The American Bar Association's Section of International Law and Practice in its Summer issues of *The International Lawyer* focuses on "International Legal Developments in Review." American Bar Association, ABA Service Center, 541 North Fairbanks Court, Chicago, IL 60611, www.abanet.org/intlaw/home.html.

Information can be obtained through memberships in organizations. Religious denominations have social action groups which publish newsletters dealing with such subjects as peacemaking and contacts with the United Nations. The United Nations Association of the United States of America (UNA-USA) publishes annually *A Global Agenda, Issues Before the General Assembly of the United Nations*, and a quarterly, *The InterDependent*.

UNA-USA, 801 Second Avenue, New York, NY 10017, www.unausa.org. Student memberships at reduced fee.

The citizen has a duty to inform elected officials on matters of importance. Letters to your congressman and senator can be written. Copies should be provided to the President of the Senate and to the Speaker of the House.

The President should know your views as well as the editor of your local newspaper. Since American corporations play a large role in establishing policies, you should write to the presidents of such companies. You should join your community's political group and, through it help to identify that party's political goals. Testifying before legislative committees, making contributions of time and money to political candidates, and serving on the program committee of a service club can be useful. Book review clubs allow for criticism of an author's views.

How can a citizen have an impact on decisions made by international organizations? In addition to the above options, there are opportunities. Look for an organization that has been designated by the U.N. as a Non-governmental Organization. Following certification they may make direct presentations to committees and working groups of the United Nations as such bodies inquire into special and often quite technical matters. One American group accorded NGO status is the UNA-USA.

Another method for obtaining the attention of governmental officials at international organizations is through presentations by scholars possessing unique professional competence. Private scholars participate in seminars with U.N. staff and delegates to explain the finer points on the subject under consideration.

In recent years private international organizations have conducted their congresses at the same time and place as important international conferences on such subjects as international trade or the human environment. They have been highly innovative.

A new educational approach to an understanding of international law has been devised by the American Society of International Law. It has consisted of seminars conducted by experts in the field for state and federal judges so that they might develop a higher degree of expertise in the field.

The International Institute of Space Law has engaged the attention of law school students in an international moot court on this special subject. The American Society of International law hosts an annual international moot court court competition. These are unrivaled learning experiences. They provide a background for participation in the formulation of the American foreign policy.

WWW RESOURCES

United Nations, Resolutions of General Assembly and Security Council, www.un.org/International Court of Justice, www.icj-cij.org/

USA, Executive Department

- www.whitehouse.gov/
- www.firstgov.gov/
- www.state.gov/
- www.DefenseLINK
- www.treas.gov/
- www.whitehouse.gov/homeland (Department of Homeland Security)

USA, Congress

- www.loc.gov/ (Library of Congress)
- www.senate.gov/ (Senate Committee on Foreign Relations)
- www.house.gov/ (House Committee on Foreign Affairs)

USA, Treaties

- www.state.gov/
- www.Fletcher.Tufts.edu (multilaterals)
- Treaties in Force: Department of State
- Millennium Summit Multilateral Treaty Framework, United Nations

Law Journals, Osgoode Hall School of Law, library.osgoode.yorku.ca/linksjournalyork.

Index